# Creutzfeldt-Jakob Disease: Managing the Risk of Transmission by Blood, Plasma, and Tissues

**PRESS**

The AABB Press publishes books and CDs on many topics of interest to those in the blood banking, transfusion medicine, and cellular therapy fields.

To purchase books or to inquire about other book services, including chapter reprints and large-quantity sales, please contact our sales department:
- 866.222.2498 (within the United States)
- +1 301.215.6499 (outside the United States)
- +1 301.951.7150 (fax)
- www.aabb.org>Bookstore

AABB customer service representatives are available by telephone from 8:30 am to 5:00 pm ET, Monday through Friday, excluding holidays.

# Creutzfeldt-Jakob Disease: Managing the Risk of Transmission by Blood, Plasma, and Tissues

Editor

Marc L. Turner, MB, ChB, PhD, FRCP, FRCPath

AABB Press
Bethesda, Maryland
2006

AABB
8101 Glenbrook Road
Bethesda, Maryland 20814-2749

ISBN NO. 1-56395-224-6
Printed in the United States

**Library of Congress Cataloging-in-Publication Data**

Creutzfeldt-Jakob disease: managing the risk of transmission by blood, plasma, and
    tissues / editor, Marc L. Turner.
        p. ; cm.
Includes bibliographical references and index.
ISBN 1-56395-224-6 (perfect bound)
    1. Creutzfeldt-Jakob disease. 2. Brain—Infections. 3. Cross infection—Prevention 4. Risk management. I. Turner, Marc L. II. AABB.
    [DNLM: 1. Creutzfeldt-Jakob Syndrome—prevention & control. 2. Biological Specimen Banks—organization & administration. 3. Creutzfeldt-Jakob Syndrome—transmission. 4. Infection Control—methods. 5. Risk Factors. 6. Risk Management. WL 300 C9255 2006]
RC394.C83C742 2006

# Contributors

**Peter Bennett, BSc, MSc, PhD**
Department of Health
London, United Kingdom

**Paul Brown, MD**
Bethesda, Maryland, United States

**Moira E. Bruce, BSc, PhD**
Institute for Animal Health
Edinburgh, United Kingdom

**Rebecca Cardigan, BSc, PhD**
National Blood Service
Brentwood/Cambridge, United Kingdom

**John Collinge, CBE, FRS**
University College London and
The National Hospital for Neurology and Neurosurgery
London, United Kingdom

**Stephen Dobra, BSc, MSc, MSc, MBA**
Department of Health
London, United Kingdom

**Peter R. Foster, BSc, MSc, PhD, CS, CSci, CEng, FIChemE**
Scottish National Blood Transfusion Service
Protein Fractionation Centre
Edinburgh, United Kingdom

**George Galea, MD(Aber), FRCP(Ed), FRCPath**
Scottish National Blood Transfusion Service Tissue Services
Edinburgh, United Kingdom

**James W. Ironside, BMSc(hons), MBChB, FRCPath, FRCP(Ed), FMedSci**
University of Edinburgh and
The National Health Service Lothian University
Hospitals Division and
Tayside University Hospitals Division
Edinburgh, United Kingdom

**Philip Minor, BA, PhD**
National Institute for Biological Standards and Control
South Mimms, United Kingdom

**Marc L. Turner, MB, ChB, PhD, FRCP, FRCPath**
University of Edinburgh and
Edinburgh Blood Transfusion Centre
Edinburgh, United Kingdom

**Jonathan D. F. Wadsworth, PhD, DIC**
University College London and
The National Hospital for Neurology and Neurosurgery
London, United Kingdom

**Lorna M. Williamson, BSc, MD, FRCP, FRCPath**
University of Cambridge and
The National Blood Service
Cambridge, United Kingdom

# Table of Contents

*Jonathan D. F. Wadsworth, PhD, DIC, and*
   *John Collinge, CBE, FRS*

*Moira E. Bruce, BSc, PhD*

# Preface

THE TRANSMISSIBLE SPONGIFORM encephalopathies (TSEs) or prion diseases make up a fascinating and challenging group of disorders. Associated with abnormal conformation of prion protein, these diseases can occur sporadically, within familial pedigrees, or through oral or parenteral transmission. Prion disorders have been described in a variety of animals, including sheep and goats (scrapie), mule deer and Rocky Mountain elk (chronic wasting disease), farmed mink (transmissible mink encephalopathy), and, most recently, cattle and a variety of other species (bovine spongiform encephalopathy).

In humans, Creutzfeldt-Jakob disease (CJD) was first described in the early 1920s, and sporadic, familial (familial CJD, fatal familial insomnia, and Gerstmann-Sträussler-Scheinker syndrome), and transmissible (kuru and iatrogenic CJD) forms have been described. However, a series of epidemiologic case-control, look-back, and surveillance studies over the past 25 years provided little evidence of transmission by blood transfusion, plasma products, or organ or tissue transplantation. Despite this, the first description of variant CJD (vCJD) in 1996 gave rise to considerable concern. It was recognized from the outset both that vCJD represented a different strain of prion disease that included the deposition of abnormal prion protein in lymphoid tissue and that the absence of evidence of transmission by blood and tissues could not, therefore, be equated with evidence of the absence of transmission. Many countries have taken a precautionary stance by deferring donors who have lived in or visited the United Kingdom (UK) and some other European countries, by excluding UK plasma from the manufacture of plasma products, and, in some countries, by implementing universal leucocyte reduction. Fortunately, many of the early predictions of the potential size of a clinical vCJD outbreak have proven unfounded. However, over the last 2 years, three clinical transmissions of vCJD prions by red cell transfusion and evidence from studies of archived tonsil and appendix samples suggesting that a high proportion of the infected population may have long-term preclinical or subclinical disease have raised further concern. In the UK and elsewhere, this concern has led to the deferral of blood and tissue recipients from donation, in an effort to reduce the incidence of higher-order transmissions and the risk of a self-sustaining outbreak. Additional risk-reduction measures under consideration include further manipulation of blood component processing, the introduction of prion-reduction filters, and vCJD testing. However, many uncertainties remain, including the prevalence of preclinical or subclinical infection among the donor population, the concentration of infectivity in peripheral blood and tissues, the temporal and spatial distribution of that infectivity, and the impact of current and future risk-reduction measures.

In the face of such uncertainty, international blood policy decisions in this field continue to be based upon risk assessments, which are built on a series of assumptions that themselves are extrapolated predominantly from experimental animal data and mathematical modeling. Additional risk-reduction measures may introduce countervailing risks, including those of blood and tissue shortages, and are often associated with substantial health economic costs.

It is therefore crucial that scientists, physicians, managers, and regulators within the international blood services community understand the science upon which risk management proposals are built and the way in which these proposals underpin the policy decision-making process. It is hoped that this volume will encourage informed debate among those involved in trying to manage the risks of transmission of these diseases by blood and tissue products.

I would like to express my gratitude to all of the contributing authors, to Paul Brown for his assistance in reviewing the book, and to the AABB Press Publications team for management of the publishing process.

Marc L. Turner, MB, ChB, PhD, FRCP, FRCPath
*Editor*

*A note on terminology:* There remains much debate among experts in the TSE/prion field as to the nature of the infectious agent and, in particular, as to the exact relationship between abnormal conformation of prion protein and infectivity. This debate is reflected in a degree of disagreement around terminology that can be confusing to those of us who are not experts in the field. For clarity, I have taken a fairly pragmatic approach in editing this volume. I have assumed rough equivalence for practical purposes between the terms "transmissible spongiform encephalopathy" and "prion disease." The abbreviations "$PrP^{Sc}$" and "$PrP^{TSE}$" are used more or less interchangeably in talking about the abnormal prion protein conformer, whereas the term "$PrP^{Res}$" is used more specifically to describe the proteinase-resistant subset of $PrP^{Sc}/PrP^{TSE}$. Finally, there are two systems in use for classifying the molecular subtypes of abnormal prion protein, that proposed by Hill et al[1] and that proposed by Parchi et al.[2] The relationship between these systems was established at a World Health Organization TSE Diagnostics Working Group—namely, that types 1 and 2 of Hill et al equate with type 1 of Parchi et al; that type 3 of Hill et al equates with type 2a of Parchi et al; and that type 4 of Hill et al equates with type 2B of Parchi et al.

# References

1. Hill AF, Joiner S, Wadsworth JD, et al. Molecular classification of sporadic Creutzfeldt-Jakob disease. Brain 2003;126:1333-46.
2. Parchi P, Giese A, Capellari S, et al. Classification of Creutzfeldt-Jakob disease based on molecular and phenotypic analysis of 300 subjects. Ann Neurol 1999;46:224-33.

# About the Editor

**Dr. Marc Turner** is Senior Lecturer in Immunohematology and Transfusion Medicine at the University of Edinburgh, Clinical Director and Consultant Hematologist at the Edinburgh Blood Transfusion Centre, and honorary Consultant Hematologist at the Royal Infirmary of Edinburgh, Edinburgh, United Kingdom. He studied medicine at the University of Manchester in 1982 and trained in general medicine and hematology before moving into transfusion medicine. He obtained his PhD in human hematopoietic stem cell biology from the University of Edinburgh in 1995. He is a Fellow of the Royal College of Physicians of London, a Fellow of the Royal College of Physicians of Edinburgh, a Fellow of the Royal College of Pathologists, and a member of the Higher Education Academy. His research interests include immunohematology, transmission of variant Creutzfeldt-Jakob disease (vCJD) by blood and tissues, and translational research in stem cell and regenerative medicine. His more general interests lie in managing the sometimes challenging interface between science, medicine, and public health policy.

Dr. Turner is Chair of the CJD Working Group of the UK Blood Services Specialist Advisory Committee on Transfusion-Transmitted Infections. He has provided specialist opinion to a number of national and international bodies on issues relating to vCJD transmission by blood and plasma products, cells, tissues, and organs. These organizations include the UK Spongiform Encephalopathy Advisory Committee; the Advisory Committee on the Microbiological Safety of Blood, Tissues, and Organs; and the CJD Incidents Panel.

In: Turner ML, ed.
*Creutzfeldt-Jakob Disease: Managing the Risk of*
*Transmission by Blood, Plasma, and Tissues*
Bethesda, MD: AABB Press, 2006

# 1

# Molecular Pathology of Prion Diseases

## JONATHAN D. F. WADSWORTH, PhD, DIC, AND JOHN COLLINGE, CBE, FRS

THE PRION DISEASES are a closely related group of neurodegenerative conditions that affect both humans and animals. They have previously been described as the subacute spongiform encephalopathies, slow virus diseases, and transmissible dementias, and they include scrapie in sheep, bovine spongiform encephalopathy (BSE) in cattle, and the human prion diseases, Creutzfeldt-Jakob disease (CJD), Gerstmann-Sträussler-Scheinker disease (GSS), fatal familial insomnia (FFI), and kuru.[1]

Although rare in humans, prion diseases are an area of intense research interest. This is, first, because of their unique bi-

*Jonathan D. F. Wadsworth, PhD, DIC, MRC Programme Lead Track Scientist, MRC Prion Unit, and Honorary Lecturer, Department of Neurodegenerative Disease; and John Collinge, CBE, FRS, Director, MRC Prion Unit, and Head, Department of Neurodegenerative Disease, Institute of Neurology, University College London and National Hospital for Neurology and Neurosurgery, London, United Kingdom*

ology, in that the transmissible agent appears to be devoid of nucleic acid and to consist of a posttranslationally modified host protein. Second, because of the ability of these and related animal diseases to cross from one species to another, sometimes by dietary exposure, there has been widespread concern that exposure to the epidemic of BSE poses a distinct and, conceivably, severe threat to public health in the United Kingdom and other countries. The occurrence of variant CJD (vCJD) and the experimental confirmation that it is caused by the same prion strain as is BSE have dramatically highlighted the need for a precise understanding of the molecular basis of prion propagation. The extremely prolonged and variable incubation periods of these diseases, particularly when they cross a species barrier, mean that it will be some years before the parameters of any human epidemic can be predicted with confidence. In the meantime, the possibility exists that significant numbers of people may be incubating this disease and that they might pass it on to others via blood transfusion, blood components, tissue and organ transplantation, and other iatrogenic routes. The recent demonstration of subclinical carrier states of prion infection in animal models is also relevant to public health, with respect to both prion zoonoses and iatrogenic transmission of human prions. Prions resist many conventional sterilization procedures, and effective methods of prion decontamination of surgical instruments and medical equipment have yet to be established.

## Aberrant Metabolism of the Prion Protein Is the Central Feature of Prion Disease

The nature of the transmissible agent in prion disease has been a subject of heated debate for many years.[2-4] The understandable initial assumption that the causative agent of "transmissible dementias" must be some form of virus was challenged by the failure to directly demonstrate such a virus (or indeed any immunologic response to it) and by the remarkable resistance of the transmissible agent to treatments that inactivate nucleic acids. These findings led to suggestions that the transmissible agent may be devoid of nucleic acid[5] and may be a protein.[6] Subsequently (1982), Prusiner[7] isolated a protease-resistant sialoglycoprotein, designated the prion protein (PrP), that was the major constituent of infective fractions and was found to accumulate in affected brain. The term prion was proposed by Prusiner to distinguish the infectious pathogen from viruses or viroids, and their definition was "small proteinaceous infectious particles that resist inactivation by procedures which [sic] modify nucleic acids."[7]

Initially, PrP was assumed to be encoded by a gene within the putative slow virus thought to be responsible for these diseases; however, amino acid sequencing of part of the PrP and the subsequent recovery of cognate cDNA clones by using an isocoding mixture of oligonucleotides led to the realization that PrP was encoded by a single-copy chromosomal gene rather than by a putative viral nucleic acid.[8-10]

After these seminal discoveries, a wealth of data firmly established that the central and unifying hallmark of the prion diseases is the aberrant metabolism of PrP, which exists in at least two conformational states with different physicochemical properties.[2-4,11] The normal cellular form of the protein, referred to as $PrP^C$, is a highly conserved cell surface glycosylphosphatidylinositol (GPI)-anchored sialoglycoprotein that is sensitive to protease treatment and soluble in detergents. In contrast, the disease-associated scrapie isoform, designated as $PrP^{Sc}$, is found only in prion-infected tissue as aggregated material, is partially resistant to protease treatment, and is insoluble in detergents. Because of its physicochemical properties, the precise atomic structure of the infectious particle or prion is still undetermined, but considerable evidence argues that prions are composed largely, if not entirely, of an abnormal isoform of PrP.[2-4,11] The essential role of host PrP for prion propagation and pathogenesis is shown by the facts that knockout mice lacking the PrP gene ($Prnp^{o/o}$ mice) are entirely resistant to prion infection[12,13] and that reintroduction of the murine PrP transgene restores susceptibility to infection.[14]

## Human Prion Diseases Are Biologically Unique

Human prion diseases are biologically unique and can be divided etiologically into inherited, sporadic, and acquired forms.[15-17] Approximately 85% of the cases of human prion disease occur sporadically as CJD (sporadic CJD, sCJD) at a rate of roughly 1 case per million population per year across the world; the incidence in men and women is equal.[18] The etiology of sCJD is unknown, although hypotheses include somatic *PRNP* mutation or the spontaneous conversion of PrP$^C$ into PrP$^{Sc}$ as a rare stochastic event.[15] Homozygosity at a common coding polymorphism at codon 129 of *PRNP* encoding either methionine or valine predisposes to the development of sCJD and acquired CJD.[19-23] In addition, a *PRNP* susceptibility haplotype has been identified, which indicates additional genetic susceptibility to sCJD at or near the *PRNP* locus.[24]

Approximately 15% of human prion diseases are associated with autosomal dominant pathogenic mutations in *PRNP*.[15,16,25] How pathogenic mutations in *PRNP* cause prion disease has yet to be resolved, but, in most cases, the mutation is thought to lead to an increased tendency of PrP$^C$ to form PrP$^{Sc}$. However, there is evidence suggesting that this may not be solely attributable to decreased thermodynamic stability of mutated PrP$^C$.[26-28] Experimentally manipulated mutations of the prion gene can lead to spontaneous neurodegeneration without the formation of detectable protease-resistant PrP.[29,30] These findings raise the question of whether all inherited forms of human prion disease invoke disease through the same mechanism; in this regard, it is currently unknown whether all are transmissible by inoculation.[16]

Although the human prion diseases are transmissible diseases, acquired forms have, until recently, been confined to rare and unusual situations. The two most frequent causes of the occurrence of iatrogenic CJD through medical procedures have been the implantation of dura mater grafts and treatment with human growth hormone derived from the pituitary glands of human cadavers.[31,32] Less frequent occurrences of human prion disease have resulted from iatrogenic transmission of CJD during corneal transplantation, contaminated electro-encephalographic electrode implantation, and surgical operations using contaminated instruments or apparatus.[31,32] The most well-known instances of acquired prion disease in humans resulting from a dietary origin have been kuru that was caused by cannibalism among the Fore linguistic group of the Eastern Highlands in Papua New Guinea[16,23,33] and, more recently, the occurrence of vCJD in the United Kingdom and other European countries that appears causally related to human exposure to BSE in cattle.[34-40] Incubation periods of acquired prion diseases in humans can be extremely prolonged, and it remains to be seen whether a substantial epidemic of vCJD will occur in the United Kingdom or elsewhere.[38]

## The Protein-Only Hypothesis of Prion Propagation

Despite extensive investigation, no evidence for a specific prion-associated nucleic acid has been found.[2-4,11,41] Instead, a wide body of data now supports the idea that infectious prions consist principally or entirely of an abnormal isoform of PrP. $PrP^{Sc}$ is derived from $PrP^{C}$ by a posttranslational mechanism, and neither amino acid sequencing nor systematic study of known covalent posttranslational modifications have shown any consistent differences between $PrP^{C}$ and $PrP^{Sc}$.[2-4,11,42] The protein-only hypothesis, in its current form, argues that prion propagation occurs through the self-replication of $PrP^{Sc}$, which takes place with high fidelity by the recruitment of endogenous $PrP^{C}$, and that this conversion involves only conformational change. However, the underlying molecular events during infection that lead to the conversion of $PrP^{C}$ to $PrP^{Sc}$ and the way in which $PrP^{Sc}$ accumulation leads to neurodegeneration remain poorly defined.

The most coherent and general model thus far proposed is that the protein, PrP, fluctuates between a dominant native state, $PrP^{C}$, and a series of minor conformations, one or a set of which can self-associate in an ordered manner to produce a stable supramolecular structure, $PrP^{Sc}$, composed of misfolded PrP monomers. Once a stable "seed" structure is formed, PrP can then be recruited, which leads to an explosive, auto-catalytic formation of $PrP^{Sc}$. Such a mechanism could underlie prion propagation and account for the transmitted, sporadic, and inherited etiologies of prion disease. The initiation of a pathogenic self-propagating conversion reaction, with the ac-cumulation of aggregated PrP, may be induced by exposure to a seed of aggregated PrP after prion inoculation, as a rare sto-chastic conformational change, or as an inevitable consequence of the expression of a pathogenic $PrP^C$ mutant that is predis-posed to form misfolded PrP. Such a system would be ex-tremely sensitive to three factors: overall $PrP^C$ concentration, the equilibrium distribution between the native conformation and the self-associating conformation, and complementarity between surfaces that come together in the aggregation step. All three of these predictions from this minimal model are manifest in the etiology of prion disease: an inversely propor-tional relationship between $PrP^C$ expression and prion incuba-tion period in transgenic mice; predisposition by relatively subtle mutations in the protein sequence; and a requirement for molecular homogeneity between $PrP^{Sc}$ and $PrP^C$ for effi-cient prion propagation.[2,3,14] It is now clear that a full under-standing of prion propagation will require knowledge of both the structure of $PrP^C$ and $PrP^{Sc}$ and the mechanism of conver-sion between them.

## Structural Properties and Putative Function of $PrP^C$

PrP is highly conserved among mammals[43]; has been identi-fied in marsupials, birds, amphibians, and fish[44-46]; and may be present in all vertebrates. It is expressed during early embryo-genesis[47] and is found in most tissues in the adult; the highest levels of expression occur in the central nervous system, in particular in association with synaptic membranes. PrP is also widely expressed in cells of the immune system.[48] Newly synthesized PrP[C] is transported to the cell surface and then internalized by either clathrin-mediated[49] or caveolae-mediated[50] mechanisms, as reviewed by Harris.[51] As a GPI-anchored cell surface glycoprotein,[52] it has been speculated that PrP may have a role in cell adhesion or signaling processes, but its precise cellular function has remained obscure.[3,53] A range of PrP[C]-interacting molecules has been identified,[53] but, despite a growing body of evidence that PrP[C] may play a role in cell survival through interaction with apoptotic pathways,[54] the in-vivo relevance of such interactions has yet to be convincingly shown. A role for PrP in copper or zinc metabolism or transport seems possible,[55] and disturbance of this function by the conformational transition from normal to disease-related isoforms of PrP may be involved in prion-related neurotoxicity.[56,57]

Mice lacking PrP as a result of gene knockout (Prnp[o/o] mice) show no gross phenotype, but these mice are completely resistant to prion disease after inoculation and do not replicate prions.[14] However, Prnp[o/o] mice do show subtle abnormalities in synaptic physiology and in circadian rhythms and sleep (for review, see Collinge[3] and Weissmann and Flechsig[14]). Whereas the relative normality of Prnp[o/o] mice was thought to result from effective adaptive changes during development, data from Prnp conditional knockout mice suggest this is not the case.[58] These mice undergo ablation of neuronal PrP expression at 9 weeks of age and remain healthy without evidence of neurodegeneration or an overt clinical phenotype. These findings show that an acute loss of neuronal PrP in adulthood is tolerated and that the pathophysiology of prion diseases is not due to loss of normal PrP function in neurons.[59,60]

The conformation of the cellular isoform of PrP was first established by nuclear magnetic resonance (NMR) measurements made on the recombinant mouse protein.[61] Since then, NMR measurements on recombinant PrP from numerous mammalian species,[62-64] including human PrP,[65-67] show that they have essentially the same conformation (for review, see

Riesner[11] and Wuthrich and Riek[68]). These data have also been supported by crystallographic determination of the structures of a human PrP dimer and sheep PrP.[69,70]

After cleavage of an N-terminal signal peptide and removal of a C-terminal peptide on the addition of a GPI anchor, the mature PrP$^C$ species consists of an N-terminal region of about 100 amino acids, which is unstructured in the isolated mol cule in solution, and a C-terminal segment, which also is about 100 amino acids in length. The C-terminal domain is folded into a largely α-helical conformation (three α-helixes and a short antiparallel β-sheet) and stabilized by a single disulfide bond linking helixes 2 and 3 (Fig 1-1). There are two asparagine-linked glycosylation sites (Figs 1-1 and 1-2). The N-terminal region contains a segment of five repeats of an eight-amino acid sequence (the octapeptide-repeat region), expansion of which by insertional mutation leads to inherited prion dis ease. Although the N-terminal region of PrP is unstructured in the isolated molecule, it seems likely that it may acquire coor

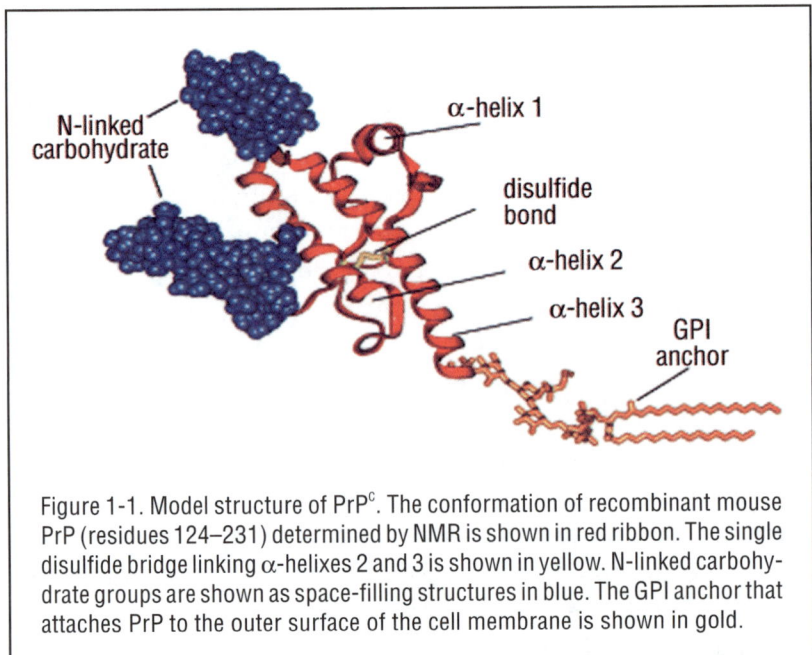

Figure 1-1. Model structure of PrP$^c$. The conformation of recombinant mouse PrP (residues 124–231) determined by NMR is shown in red ribbon. The single disulfide bridge linking α-helixes 2 and 3 is shown in yellow. N-linked carbohydrate groups are shown as space-filling structures in blue. The GPI anchor that attaches PrP to the outer surface of the cell membrane is shown in gold.

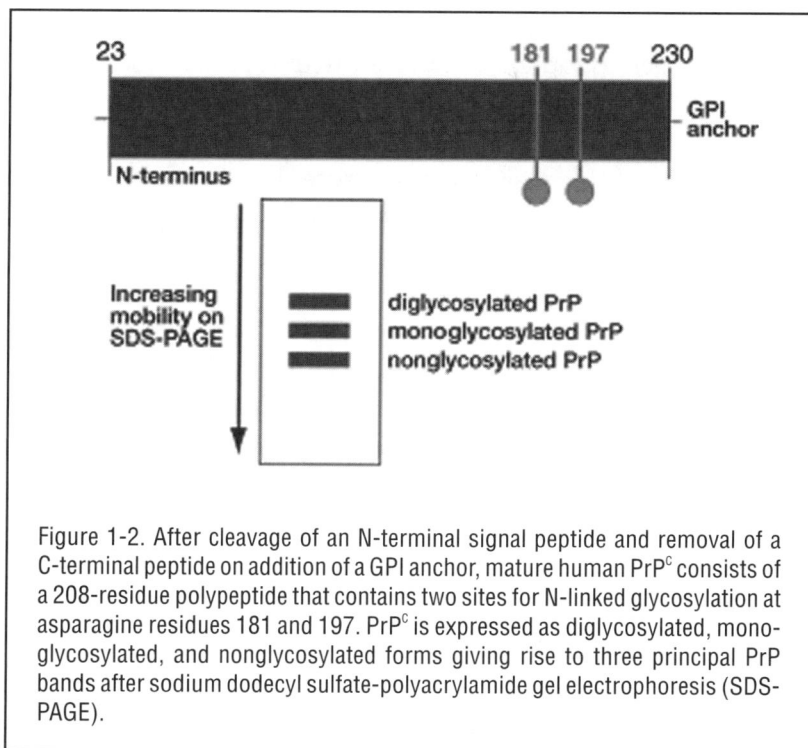

Figure 1-2. After cleavage of an N-terminal signal peptide and removal of a C-terminal peptide on addition of a GPI anchor, mature human PrP$^c$ consists of a 208-residue polypeptide that contains two sites for N-linked glycosylation at asparagine residues 181 and 197. PrP$^c$ is expressed as diglycosylated, monoglycosylated, and nonglycosylated forms giving rise to three principal PrP bands after sodium dodecyl sulfate-polyacrylamide gel electrophoresis (SDS-PAGE).

dinated structure in vivo through coordination of either $Cu^{2+}$ or $Zn^{2+}$ ions.[3,71] The structured C-terminal domain of PrP folds and unfolds reversibly in response to chaotropic denaturants, and it appears that there are no equilibrium intermediates[66] or kinetic intermediates[72] in the folding reaction and that the protein displays unusually rapid rates of folding and unfolding.[72] These data suggest that PrP$^{Sc}$ is unlikely to be formed from a kinetic folding intermediate, as has been hypothesized in the case of amyloid formation in other systems, and that it is more likely to be formed from the unfolded state of PrP (for review, see Collinge[3] and Jackson and Clarke[73]).

## Structural Properties of PrP$^{Sc}$

PrP$^{Sc}$ is extracted from affected brains as highly aggregated, detergent-insoluble material that is not amenable to high-resolution structural techniques. However, Fourier transform infrared spectroscopic methods show that PrP$^{Sc}$, in sharp contrast to PrP$^C$, has a high β-sheet content.[74,75] PrP$^{Sc}$ is covalently indistinguishable from PrP$^C$ [42] but can be distinguished from PrP$^C$ by its partial resistance to proteolysis and its marked insolubility in detergents (for review, see Prusiner[2] and Riesner[11]). Under conditions in which PrP$^C$ exists as a detergent-soluble monomer and is completely degraded by the nonspecific protease proteinase K, PrP$^{Sc}$ exists in an aggregated form, with the C-terminal two-thirds of the protein showing marked resistance to proteolytic degradation, which lead to the generation of amino-terminus-truncated fragments of diglycosylated, monoglycosylated, and nonglycosylated PrP (Figs 1-2 and 1-3A). For a particular PrP$^{Sc}$ isoform, all three

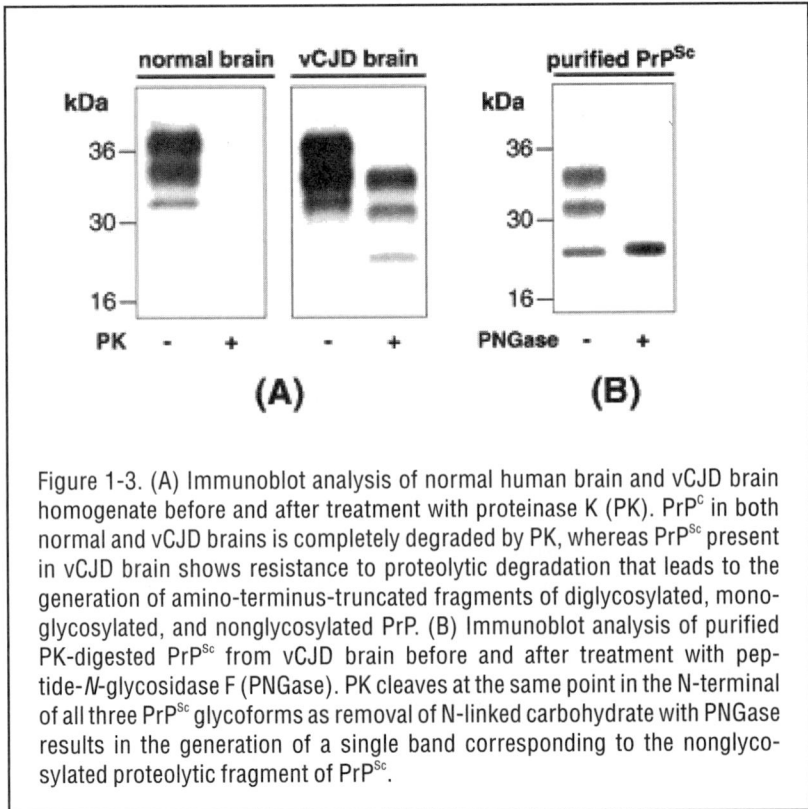

Figure 1-3. (A) Immunoblot analysis of normal human brain and vCJD brain homogenate before and after treatment with proteinase K (PK). PrP$^c$ in both normal and vCJD brains is completely degraded by PK, whereas PrP$^{Sc}$ present in vCJD brain shows resistance to proteolytic degradation that leads to the generation of amino-terminus-truncated fragments of diglycosylated, monoglycosylated, and nonglycosylated PrP. (B) Immunoblot analysis of purified PK-digested PrP$^{Sc}$ from vCJD brain before and after treatment with peptide-*N*-glycosidase F (PNGase). PK cleaves at the same point in the N-terminal of all three PrP$^{Sc}$ glycoforms as removal of N-linked carbohydrate with PNGase results in the generation of a single band corresponding to the nonglycosylated proteolytic fragment of PrP$^{Sc}$.

PrP[Sc] glycoforms show equivalent accessibility to proteinase K and are cleaved at the same point in the N-terminus of the protein (Fig 1-3B). There is no evidence for a specific prion-associated nucleic acid or other protein components,[2-4,11,41] but purified prion rods do contain an inert polysaccharide scaffold.[11,76]

Defining the precise molecular events that occur during the conversion of PrP[C] to the infectious isoform of PrP is of paramount importance, because this process is a prime target for therapeutic intervention. Direct in-vitro mixing experiments have been performed in an attempt to produce PrP[Sc].[77,78] In such experiments, PrP[Sc] is used in excess as a seed to convert PrP[C] to a protease-resistant form, designated PrP[Res]. Whereas there are many examples in the literature of conditions that generate PrP[Res],[77,79-81] historically, such reactions have not been able to show de novo production of prion infectivity.[78] Recently, however, a protein-misfolding cyclic amplification system[82] has shown substantial amplification of PrP[Res].[83] After serial cycles of amplification in which the seeding PrP[Sc] brain homogenate was diluted $10^{-20}$-fold, amplified PrP[Res] remained infectious, albeit with a specific infectivity considerably lower than that of the original hamster prion strain.[83] Despite the significance of this experiment, it does not constitute proof of the protein-only hypothesis, because brain homogenate, rather than purified PrP, was used as the substrate for amplification. Nevertheless, protein-misfolding cyclic amplification may provide the means for systematic investigation of whether the generation of an infectious PrP isoform requires additional, as yet unknown, cofactors for the acquisition of infectivity.[78] This method also provides a platform for the development of preclinical diagnostic tests for human and animal prion diseases.[84,85]

The difficulty of performing structural studies on native PrP[Sc] has led to attempts to produce soluble β-sheet-rich forms of recombinant PrP that may be amenable to NMR or crystallographic structure determination.[86-88] Conditions have been identified in which the PrP polypeptide can be converted between alternative folded conformations that are representative of $PrP^C$ and $PrP^{Sc}$. At neutral or basic pH, PrP adopts an α-helical fold representative of $PrP^C$, and this conformation is locked by the presence of the native disulphide bond. Upon reduction of the disulphide bond, $PrP^C$ rearranges to a predominantly β-sheet structure.[87] This alternative conformation, designated β-PrP, is only present at acidic pH with the $PrP^C$ conformation predominating at neutral pH. It is important that β-PrP shares overlapping properties with $PrP^{Sc}$, including partial resistance to proteolysis and a propensity to aggregate into fibrils.[87] This work suggests that β-PrP may be an intermediate on the pathway to formation of $PrP^{Sc}$, and the conditions required to form β-PrP may be relevant to the conditions $PrP^C$ would encounter within the cell during internalization and recycling. The low pH and reducing environment of the endosomal pathway would be a likely candidate and, although it remains to be shown, evidence implicates either late-endosome-like organelles or lysosomes as sites for $PrP^{Sc}$ replication.[89-92] Success in producing in experimental animals disease that can be serially propagated after inoculation with $PrP^{Sc}$-like forms derived from recombinant PrP would not only prove the protein-only hypothesis but would also provide an essential model by which the mechanism of prion propagation can be understood in molecular detail. In this regard, it was recently reported that intracerebral injection of a β-sheet-rich fibrillar preparation of amino-terminus-truncated recombinant mouse PrP (comprising residues 89 to 230) into mice overexpressing PrP with the same deletion caused neurologic disease after about 520 days.[93]

Whereas $Prnp^{o/o}$ mice are completely resistant to prion infection, reconstitution of such mice with PrP transgenes restores susceptibility to prion infection in a species-specific manner and allows a reverse genetics approach to study structure-function relationships in PrP (for review, see Weissmann and Flechsig[14] and Asante and Collinge[94]). Expression of PrP N-terminal deletion mutants to residue 106 is tolerated and supports prion propagation.[95,96] However, deletion beyond this leads to severe ataxia and neuronal loss in the granular cell layer of the cerebellum.[14,97] PrP in its entirety is unnecessary for prion propagation. Not only can the unstructured N-terminal 90 amino acids be deleted, but also the first α-helix, the second β-strand, and part of helix 2. In transgenic animals, a 106-amino-acid fragment of the protein comprising PrPΔ23-88Δ141-176 conferred susceptibility to and propagation of prions.[98,99]

## Prion Disease Pathology and Pathogenesis

Although the pathologic consequences of prion infection occur in the central nervous system (CNS), and although experimental transmission of these diseases is most efficiently accomplished by intracerebral inoculation, most natural infections do not occur by these means. Indeed, administration to sites other than the CNS is known to be associated with much longer incubation periods, which may extend to 20 years or more.[3,32] Experimental evidence suggests that this latent period is associated with clinically silent prion replication in lymphoreticular tissue, whereas neuroinvasion takes place later.[100-102] The M cells in the intestinal epithelium appear to mediate prion entry from the gastrointestinal lumen into the body,[103,104] and follicular dendritic cells (FDCs) are thought to be essential for prion replication and for the accumulation of disease-associated PrP^Sc within secondary lymphoid organs.[101,102,105] B-cell-deficient mice are resistant to intraperitoneal inoculation with prions,[106] probably because of their involvement with FDC maturation and maintenance.[102,105,107,108] However, neuroinvasion is possible without FDCs, which indicates that other types of peripheral cells can replicate prions.[109,110]

The interface between FDCs and sympathetic nerves represents a critical site for the transfer of lymphoid prions into the nervous system,[111,112] but the mechanism by which this is achieved remains unknown. Distinct forms of prion disease show differences in lymphoreticular involvement that may be related to the etiology of the disease or to divergent properties of distinct prion strains.[102] For example, the tissue distribution of PrP$^{Sc}$ in vCJD differs strikingly from that in classical CJD,[113-117] with uniform and prominent involvement of lymphoreticular tissues and with the highest amounts (up to 10% of brain concentrations) in tonsil[113,114] (Fig 1-4A,D). In contrast, in sCJD, PrP$^{Sc}$ has only been irregularly detected by immunoblotting in non-CNS tissues at much lower levels.[118] Tonsil biopsy is used for diagnosis of vCJD and, to date, has shown 100% sensitivity and specificity for diagnosis of vCJD at an early clinical stage[17,113,114]; moreover, tonsil is the tissue of choice for prospective studies investigating the prevalence of vCJD prion infection in the Uniked Kingdom and in other populations.[119,120]

The demonstration of extensive lymphoreticular involvement in the peripheral pathogenesis of vCJD raises concerns that iatrogenic transmission of vCJD prions through medical procedures may be a major public health issue.[3,17,117] Prions resist many conventional sterilization procedures, and surgical stainless steel-bound prions transmit disease with remarkable efficiency when implanted into mice.[121,122] Cases of transfusion-associated vCJD prion infection have also now been reported.[123,124] In contrast, there is no epidemiologic evidence of transmission of classical CJD via blood transfusion.[125,126]

The brains of patients or animals with prion disease frequently show no recognizable abnormalities on gross examination at necropsy, but microscopic examination of the CNS typically reveals characteristic histopathologic changes, consisting of neuronal vacuolation and degeneration, which give the cerebral gray matter a microvacuolated or "spongiform" appearance, and a reactive proliferation of astroglial cells (for review, see Budka et al[127] and Budka[128]). Although spongiform degeneration is frequently detected, it is not an obligatory neuropathologic feature of prion disease; astrocytic gliosis, although not specific to the prion diseases, is seen more often. The lack of an inflammatory response is also an important characteristic. Demonstration of abnormal PrP immunoreactivity—or, more specifically, biochemical detection of

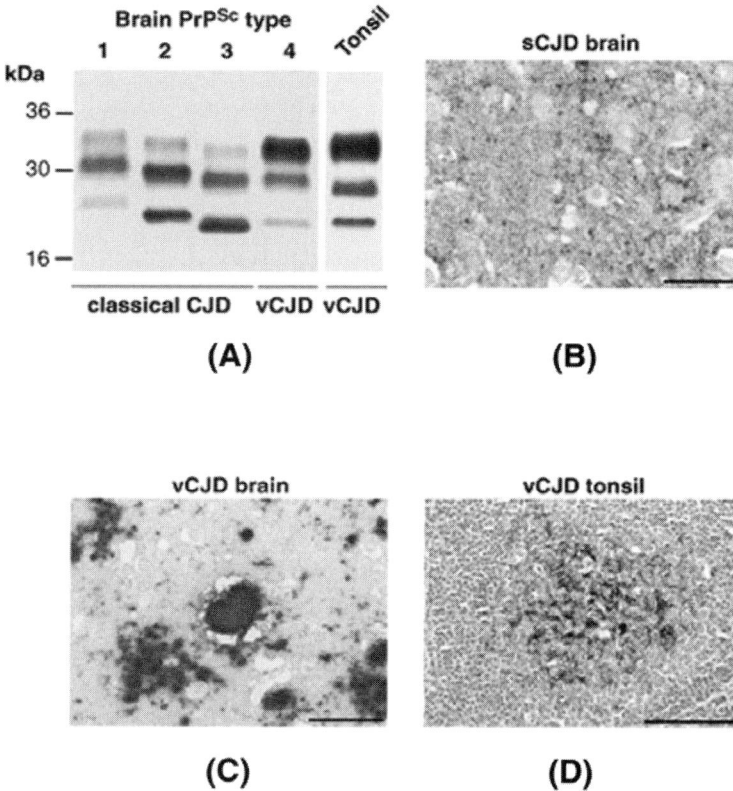

Figure 1-4. Characterization of disease-related prion protein in human prion disease. (A) Immunoblots of proteinase K-digested tissue homogenate with monoclonal antibody 3F4 showing PrP$^{Sc}$ types 1 to 4 in human brain and PrP$^{Sc}$ type 4t in vCJD tonsil. Types 1 to 3 PrP$^{Sc}$ are seen in the brain of classical forms of CJD (either sCJD or iatrogenic CJD), whereas types 4 and 4t PrP$^{Sc}$ are uniquely seen in vCJD brain or tonsil, respectively. Brain from patients with sCJD or vCJD show abnormal PrP immunoreactivity after immunohisto-chemistry analysis using an anti-PrP monoclonal antibody. Abnormal PrP deposition in sCJD brain most commonly presents as diffuse, synaptic staining (B), whereas vCJD brain is distinguished by the presence of florid PrP plaques consisting of a round amyloid core of PrP surrounded by a ring of spongiform vacuoles (C). (D) Tonsil from a vCJD patient showing abnormal PrP immuno-reactivity after immunohistochemistry analysis using an anti-PrP monoclonal antibody. Abnormal PrP immunoreactivity in vCJD tonsil is confined to lym-phatic follicles with deposition mainly in dendritic cells. Scale bars: B and C, 50 microns; D, 100 microns.

PrP$^{Sc}$ in brain material by immunoblotting techniques (Figs 1-3A, 1-4A)—is diagnostic of prion disease, and some forms of prion disease are characterized by deposition of amyloid plaques composed of insoluble aggregates of PrP.[127,128] Amyloid plaques are a notable feature of kuru and GSS,[127,129] but they are less frequently found in the brains of patients with sCJD, which typically show a diffuse pattern of abnormal PrP deposition[127,130] (Fig 1-4B). The histopathologic features of vCJD are remarkably consistent. They distinguish vCJD from other human prion diseases with large numbers of PrP-positive amyloid plaques that differ in morphology from the plaques seen in kuru and GSS in that, with vCJD, the surrounding tissue takes on a microvacuolated appearance, which gives the plaques a florid appearance[34,131] (Fig 1-4C). Abundant florid plaques are established as the neuropathologic hallmark of vCJD,[131] and, to date, they have been found only in association with BSE-derived prions in hosts with PrP M129 homozygosity (humans, primates, or transgenic mice[34,39,40,132]).

## Cell Death in Prion Disease

The precise structure of the infectious agent and the cause of neuronal cell death in prion disease remain unclear. The current working hypothesis is that an abnormal isoform of PrP is the infectious agent. To date, the most highly enriched preparations contain a large excess of PrP monomers per infectious unit,[41,133] but it is unclear whether only a single one of these PrP$^{Sc}$ molecules is actually infectious or whether PrP aggregates are necessary for infectivity.[134] However, the relationship of PrP$^{Sc}$ molecules to infectivity could merely relate to the rapid clearance of prions from the brain known to occur on intracerebral challenge.[12,13,41]

Various mechanisms have been proposed to explain neuronal death in prion disease (for review, see Mallucci and Collinge,[60] Brandner,[135] and Weissmann and Aguzzi[136]), which is thought to occur via an apoptotic mechanism.[137-139] In-vitro studies have suggested that both full-length PrP$^{Sc}$ [140,141] and shorter peptide fragments[142] are toxic when applied to primary cultured neurons. Other suggested mechanisms relate to altered PrP$^C$ trafficking.[51] It has been reported that PrP$^C$ may assume a transmembrane topology ($^{Ctm}$PrP) with a concentration suggested to correlate with neurotoxicity.[30,51] More recently, it was proposed that prion-associated toxicity involves altered trafficking of PrP$^C$, where inhibition of the ubiquitin-proteasome system (UPS) results in extensive PrP$^C$ accumulation in the cytoplasm and associated neuronal cell death.[143] However, the data are conflicting, and there is evidence both for and against the possibility that this cytoplasmic accumulation of PrP$^C$ has neurotoxic sequelae (for review, see Castilla et al[138] and Kristiansen et al[139]). Recently, however, it has been shown that prion propagation can invoke a neurotoxic mechanism involving intracellular formation of PrP$^{Sc}$ aggresome structures and that formation of these structures is associated with induction of caspase-mediated apoptosis.[139]

Whereas PrP$^C$ is absolutely required for prion propagation and neurotoxicity,[12] knockout of PrP$^C$ in adult brain[58] and embryonic models[144,145] has no overt phenotypic effect, which effectively excludes the loss of PrP$^C$ function in neurons as a significant mechanism in prion neurodegeneration.[60] Notably, there is also considerable evidence that PrP$^{Sc}$ and indeed prions (whether or not they are identical) may not themselves be highly neurotoxic. PrP$^C$-null tissue remains healthy and free of pathology when exposed to PrP$^{Sc}$,[59,146] and there is no direct correlation between neuronal loss and PrP$^{Sc}$ plaques in CJD brain.[147] Mice with reduced levels of PrP$^C$ expression have extremely high levels of PrP$^{Sc}$ and prions in the brain, and yet they remain well for several months after their wild-type counterparts have succumbed. Conversely, transgenic mice, which have high levels of murine PrP$^C$, have short incubation periods and yet produce low levels of PrP$^{Sc}$ after inoculation with mouse prions.[14] There are also reports of prion diseases in which PrP$^{Sc}$ is barely detectable.[37,148-150] The evidence that animals with subclinical prion infection can harbor high levels of prion infectivity and detectable PrP$^{Sc}$ without exhibiting any clinical signs of prion disease challenges our understanding of the pathogenic mechanisms involved in these diseases.[3,151-153]

On the basis of these collective data, it is possible to hypothesize that the neurotoxic prion molecule may not be $PrP^{Sc}$ itself but, rather, a toxic intermediate that is produced in the process of conversion of $PrP^C$ to $PrP^{Sc}$ and that $PrP^{Sc}$, which is present as highly aggregated material, is a relatively inert end-product.[3,60,153] The steady-state level of such a toxic monomeric or oligomeric PrP intermediate could determine the rate of neurodegeneration. Subclinical prion infection states may generate the toxic intermediate at extremely low levels that are below the threshold required for neurotoxicity.[3,153] Recently, direct support for this hypothesis has been shown by depleting endogenous neuronal $PrP^C$ in mice with established neuroinvasive prion infection. This depletion of $PrP^C$ reverses early spongiform change and prevents neuronal loss and progression to clinical prion disease, despite the accumulation of extraneuronal $PrP^{Sc}$ to levels seen in terminally ill wild-type mice.[59] These data establish that propagation of nonneuronal $PrP^{Sc}$ is not pathogenic but that arresting the continued conversion of $PrP^C$ to $PrP^{Sc}$ within neurons during scrapie infection prevents prion neurotoxicity. Notably, this model also validates $PrP^C$ as a key therapeutic target in prion disease.[60]

## The Molecular Basis of Prion Strain Diversity

A major problem with the protein-only hypothesis of prion propagation has been the explanation of the existence of multiple isolates, or strains, of prions. Prion strains are distinguished by their biologic properties: they produce distinct incubation periods and patterns of neuropathologic targeting (so-called lesion profiles) in defined inbred mouse lines (for review, see Bruce[154]). Because they can be serially propagated in inbred mice with the same *Prnp* genotype, they cannot be encoded by differences in PrP primary structure. Usually, distinct strains of conventional pathogen are explained by differences in their nucleic acid genome. However, in the absence of such a scrapie genome, alternative possibilities must be considered. Weissmann[155] proposed a "unified hypothesis" in which, although the protein alone was argued to be sufficient to account for infectivity, strain characteristics could be encoded by a small cellular nucleic acid, or "co-prion." Although this hypothesis leads to the testable prediction that strain characteristics, unlike infectivity, would be sensitive to ultraviolet irradiation, no such test has been reported. At the other extreme, the protein-only hypothesis would have to explain how a single polypeptide chain could encode multiple disease phenotypes.

Support for the contention that strain specificity may be encoded by PrP itself was provided by the study of two distinct strains of transmissible mink encephalopathy prions that can be serially propagated in hamsters, designated "hyper" and "drowsy." These strains can be distinguished by the differing physicochemical properties of the accumulated $PrP^{Sc}$ in the brains of affected hamsters. After limited proteolysis, strain-specific migration patterns of $PrP^{Sc}$ are seen on Western blots that relate to different N-terminal ends of $PrP^{Sc}$ after protease treatment, which imply differing conformations of $PrP^{Sc}$.[156] Distinct $PrP^{Sc}$ conformations are now recognized to be associated with other prion strains,[157,158] and, similarly, different human $PrP^{Sc}$ isoforms have been found to propagate in the brain of patients with phenotypically distinct forms of CJD.[35,56,130,147,157,159-162]

The different fragment sizes seen on Western blots after treatment with proteinase K suggest that there are several different human $PrP^{Sc}$ conformations [Fig 1-4(A)], referred to as molecular strain types. These types can be further classified by the ratio of the three PrP bands seen after protease digestion, corresponding to amino-terminus-truncated cleavage products generated from di-, mono-, or nonglycosylated $PrP^{Sc}$. Four types of human $PrP^{Sc}$ have been commonly identified by using molecular strain typing [3,17,35,130] (Fig 1-4A), although much greater heterogeneity seems likely.[17] Sporadic and iatrogenic CJD are associated with $PrP^{Sc}$ types 1 to 3, whereas type 4

$PrP^{Sc}$ is uniquely associated with vCJD and is characterized by a fragment size and glycoform ratio that are distinct from those of $PrP^{Sc}$ types 1 to 3 but similar to those of $PrP^{Sc}$ seen in BSE and BSE when transmitted to several other species. An earlier classification of $PrP^{Sc}$ types seen in classical CJD described only two banding patterns[147]: $PrP^{Sc}$ types 1 and 2 that the authors describe corresponded to the type 1 pattern described by Gambetti (Parchi et al[160,163]) and the authors' type 3 fragment size corresponded to Gambetti's type 2 pattern. Whereas type 4 $PrP^{Sc}$ is readily distinguished from the $PrP^{Sc}$ types seen in classical CJD by a predominance of the diglycosylated PrP glycoform, type 4 $PrP^{Sc}$ also has a distinct proteolytic fragment size,[130] although it is not recognized by the alternative classification that designates type 4 $PrP^{Sc}$ as type 2b.[163]

Efforts to produce a unified international classification and nomenclature of human $PrP^{Sc}$ types have been complicated by the fact that the N-terminal conformation of some $PrP^{Sc}$ subtypes seen in sCJD can be altered in vitro via changes in metal-ion occupancy[56,130] or solvent pH.[164,165] It was recently proposed that pH alone determines $PrP^{Sc}$ N-terminal structure,[165] but this interpretation has not been supported by other studies,[166,167] and strain-specific $PrP^{Sc}$ conformations show critical dependence upon the presence of copper or zinc ions under conditions in which pH 7.4 is strictly controlled.[56] Although agreement has yet to be reached on methodologic differences, nomenclature, and the biological importance of relatively subtle biochemical differences in $PrP^{Sc}$, there is strong agreement between laboratories that phenotypic diversity in human prion disease relates to the propagation of disease-related PrP isoforms with distinct physicochemical properties.[35,56,130,147,157,159-162] Polymorphism at PRNP residue 129 appears to dictate the propagation of distinct $PrP^{Sc}$ types in humans,[3,17] and it has now become clear that prion strain selection and the propagation of distinct $PrP^{Sc}$ types may also be crucially influenced by other genetic loci of the host genome.[39,168,169]

The hypothesis that alternative conformations or assembly states of PrP[Sc] provide the molecular substrate for clinico-pathological heterogeneity seen in human prion diseases (and that this relates to the existence of distinct human prion strains) has been strongly supported by transmission experiments in conventional and transgenic mice. Transgenic mice expressing only human PrP with either valine (V) or methionine (M) at residue 129 have shown that this polymorphism constrains both the propagation of distinct human PrP[Sc] conformers and the occurrence of associated patterns of neuropathology.[3,35,37,39,40] Biophysical measurements suggest that this powerful effect of residue 129 on prion strain selection is likely to be mediated via its effect on the conformation of PrP[Sc] or its precursors or on the kinetics of their formation, because it has no measurable effect on the folding, dynamics, or stability of PrP[C].[67] These data are consistent with a conformational selection model of prion transmission barriers[3,38,40,153] (see below) and strongly support the protein-only hypothesis of infectivity by suggesting that prion strain variation is encoded by a combination of PrP conformation and glycosylation.[3] These findings also provide a molecular basis for *PRNP* codon 129 as a major locus influencing both prion disease susceptibility and phenotype in humans.[3,23]

Notably, there appear to be no overlapping preferred PrP[Sc] conformations for V129 and M129 human PrP that can be generated as a result of exposure to the vCJD/BSE prion strain.[40] Depending on the origin of the inoculum and the PrP codon 129 genotype of the host, primary or secondary transmission of BSE-derived prions can result in four distinct prion disease phenotypes. Transgenic mice homozygous for human PrP M129 propagate either type 2 or 4 PrP[Sc] whose respective neuropathologies are consistent with human sCJD or vCJD,[39,40] whereas transgenic mice homozygous for human PrP V129 either propagate type 5 PrP[Sc] and a distinct pattern of neuropathology or develop clinical prion disease in the absence of detectable PrP[Sc].[37,40] Whereas caution must be exercised in extrapolating from animal models, even when faithful recapitulation of molecular and pathologic phenotypes is possible (Fig 1-5), these findings argue that primary human BSE prion infection and secondary infection with vCJD prions by iatrogenic routes may not be restricted to a single disease phenotype.

The identification of strain-specific $PrP^{Sc}$ structural properties now allows an etiology-based classification of human prion disease by typing of the infectious agent itself. Molecular strain typing of prion isolates is being applied in the molecular diagnosis of sCJD and vCJD and to produce a new classification of human prion diseases with implications for epidemiologic studies of the etiologies of sCJD and BSE-related human prion disease.[3,39,40] Stratification of all human prion disease cases by $PrP^{Sc}$ type will enable the rapid recognition of any change in relative frequencies of particular $PrP^{Sc}$ subtypes in relation to either BSE exposure patterns or iatrogenic

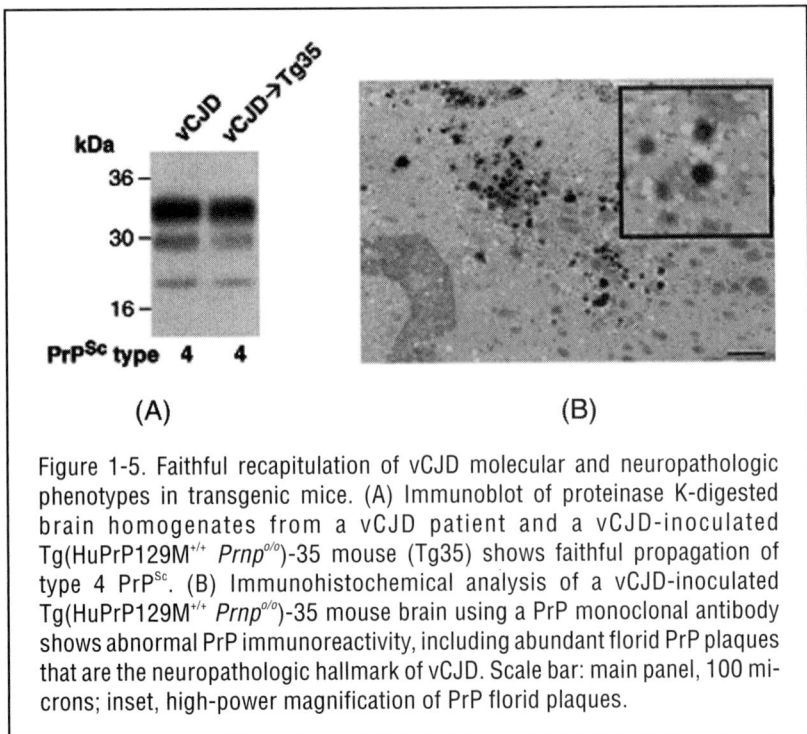

Figure 1-5. Faithful recapitulation of vCJD molecular and neuropathologic phenotypes in transgenic mice. (A) Immunoblot of proteinase K-digested brain homogenates from a vCJD patient and a vCJD-inoculated Tg(HuPrP129M$^{+/+}$ Prnp$^{o/o}$)-35 mouse (Tg35) shows faithful propagation of type 4 $PrP^{Sc}$. (B) Immunohistochemical analysis of a vCJD-inoculated Tg(HuPrP129M$^{+/+}$ Prnp$^{o/o}$)-35 mouse brain using a PrP monoclonal antibody shows abnormal PrP immunoreactivity, including abundant florid PrP plaques that are the neuropathologic hallmark of vCJD. Scale bar: main panel, 100 microns; inset, high-power magnification of PrP florid plaques.

sources of vCJD prions. Such methods allow strain typing to be performed in days rather than in the 1 to 2 years required for classic biologic strain typing. This technique may also be applicable in ascertaining whether BSE has been transmitted to other species and thereby poses a threat to human health.[3]

## A Conformational Selection Model of Prion Transmission Barriers

Prion transmission between species is limited by a species barrier that restricts transmission of prion disease between different mammalian species. On primary passage of prions from species A to species B, usually not all of the inoculated animals of species B develop disease, and those that do have much longer and more variable incubation periods than do those seen with transmission of prions within the same species. On second passage of infectivity to further animals of species B, the transmission parameters resemble within-species transmissions, in which most if not all animals develop the disease with short and consistent incubation periods. Therefore, species barriers can be quantified by measuring the shortening of the mean incubation period on primary and second passage, or, perhaps more rigorously, by a comparative titration study. The effect of a very substantial species barrier is that few, if any, animals succumb to clinical prion disease at all on primary passage or after incubation periods approaching the natural lifespan of the species concerned.[3,153]

Early studies of the molecular basis of the species barrier argued that it principally resided in differences in PrP primary structure between the species from which the inoculum was derived and the inoculated host. However, it has been clear for many years that the prion strain type also has a crucial effect on species barriers. For example, the natural transmission of BSE to a wide variety of hosts, and the subsequent demonstration that transmission of BSE from these different species (all with varied PrP primary amino acid sequences) to mice results in the maintenance of a "BSE-like" strain, provides a key example of where effects from a prion strain appear to be more important than PrP primary sequence homology to such barriers.[170] Similarly, after transmission to transgenic mice expressing only human PrP, there is disparity in the behavior of sCJD or vCJD prions that have originated in humans expressing wild-type PrP of identical primary sequence.[35,37,39] Whereas sCJD prions have transmission characteristics consistent with the complete absence of a species barrier, vCJD prions have transmission properties that are completely distinct from other human prions but closely similar to those of cattle BSE and consistent with the presence of a barrier.[3,37,39,40] The term "species barrier" does not seem appropriate to describe such effects, and the general term "transmission barrier" now seems preferable.[3,38,153]

Recent data have also further challenged our understanding of prion transmission barriers. The assessment of species barriers has historically relied on the development of a clinical disease in inoculated animals; however, during infection with prion diseases, infectious titers in the brain rise progressively throughout prolonged, clinically silent incubation periods. Therefore, asymptomatic animals can have significant infectious titers in the brain and other tissues. However, subclinical forms of prion infection that are distinct from preclinical forms, in which animals become asymptomatic carriers of infectivity and do not develop clinical disease during a normal lifespan, have now been recognized.[39,40,151,152,171] Such carrier states are well recognized in other infectious diseases, and these data indicate that current definitions of transmission barriers (conventionally assessed on the basis of occurrence of clinical disease in inoculated animals) must be reassessed.[3,153] Subclinical or carrier states of prion disease have major implications for public health, most notably with respect to iatrogenic transmission from apparently healthy persons.

The conformational selection model of prion transmission barriers encompasses contributions from both PrP sequence and strain-specific $PrP^{Sc}$ structural properties.[3,38,153] Both PrP amino acid sequence and strain type will affect the three-dimensional structure of glycosylated PrP, which will presumably, in turn, affect the efficiency of the protein–protein interactions thought to determine prion propagation. Mammalian PrP genes are highly conserved, and presumably only a restricted number of different $PrP^{Sc}$ conformations (that are highly stable and can therefore be serially propagated) will be permissible thermodynamically and will constitute the range of prion strains seen. PrP glycosylation may be important in stabilizing particular $PrP^{Sc}$ conformations. Whereas a significant number of different $PrP^{Sc}$ conformations may be possible among the range of mammalian PrPs, only a subset of these conformations would be allowable for any given single mammalian PrP sequence. Substantial overlap between the favored conformations for $PrP^{Sc}$ derived from species A and species B may result in relatively easy transmission of prion diseases between these two species, whereas two species with no preferred $PrP^{Sc}$ conformations in common would have a large barrier to transmission (and, indeed, transmission would necessitate a change of strain type). According to such a model of a prion transmission barrier, BSE may represent a thermodynamically highly favored $PrP^{Sc}$ conformation that is permissive for PrP expressed in a wide range of different species and that may account for the remarkable promiscuity of this strain in mammals.[3,38,153] The transmission properties of the BSE/vCJD prion strain in transgenic mice expressing human PrP with either valine or methionine at residue 129 can be readily interpreted within the conformational selection model,[40] and this model has recently been supported by work with yeast prions.[172,173] Contributions of other components to the species barrier are possible and may involve interacting cofactors that mediate the efficiency of prion propagation,[174] although no such factors have yet been convincingly identified.[78]

## Future Perspective

The novel pathogenic mechanisms involved in prion propagation are likely to be of wider significance and may be relevant to other neurologic and nonneurologic illnesses; indeed, other prion-like mechanisms have been described, and the field of yeast and fungal prions has emerged.[175-177] A number of advances in understanding prion neurodegeneration are already casting considerable light on related mechanisms in other, more common neurodegenerative diseases such as Alzheimer's, Parkinson's, and Huntington's diseases. Intriguingly, misfolding and aggregation of proteins seem to be central themes in neurodegenerative disease. Whereas the protein-only hypothesis of prion propagation is supported by compelling experimental data and appears able to encompass the phenomenon of prion strain diversity, the goal of systematically producing prions in vitro remains unreached. Success in producing disease in experimental animals that can be serially propagated after inoculation with $PrP^{Sc}$-like forms derived from recombinant PrP not only would prove the protein-only hypothesis but also would provide an essential model by which the mechanism of prion propagation can be understood in molecular detail. The molecular characterization of the transmissible agent and the development of prion-specific molecular markers, together with the development of a blood-based presymptomatic diagnostic test, will be extremely challenging, but such advances are essential to the management of this serious public health concern.

# References

1. Collinge J. Molecular neurology of prion disease. J Neurol Neurosurg Psychiatry 2005;76:906-19.
2. Prusiner SB. Prions. Proc Natl Acad Sci U S A 1998;95:13363-83.
3. Collinge J. Prion diseases of humans and animals: Their causes and molecular basis. Annu Rev Neurosci 2001;24:519-50.
4. Weissmann C. The state of the prion. Nat Rev Microbiol 2004;2: 861-71.
5. Alper T, Cramp WA, Haig DA, Clarke MC. Does the agent of scrapie replicate without nucleic acid? Nature 1967;214:764-6.
6. Griffith JS. Self replication and scrapie. Nature 1967;215:1043-4.
7. Prusiner SB. Novel proteinaceous infectious particles cause scrapie. Science 1982;216:136-44.

8. Oesch B, Westaway D, Walchli M, et al. A cellular gene encodes scrapie PrP 27-30 protein. Cell 1985;40:735-46.

9. Chesebro B, Race R, Wehrly K, et al. Identification of scrapie prion protein-specific mRNA in scrapie-infected and uninfected brain. Nature 1985;315:331-3.

10. Basler K, Oesch B, Scott M, et al. Scrapie and cellular PrP isoforms are encoded by the same chromosomal gene. Cell 1986;46:417-28.

11. Riesner D. Biochemistry and structure of $PrP^C$ and $PrP^{Sc}$. Br Med Bull 2003;66:21-33.

12. Bueler H, Aguzzi A, Sailer A, et al. Mice devoid of PrP are resistant to scrapie. Cell 1993;73:1339-47.

13. Sailer A, Bueler H, Fischer M, et al. No propagation of prions in mice devoid of PrP. Cell 1994;77:967-8.

14. Weissmann C, Flechsig E. PrP knock-out and PrP transgenic mice in prion research. Br Med Bull 2003;66:43-60.

15. Collinge J. Human prion diseases and bovine spongiform encephalopathy (BSE). Hum Mol Genet 1997;6:1699-705.

16. Collinge J, Palmer MS. Prion diseases. Oxford, UK: Oxford University Press, 1997.

17. Wadsworth JD, Hill AF, Beck JA, Collinge J. Molecular and clinical classification of human prion disease. Br Med Bull 2003;66:241-54.

18. Brown P, Cathala F, Raubertas RF, et al. The epidemiology of Creutzfeldt-Jakob disease: Conclusion of a 15-year investigation in France and review of the world literature. Neurology 1987;37:895-904.

19. Collinge J, Palmer MS, Dryden AJ. Genetic predisposition to iatrogenic Creutzfeldt-Jakob disease. Lancet 1991;337:1441-2.

20. Palmer MS, Dryden AJ, Hughes JT, Collinge J. Homozygous prion protein genotype predisposes to sporadic Creutzfeldt-Jakob disease. Nature 1991;352:340-2.

21. Windl O, Dempster M, Estibeiro JP, et al. Genetic basis of Creutzfeldt-Jakob disease in the United Kingdom: A systematic analysis of predisposing mutations and allelic variation in the PRNP gene. Hum Genet 1996;98:259-64.

22. Lee HS, Brown P, Cervenáková L, et al. Increased susceptibility to kuru of carriers of the PRNP 129 methionine/methionine genotype. J Infect Dis 2001;183:192-6.

23. Mead S, Stumpf MP, Whitfield J, et al. Balancing selection at the prion protein gene consistent with prehistoric kuru-like epidemics. Science 2003;300:640-3.

24. Mead S, Mahal SP, Beck J, et al. Sporadic—but not variant—Creutzfeldt-Jakob disease is associated with polymorphisms upstream of PRNP exon 1. Am J Hum Genet 2001;69:1225-35.

25. Kovacs GG, Trabattoni G, Hainfellner JA, et al. Mutations of the prion protein gene; phenotypic spectrum. J Neurol 2002;249:1567-82.

26. Riek R, Wider G, Billeter M, et al. Prion protein NMR structure and familial human spongiform encephalopathies. Proc Natl Acad Sci U S A 1998;95:11667-72.

27. Swietnicki W, Petersen RB, Gambetti P, Surewicz WK. Familial mutations and the thermodynamic stability of the recombinant human prion protein. J Biol Chem 1998;273:31048-52.
28. Liemann S, Glockshuber R. Influence of amino acid substitutions related to inherited human prion diseases on the thermodynamic stability of the cellular prion protein. Biochemistry 1999;38:3258-67.
29. Muramoto T, DeArmond SJ, Scott M, et al. Heritable disorder resembling neuronal storage disease in mice expressing prion protein with deletion of an α-helix. Nat Med 1997;3:750-5.
30. Hegde RS, Mastrianni JA, Scott MR, et al. A transmembrane from of the prion protein in neurodegenerative disease. Science 1998;279:827-34.
31. Brown P, Preece MA, Will RG. "Friendly fire" in medicine: Hormones, homografts, and Creutzfeldt-Jakob disease. Lancet 1992;340: 24-7.
32. Brown P, Preece M, Brandel JP, et al. Iatrogenic Creutzfeldt-Jakob disease at the millennium. Neurology 2000;55:1075-81.
33. Alpers MP. Epidemiology and clinical aspects of kuru. In: Prusiner SB, McKinley MP, eds. Prions: Novel infectious pathogens causing scrapie and Creutzfeldt-Jakob disease. San Diego: Academic Press, 1987:451-65.
34. Will RG, Ironside JW, Zeidler M, et al. A new variant of Creutzfeldt-Jakob disease in the UK. Lancet 1996;347:921-5.
35. Collinge J, Sidle KCL, Meads J, et al. Molecular analysis of prion strain variation and the aetiology of "new variant" CJD. Nature 1996;383:685-90.
36. Bruce ME, Will RG, Ironside JW, et al. Transmissions to mice indicate that "new variant" CJD is caused by the BSE agent. Nature 1997;389:498-501.
37. Hill AF, Desbruslais M, Joiner S, et al. The same prion strain causes vCJD and BSE. Nature 1997;389:448-50.
38. Collinge J. Variant Creutzfeldt-Jakob disease. Lancet 1999;354:317-23.
39. Asante EA, Linehan JM, Desbruslais M, et al. BSE prions propagate as either variant CJD-like or sporadic CJD-like prion strains in transgenic mice expressing human prion protein. EMBO J 2002;21:6358-66.
40. Wadsworth JD, Asante EA, Desbruslais M, et al. Human prion protein with valine 129 prevents expression of variant CJD phenotype. Science 2004;306:1793-6.
41. Safar JG, Kellings K, Serban A, et al. Search for a prion-specific nucleic acid. J Virol 2005;79:10796-806.
42. Stahl N, Baldwin MA, Teplow DB, et al. Structural studies of the scrapie prion protein using mass spectrometry and amino acid sequencing. Biochemistry 1993;32:1991-2002.
43. Wopfner F, Weidenhöfer G, Schneider R, et al. Analysis of 27 mammalian and 9 avian PrPs reveals high conservation of flexible regions of the prion protein. J Mol Biol 1999;289:1163-78.

44. Windl O, Dempster M, Estibeiro P, Lathe R. A candidate marsupial *PrP* gene reveals two domains conserved in mammalian PrP proteins. Gene 1995;159:181-6.
45. Calzolai L, Lysek DA, Perez DR, et al. Prion protein NMR structures of chickens, turtles, and frogs. Proc Natl Acad Sci U S A 2005;102: 651-5.
46. Cotto E, Andre M, Forgue J, et al. Molecular characterization, phylogenetic relationships, and developmental expression patterns of prion genes in zebrafish (*Danio rerio*). FEBS J 2005;272:500-13.
47. Manson J, West JD, Thomson V, et al. The prion protein gene: A role in mouse embryogenesis? Development 1992;115:117-22.
48. Dodelet VC, Cashman NR. Prion protein expression in human leukocyte differentiation. Blood 1998;91:1556-61.
49. Shyng S-L, Heuser JE, Harris DA. A glycolipid-anchored prion protein is endocytosed via clathrin-coated pits. J Cell Biol 1994;125: 1239-50.
50. Peters PJ, Mironov A Jr, Peretz D, et al. Trafficking of prion proteins through a caveolae-mediated endosomal pathway. J Cell Biol 2003; 162:703-17.
51. Harris DA. Trafficking, turnover and membrane topology of PrP. Br Med Bull 2003;66:71-85.
52. Stahl N, Baldwin MA, Hecker R, et al. Glycosylinositol phospholipid anchors of the scrapie and cellular prion proteins contain sialic acid. Biochemistry 1992;50:43-53.
53. Lasmezas CI. Putative functions of PrP$^C$. Br Med Bull 2003;66:61-70.
54. Solforosi L, Criado JR, McGavern DB, et al. Cross-linking cellular prion protein triggers neuronal apoptosis in vivo. Science 2004;303: 1514-6.
55. Pauly PC, Harris DA. Copper stimulates endocytosis of the prion protein. J Biol Chem 1998;273:33107-10.
56. Wadsworth JDF, Hill AF, Joiner S, et al. Strain-specific prion-protein conformation determined by metal ions. Nat Cell Biol 1999;1:55-9.
57. Bush AI. Metals and neuroscience. Curr Opin Chem Biol 2000;4: 184-91.
58. Mallucci GR, Ratté S, Asante EA, et al. Post-natal knockout of prion protein alters hippocampal CA1 properties, but does not result in neurodegeneration. EMBO J 2002;21:202-10.
59. Mallucci G, Dickinson A, Linehan J, et al. Depleting neuronal PrP in prion infection prevents disease and reverses spongiosis. Science 2003;302:871-4.
60. Mallucci G, Collinge J. Rational targeting for prion therapeutics. Nat Rev Neurosci 2005;6:23-34.
61. Riek R, Hornemann S, Wider G, et al. NMR structure of the mouse prion protein domain PrP (121-231). Nature 1996;382:180-2.
62. James TL, Liu H, Ulyanov NB, et al. Solution structure of a 142-residue recombinant prion protein corresponding to the infectious frag-

ment of the scrapie isoform. Proc Natl Acad Sci U S A 1997;94: 10086-91.

63. Lysek DA, Schorn C, Nivon LG, et al. Prion protein NMR structures of cats, dogs, pigs, and sheep. Proc Natl Acad Sci U S A 2005;102: 640-5.

64. Gossert AD, Bonjour S, Lysek DA, et al. Prion protein NMR structures of elk and of mouse/elk hybrids. Proc Natl Acad Sci U S A 2005;102: 646-50.

65. Zahn R, Liu AZ, Lührs T, et al. NMR solution structure of the human prion protein. Proc Natl Acad Sci U S A 2000;97:145-50.

66. Hosszu LLP, Baxter NJ, Jackson GS, et al. Structural mobility of the human prion protein probed by backbone hydrogen exchange. Nat Struct Biol 1999;6:740-3.

67. Hosszu LL, Jackson GS, Trevitt CR, et al. The residue 129 polymorphism in human prion protein does not confer susceptibility to CJD by altering the structure or global stability of $PrP^C$. J Biol Chem 2004;279:28515-21.

68. Wuthrich K, Riek R. Three-dimensional structures of prion proteins. Adv Protein Chem 2001;57:55-82.

69. Knaus KJ, Morillas M, Swietnicki W, et al. Crystal structure of the human prion protein reveals a mechanism for oligomerization. Nat Struct Biol 2001;8:770-4.

70. Haire LF, Whyte SM, Vasisht N, et al. The crystal structure of the globular domain of sheep prion protein. J Mol Biol 2004;336:1175-83.

71. Jackson GS, Murray I, Hosszu LLP, et al. Location and properties of metal-binding sites on the human prion protein. Proc Natl Acad Sci U S A 2001;98:8531-5.

72. Wildegger G, Liemann S, Glockshuber R. Extremely rapid folding of the C-terminal domain of the prion protein without kinetic intermediates. Nat Struct Biol 1999;6:550-3.

73. Jackson GS, Clarke AR. Mammalian prion proteins. Curr Opin Struct Biol 2000;10:69-74.

74. Pan K-M, Baldwin MA, Nguyen J, et al. Conversion of alpha-helices into beta-sheets features in the formation of the scrapie prion proteins. Proc Natl Acad Sci U S A 1993;90:10962-6.

75. Caughey B, Raymond GJ, Bessen RA. Strain-dependent differences in beta-sheet conformations of abnormal prion protein. J Biol Chem 1998;273:32230-5.

76. Appel TR, Dumpitak C, Matthiesen U, Riesner D. Prion rods contain an inert polysaccharide scaffold. Biol Chem 1999;380:1295-306.

77. Kocisko DA, Come JH, Priola SA, et al. Cell-free formation of protease-resistant prion protein. Nature 1994;370:471-4.

78. Caughey B. Prion protein conversions: Insight into mechanisms, TSE transmission barriers and strains. Br Med Bull 2003;66:109-20.

79. Bessen RA, Kocisko DA, Raymond GJ, et al. Non-genetic propagation of strain-specific properties of scrapie prion protein. Nature 1995;375: 698-700.

80. Raymond GJ, Hope J, Kocisko DA, et al. Molecular assessment of the potential transmissibilities of BSE and scrapie to humans. Nature 1997;388:285-8.

81. Hill AF, Antoniou M, Collinge J. Protease-resistant prion protein produced in vitro lacks detectable infectivity. J Gen Virol 1999;80:11-4.

82. Saborio GP, Permanne B, Soto C. Sensitive detection of pathological prion protein by cyclic amplification of protein misfolding. Nature 2001;411:810-3.

83. Castilla J, Saa P, Hetz C, Soto C. In vitro generation of infectious scrapie prions. Cell 2005;121:195-206.

84. Soto C. Diagnosing prion diseases: Needs, challenges and hopes. Nat Rev Microbiol 2004;2:809-19.

85. Castilla J, Saa P, Soto C. Detection of prions in blood. Nat Med 2005;11:982-5.

86. Hornemann S, Glockshuber R. A scrapie-like unfolding intermediate of the prion protein domain PrP(121-231) induced by acidic pH. Proc Natl Acad Sci U S A 1998;95:6010-4.

87. Jackson GS, Hosszu LLP, Power A, et al. Reversible conversion of monomeric human prion protein between native and fibrilogenic conformations. Science 1999;283:1935-7.

88. Bocharova OV, Breydo L, Parfenov AS, et al. In vitro conversion of full-length mammalian prion protein produces amyloid form with physical properties of PrP$^{Sc}$. J Mol Biol 2005;346:645-59.

89. Arnold JE, Tipler C, Laszlo L, et al. The abnormal isoform of the prion protein accumulates in late-endosome-like organelles in scrapie-infected mouse brain. J Pathol 1995;176:403-11.

90. Mayer RJ, Landon M, Laszlo L, et al. Protein processing in lysosomes: The new therapeutic target in neurodegenerative disease. Lancet 1992;340:156-9.

91. Taraboulos A, Raeber A, Borchelt DR, et al. Synthesis and trafficking of prion proteins in cultured cells. Mol Biol Cell 1992;3:851-63.

92. Laszlo L, Lowe J, Self T, et al. Lysosomes as key organelles in the pathogenesis of prion encephalopathies. J Pathol 1992;166:333-41.

93. Legname G, Baskakov IV, Nguyen HO, et al. Synthetic mammalian prions. Science 2004;305:673-6.

94. Asante E, Collinge J. Transgenic studies of the influence of the PrP structure on TSE diseases. Advances in protein chemistry. San Diego: Academic Press, 2000:273-311.

95. Fischer M, Rulicke T, Raeber A, et al. Prion protein (PrP) with amino-proximal deletions restoring susceptibility of PrP knockout mice to scrapie. EMBO J 1996;15:1255-64.

96. Flechsig E, Shmerling D, Hegyi I, et al. Prion protein devoid of the octapeptide repeat region restores susceptibility to scrapie in PrP knockout mice. Neuron 2000;27:399-408.

97. Shmerling D, Hegyi I, Fischer M, et al. Expression of amino-terminally truncated PrP in the mouse leading to ataxia and specific cerebellar lesions. Cell 1998;93:203-14.

98. Muramoto T, Scott M, Cohen FE, Prusiner SB. Recombinant scrapie-like prion protein of 106 amino acids is soluble. Proc Natl Acad Sci U S A 1996;93:15457-62.

99. Supattapone S, Bosque P, Muramoto T, et al. Prion protein of 106 residues creates an artificial transmission barrier for prion replication in transgenic mice. Cell 1999;96:869-78.

100. Kimberlin RH, Walker CA. Pathogenesis of experimental scrapie. Ciba Found Symp 1988;135:37-62.

101. Fraser H, Bruce ME, Davies D, et al. The lymphoreticular system in the pathogenesis of scrapie. In: Prusiner SB, Collinge J, Powell J, Anderton B, eds. Prion diseases of humans and animals. London, UK: Ellis Horwood, 1992:308-17.

102. Aguzzi A. Prions and the immune system: A journey through gut, spleen, and nerves. Adv Immunol 2003;81:123-71.

103. Heppner FL, Christ AD, Klein MA, et al. Transepithelial prion transport by M cells. Nat Med 2001;7:976-7.

104. Ghosh S. Mechanism of intestinal entry of infectious prion protein in the pathogenesis of variant Creutzfeldt-Jakob disease. Adv Drug Deliv Rev 2004;56:915-20.

105. Mabbott N, Turner M. Prions and the blood and immune systems. Haematologica 2005;90:542-8.

106. Klein MA, Frigg R, Flechsig E, et al. A crucial role for B cells in neuroinvasive scrapie. Nature 1997;390:687-90.

107. Klein M, Frigg R, Raeber A, et al. PrP expression in B-lymphocytes is not required for prion neuroinvasion. Nat Med 1998;4:1429-33.

108. Mabbott NA, Young J, McConnell I, Bruce ME. Follicular dendritic cell dedifferentiation by treatment with an inhibitor of the lymphotoxin pathway dramatically reduces scrapie susceptibility. J Virol 2003;77:6845-54.

109. Prinz M, Montrasio F, Klein MA, et al. Lymph nodal prion replication and neuroinvasion in mice devoid of follicular dendritic cells. Proc Natl Acad Sci U S A 2002;99:919-24.

110. Oldstone MB, Race R, Thomas D, et al. Lymphotoxin-alpha- and lymphotoxin-beta-deficient mice differ in susceptibility to scrapie: Evidence against dendritic cell involvement in neuroinvasion. J Virol 2002;76:4357-63.

111. Mabbott NA, Bruce ME. Prion disease: Bridging the spleen-nerve gap. Nat Med 2003;9:1463-4.

112. Prinz M, Heikenwalder M, Junt T, et al. Positioning of follicular dendritic cells within the spleen controls prion neuroinvasion. Nature 2003;425:957-62.

113. Hill AF, Butterworth RJ, Joiner S, et al. Investigation of variant Creutzfeldt-Jakob disease and other human prion diseases with tonsil biopsy samples. Lancet 1999;353:183-9.

114. Wadsworth JDF, Joiner S, Hill AF, et al. Tissue distribution of protease resistant prion protein in variant CJD using a highly sensitive immuno-blotting assay. Lancet 2001;358:171-80.

115. Hilton DA, Sutak J, Smith ME, et al. Specificity of lymphoreticular accumulation of prion protein for variant Creutzfeldt-Jakob disease. J Clin Pathol 2004;57:300-2.

116. Head MW, Ritchie D, Smith N, et al. Peripheral tissue involvement in sporadic, iatrogenic, and variant Creutzfeldt-Jakob disease: An immunohistochemical, quantitative, and biochemical study. Am J Pathol 2004;64:143-53.

117. Joiner S, Linehan JM, Brandner S, et al. High levels of disease related prion protein in the ileum in variant Creutzfeldt-Jakob disease. Gut 2005;54:1506-8.

118. Glatzel M, Abela E, Maissen M, Aguzzi A. Extraneural pathologic prion protein in sporadic Creutzfeldt-Jakob disease. N Engl J Med 2003;349:1812-20.

119. Hilton DA, Ghani AC, Conyers L, et al. Prevalence of lymphoreticular prion protein accumulation in UK tissue samples. J Pathol 2004;203:733-9.

120. Frosh A, Smith LC, Jackson CJ, et al. Analysis of 2000 consecutive UK tonsillectomy specimens for disease-related prion protein. Lancet 2004;364:1260-2.

121. Flechsig E, Hegyi I, Enari M, et al. Transmission of scrapie by steel-surface-bound prions. Mol Med 2001;7:679-84.

122. Jackson GS, McKintosh E, Flechsig E, et al. An enzyme-detergent method for effective prion decontamination of surgical steel. J Gen Virol 2005;86:869-78.

123. Llewelyn CA, Hewitt PE, Knight RS, et al. Possible transmission of variant Creutzfeldt-Jakob disease by blood transfusion. Lancet 2004; 363:417-21.

124. Peden AH, Head MW, Ritchie DL, et al. Preclinical vCJD after blood transfusion in a PRNP codon 129 heterozygous patient. Lancet 2004; 364:527-9.

125. Esmonde TFG, Will RG, Slattery JM, et al. Creutzfeldt-Jakob disease and blood transfusion. Lancet 1993;341:205-7.

126. Wilson K, Code C, Ricketts MN. Risk of acquiring Creutzfeldt-Jakob disease from blood transfusions: Systematic review of case-control studies. Br Med J 2000;321:17-9.

127. Budka H, Aguzzi A, Brown P, et al. Neuropathological diagnostic criteria for Creutzfeldt-Jakob disease (CJD) and other human spongiform encephalopathies (prion diseases). Brain Pathol 1995;5:459-66.

128. Budka H. Neuropathology of prion diseases. Br Med Bull 2003;66: 121-30.

129. Hainfellner JA, Brantner-Inthaler S, Cervenáková L, et al. The original Gerstmann-Sträussler-Scheinker family of Austria: Divergent clinicopathological phenotypes but constant PrP genotype. Brain Pathol 1995;5:201-11.

130. Hill AF, Joiner S, Wadsworth JD, et al. Molecular classification of sporadic Creutzfeldt-Jakob disease. Brain 2003;126:1333-46.

131. Ironside JW, Head MW. Neuropathology and molecular biology of variant Creutzfeldt-Jakob disease. Curr Top Microbiol Immunol 2004; 284:133-59.

132. Lasmezas CI, Fournier JG, Nouvel V, et al. Adaptation of the bovine spongiform encephalopathy agent to primates and comparison with Creutzfeldt-Jakob disease: Implications for human health. Proc Natl Acad Sci U S A 2001;98:4142-7.

133. Prusiner SB, McKinley MP, Bowman K, et al. Scrapie prions aggregate to form amyloid-like birefringent rods. Cell 1983;35:349-58.

134. Silveira JR, Raymond GJ, Hughson AG, et al. The most infectious prion protein particles. Nature 2005;437:257-61.

135. Brandner S. CNS pathogenesis of prion diseases. Br Med Bull 2003;66: 131-9.

136. Weissmann C, Aguzzi A. Approaches to therapy of prion diseases. Annu Rev Med 2005;56:321-44.

137. Cronier S, Laude H, Peyrin JM. Prions can infect primary cultured neurons and astrocytes and promote neuronal cell death. Proc Natl Acad Sci U S A 2004;101:12271-6.

138. Castilla J, Hetz C, Soto C. Molecular mechanisms of neurotoxicity of pathological prion protein. Curr Mol Med 2004;4:397-403.

139. Kristiansen M, Messenger MJ, Klohn PC, et al. Disease-related prion protein forms aggresomes in neuronal cells leading to caspase-activation and apoptosis. J Biol Chem 2005;280:38851-61.

140. Muller WE, Ushijima H, Schroder HC, et al. Cytoprotective effect of NMDA receptor antagonists on prion protein (Prion$^{Sc}$)-induced toxicity in rat cortical cell cultures. Eur J Pharmacol 1993;246:261-7.

141. Hetz C, Russelakis-Carneiro M, Maundrell K, et al. Caspase-12 and endoplasmic reticulum stress mediate neurotoxicity of pathological prion protein. EMBO J 2003;22:5435-45.

142. Forloni G, Angeretti N, Chiesa R, et al. Neurotoxicity of a prion protein fragment. Nature 1993;362:543-6.

143. Ma J, Lindquist S. Conversion of PrP to a self-perpetuating PrP$^{Sc}$-like conformation in the cytosol. Science 2002;298:1785-8.

144. Bueler H, Fischer M, Lang Y, et al. Normal development and behaviour of mice lacking the neuronal cell-surface PrP protein. Nature 1992;356:577-82.

145. Manson JC, Clarke AR, Hooper ML, et al. 129/Ola mice carrying a null mutation in PrP that abolishes mRNA production are developmentally normal. Mol Neurobiol 1994;8:121-7.

146. Brandner S, Isenmann S, Raeber A, et al. Normal host prion protein necessary for scrapie-induced neurotoxicity. Nature 1996;379:339-43.

147. Parchi P, Castellani R, Capellari S, et al. Molecular basis of phenotypic variability in sporadic Creutzfeldt-Jakob disease. Ann Neurol 1996;39:767-78.

148. Collinge J, Palmer MS, Sidle KCL, et al. Transmission of fatal familial insomnia to laboratory animals. Lancet 1995;346:569-70.

149. Medori R, Montagna P, Tritschler HJ, et al. Fatal familial insomnia: A second kindred with mutation of prion protein gene at codon 178. Neurology 1992;42:669-70.

150. Lasmezas CI, Deslys J-P, Robain O, et al. Transmission of the BSE agent to mice in the absence of detectable abnormal prion protein. Science 1997;275:402-5.

151. Hill AF, Joiner S, Linehan J, et al. Species barrier independent prion replication in apparently resistant species. Proc Natl Acad Sci U S A 2000;97:10248-53.

152. Race R, Raines A, Raymond GJ, et al. Long-term subclinical carrier state precedes scrapie replication and adaptation in a resistant species: Analogies to bovine spongiform encephalopathy and variant Creutzfeldt-Jakob disease in humans. J Virol 2001;75:10106-12.

153. Hill AF, Collinge J. Subclinical prion infection. Trends Microbiol 2003;11:578-84.

154. Bruce ME. TSE strain variation. Br Med Bull 2003;66:99-108.

155. Weissmann C. A "unified theory" of prion propagation. Nature 1991; 352:679-83.

156. Bessen RA, Marsh RF. Distinct PrP properties suggest the molecular basis of strain variation in transmissible mink encephalopathy. J Virol 1994;68:7859-68.

157. Telling GC, Parchi P, DeArmond SJ, et al. Evidence for the conformation of the pathologic isoform of the prion protein enciphering and propagating prion diversity. Science 1996;274:2079-82.

158. Safar J, Wille H, Itri V, et al. Eight prion strains have PrP$^{Sc}$ molecules with different conformations. Nat Med 1998;4:1157-65.

159. Gambetti P, Kong Q, Zou W, et al. Sporadic and familial CJD: Classification and characterisation. Br Med Bull 2003;66:213-39.

160. Parchi P, Giese A, Capellari S, et al. Classification of sporadic Creutzfeldt-Jakob disease based on molecular and phenotypic analysis of 300 subjects. Ann Neurol 1999;46:224-33.

161. Zanusso G, Farinazzo A, Prelli F, et al. Identification of distinct N-terminal truncated forms of prion protein in different Creutzfeldt-Jakob disease subtypes. J Biol Chem 2004;279:38936-42.

162. Parchi P, Zou WQ, Wang W, et al. Genetic influence on the structural variations of the abnormal prion protein. Proc Natl Acad Sci U S A 2000;97:10168-72.

163. Parchi P, Capellari S, Chen SG, et al. Typing prion isoforms. Nature 1997;386:232-3.

164. Zanusso G, Farinazzo A, Fiorini M, et al. pH-dependent prion protein conformation in classical Creutzfeldt-Jakob disease. J Biol Chem 2001;276:40377-80.

165. Notari S, Capellari S, Giese A, et al. Effects of different experimental conditions on the PrP$^{Sc}$ core generated by protease digestion: Implications for strain typing and molecular classification of CJD. J Biol Chem 2004;279:16797-804.

166. Lewis V, Hill AF, Klug GM, et al. Australian sporadic CJD analysis supports endogenous determinants of molecular-clinical profiles. Neurology 2005;65:113-8.

167. Polymenidou M, Stoeck K, Glatzel M, et al. Coexistence of multiple PrP$^{Sc}$ types in individuals with Creutzfeldt-Jakob disease. Lancet Neurol 2005;4:805-14.

168. Stephenson DA, Chiotti K, Ebeling C, et al. Quantitative trait loci affecting prion incubation time in mice. Genomics 2000;69:47-53.

169. Lloyd SE, Onwuazor ON, Beck JA, et al. Identification of multiple quantitative trait loci linked to prion disease incubation period in mice. Proc Natl Acad Sci U S A 2001;98:6279-83.

170. Bruce M, Chree A, McConnell I, et al. Transmission of bovine spongiform encephalopathy and scrapie to mice: Strain variation and the species barrier. Philos Trans R Soc Lond Biol 1994;343:405-11.

171. Thackray AM, Klein MA, Aguzzi A, Bujdoso R. Chronic subclinical prion disease induced by low-dose inoculum. J Virol 2002;76:2510-7.

172. King CY, Diaz-Avalos R. Protein-only transmission of three yeast prion strains. Nature 2004;428:319-23.

173. Tanaka M, Chien P, Yonekura K, Weissman JS. Mechanism of cross-species prion transmission an infectious conformation compatible with two highly divergent yeast prion proteins. Cell 2005;121:49-62.

174. Telling GC, Scott M, Mastrianni J, et al. Prion propagation in mice expressing human and chimeric PrP transgenes implicates the interaction of cellular PrP with another protein. Cell 1995;83:79-90.

175. Wickner RB, Edskes HK, Ross ED, et al. Prion genetics: New rules for a new kind of gene. Annu Rev Genet 2004;38:681-707.

176. Chien P, Weissman JS, DePace AH. Emerging principles of conformation-based prion inheritance. Annu Rev Biochem 2004;73:617-56.

177. Shorter J, Lindquist S. Prions as adaptive conduits of memory and inheritance. Nat Rev Genet 2005;6:435-50.

In: Turner ML, ed.
*Creutzfeldt-Jakob Disease: Managing the Risk of*
*Transmission by Blood, Plasma, and Tissues*
Bethesda, MD: AABB Press, 2006

# 2

# Pathogenesis of Peripherally Transmitted Transmissible Spongiform Encephalopathies

MOIRA E. BRUCE, BSC, PHD

TRANSMISSIBLE SPONGIFORM encephalopathies (TSEs or prion diseases) may be acquired by dietary, environmental, or iatrogenic exposure to infection. For example, the bovine spongiform encephalopathy (BSE) epidemic was almost certainly maintained by the consumption by cattle of contaminated meat and bone meal.[1] BSE subsequently spread to several other animal species and to humans (as variant Creutzfeldt-Jakob disease or vCJD), probably also by a dietary route.[2,3] Recently, there have been three probable secondary human-to-human transmissions of vCJD by blood transfusion.[4-6] Furthermore, there have been several instances of iatrogenic transmission of sporadic CJD (sCJD) in humans, which were associated with the injection of contami-

*Moira E. Bruce, BSc, PhD, Head of Pathology and Pathogenesis Section, Institute for Animal Health, Neuropathogenesis Unit, Edinburgh, United Kingdom*

nated pharmaceuticals.[7] To assess the risks of further infections by these routes, to underpin approaches to diagnosis, and to develop strategies for prevention and treatment, it is important to understand the pathogenesis of TSE disease after such peripheral exposures.

## TSE Agent Accumulation in Lymphoid Tissues

The major sites of accumulation of TSE agents outside the central nervous system (CNS) are the spleen, lymph nodes, and other secondary lymphoid tissues. However, a prominent lymphoid involvement is seen in only some of the naturally occurring TSEs: in many sheep with natural scrapie,[8,9] in deer with chronic wasting disease,[10] and in patients with vCJD.[11,12] In other TSEs, such as BSE in cattle[13] and sCJD or iatrogenically transmitted sCJD in humans,[12] there is little, if any, involvement of the lymphoid or other nonnervous tissues. The reasons for these differences are not understood, but the differences are likely to depend on the strain of TSE, genetic factors in the host, the route of infection, and the level of exposure to infection. The practical implication for the human TSEs is that the wide tissue distribution of infectivity in vCJD is likely to present greater risks for iatrogenic spread than exist for sCJD. Because a prominent lymphoid involvement is seen in experimental rodent TSEs[14] and in sheep experimentally infected with BSE,[15,16] these models can be used to understand the risks of iatrogenic spread that are associated with blood transfusion, tissue transplantation, and contaminated surgical instruments.

Most of our basic understanding of the pathogenesis of TSEs has come from experimental studies of scrapie isolates in rodents. These studies have shown that the intravenous route of infection is only about ten times less efficient than direct intracerebral injection.[17] Infection can also be transmitted readily but somewhat less efficiently by intraperitoneal injection and less efficiently still via the skin or gastrointestinal tract. After TSE infection by any of these peripheral routes, the infectious agent usually replicates and accumulates in the lymphoid tissues at an early stage, long before it spreads to the brain and causes neurologic disease.[14] In these models, there is typically a rapid replication phase in the lymphoid tissues over the first few weeks, up to a plateau level that is maintained throughout the remainder of the long incubation period. The length of this incubation period is controlled by the strain of the TSE agent and the host prion protein (PrP) genotype,[18] together with the dose and route of infection. In some models, the asymptomatic phase can extend beyond the natural life span of the animal.[19] Infection of the lymphoid tissues and, later, the nervous system is accompanied by the accumulation of abnormally folded, relatively protease-resistant forms of PrP.[20] Therefore, the presence of this "pathologic" PrP is widely used as a marker for TSE infection in peripheral tissues.

For vCJD in humans, detection of pathologic PrP gives evidence of a widespread lymphoid tissue infection at the end stage of disease,[12,21] and this involvement has been substantiated directly for spleen and tonsil by bioassay in mice.[11] Moreover, abnormal accumulations of PrP have been detected in appendix samples surgically removed from two patients who went on to develop clinical vCJD 8 months or 2 years later.[22,23] Further evidence of preclinical vCJD infection of lymphoid tissues has come from a survey of anonymized, surgically removed appendix and tonsil samples, in which 3 of about 13,000 samples showed pathologic PrP accumulations.[24] These observations suggest that, as in the rodent models, vCJD infectivity is widespread in lymphoid tissues long before patients show any clinical signs of disease and that there is the potential for iatrogenic spread of infection from these apparently healthy individuals.

Rodent TSE models have been used for many years to study the details of pathogenesis after peripheral exposure to infection by tracking the progress of the infection from its site of entry into the animal to its ultimate targets in the CNS. Many of these studies have focused on the significance of the replication phase in the lymphoid tissues and on the identification of the lymphoid cells involved in acquiring and maintaining infection. Early studies established that genetic asplenia or splenectomy performed before a peripheral TSE injection substantially extended the incubation period. This shows, first, that lymphoid tissues are relevant to overall disease progression and, second, that the quickest route from the periphery to the CNS is via the spleen, at least in some models.[25] Later studies that began to explore the involvement of lymphoid cell populations showed that whole-body γ-radiation doses that would ablate short-lived marrow-derived cells had no effect on either agent replication in the spleen or the incubation period leading up to clinical disease.[26] This finding implies that pathogenesis depends on long-lived, radiation- resistant cells and effectively excludes a critical role for most lymphocyte and myeloid cell populations.

## Normal and Pathologic PrP in Lymphoid Tissues

In the lymphoid tissues of mice experimentally infected with TSEs, pathologic PrP accumulation is seen prominently in discrete areas of the lymphoid follicles, which correspond exactly to the sites occupied by follicular dendritic cells (FDCs) and their processes.[27,28] This pattern of pathologic PrP deposition is also seen in experimental sheep BSE,[16] in natural sheep scrapie,[29] and in vCJD in humans,[12] giving us confidence that the mouse and sheep TSEs are valid experimental models for vCJD lymphoid infection. Another reason for suspecting a role for FDCs in TSE pathogenesis is that high levels of the normal form of PrP can be detected on networks of FDC processes in uninfected mice.[28,30] Studies in transgenic "PrP knockout" mice in which the PrP gene has been disrupted, completely preventing the production of the protein, have shown that expression of PrP is required for an animal to be susceptible to TSE infection.[31] It therefore follows that the cells in the spleen most likely to support scrapie replication in ordinary mice are those expressing PrP. However, although FDCs are strong candidates, other cell types in the lymphoid tissues (eg, lymphocytes and dendritic cells) have also been shown to express normal PrP.[32-34] Furthermore, pathologic PrP accumulates in macrophages as well as on FDC networks in the lymphoid follicles of scrapie-infected mice.[35] Therefore, the presence of normal and abnormal PrP on FDCs does not necessarily mean that these cells are producing the protein, because they could be retaining and concentrating PrP produced by other cell types.

Following on from these observations, a series of studies has strongly supported a central role for FDCs in pathogenesis. FDCs, unlike many other cells of the lymphoid system, are long-lived, resistant to γ-radiation, and not replaced from the marrow.[36] The availability of PrP knockout mice therefore made it possible to produce radiation chimeras by marrow grafting between PrP-expressing and PrP-deficient mice.[30] In these chimeric mice, there is a PrP genetic mismatch between FDCs and marrow-derived cells such as lymphocytes, macrophages, and dendritic cells. In these models, normal PrP was seen on FDCs only in mice in which the FDCs themselves carried a PrP gene. It was not seen on FDCs in mice with PrP-deficient FDCs, even in the presence of marrow-derived cell populations expressing PrP. Furthermore, when these PrP-chimeric mice were challenged with scrapie, replication in the spleen depended only on the PrP genetic status of the FDCs and not on whether marrow-derived cells were expressing PrP.[30] These observations strongly suggest that FDCs themselves produce normal PrP and are the site of scrapie replication in the spleen, although the results do not rule out a role for other cell types that are not of marrow origin, such as peripheral nerves and stromal cells.

## Role of FDCs in Lymphoid Tissue Infection

Further evidence that FDCs themselves are critical in pathogenesis has come from studies in mice that are deficient in

FDCs as a result of spontaneous genetic defects or transgenic manipulations. These models depend on the fact that FDC precursors, resident in the lymphoid tissues, require signals produced by lymphocytes, in particular B cells, to mature into fully functional FDCs.[37] Therefore, any mouse lacking these maturation signals or their receptors will also lack FDCs. The first studies of this type were in mice with severe combined immunodeficiency (SCID), in which there is a spontaneous mutation that leads to a lack of both B and T lymphocytes; as a secondary result of the B-cell deficiency, these mice also lack FDCs.[38] When injected peripherally with scrapie, SCID mice failed to accumulate the infective agent in their spleens; consequently, they were relatively resistant to infection.[39-41] Marrow transplants from immunocompetent normal or PrP knockout mice restored lymphocyte populations, led to maturation of FDCs, and made the mice fully susceptible to scrapie.[30,39,40]

Later studies exploited a series of transgenic mouse lines lacking specific immune system cells to define the separate roles of lymphocytes and FDCs in TSE pathogenesis. These studies showed that mice specifically deficient in T cells are fully susceptible to peripherally injected scrapie,[42] an observation which confirmed the conclusions of an earlier study in neonatally thymectomized mice.[25] However, transgenic mice lacking B cells and, indirectly, FDCs are relatively resistant.[42] To separate the roles of B cells and FDCs, scrapie susceptibility has been studied in transgenic mice that have normal B-lymphocyte populations but that are deficient in FDCs as a result of disruption of the maturation signaling between B cells and FDCs. Tumor necrosis factor α (TNFα) and membrane lymphotoxin (LTαβ) are produced by B cells and are recognized by FDCs or their precursors via specific cell surface receptors.[43,44] In the absence of either of these cytokines or their receptors, FDCs fail to mature. The accumulation of TSE agents in the spleens of transgenic mice with such deficiencies is indeed impaired, and the mice are relatively resistant to TSE infection and have a slower disease course.[30,45-48] These observations again implicate FDCs as critical cells in pathogenesis in a range of models. However, the studies also suggest that, for certain TSE strains, other cell types may support lymphoid replication and/or neuroinvasion in the absence of FDCs.[46,47]

## Effects of Temporary Ablation of FDCs

Temporary disruption of signaling via TNFα or LTαβ can also be achieved by treating mice with soluble forms of their respective receptors, in the form of the fusion proteins huTNFR:Fc or LTβR-Ig.[49,50] Treatment with either of these reagents results in the rapid disappearance of FDC markers, including normal PrP. The duration of FDC depletion is about 2 weeks for huTNFR:Fc and more than a month for LTβR-Ig. Treatment of mice with either reagent shortly before an intraperitoneal scrapie injection significantly delayed the onset of neurologic disease.[51-53] However, as would be expected from its more prolonged effect on FDCs, LTβR-Ig had the more profound effect, which led to a marked reduction in susceptibility to infection, a delay in the accumulation of infectivity and pathologic PrP in the spleen, and a dramatic extension of the incubation period of the disease.[51,53,54] As well as providing further evidence for the importance of FDCs, the latter treatment can be used to investigate the timing of FDC involvement after scrapie exposure by different routes.

Treatment of mice with a single dose of LTβR-Ig as late as 6 weeks after an intraperitoneal scrapie injection led to a significant extension of the incubation period, implying that FDCs continue to make some contribution to pathogenesis for several weeks after injection.[51] In contrast, although a single LTβR-Ig injection 3 days before oral scrapie exposure completely protected the mice from infection, treatment 2 weeks after exposure had absolutely no effect.[54] This shows that FDCs are required for infection to be established in the animal after oral exposure but also that they are critical for only a very short time. The implication is that infectivity spreads rapidly to a cell type that is insensitive to LTβR-Ig treatment, such as neurons of the peripheral or enteric nervous systems. LTβR-Ig treatment also impaired pathogenesis in mice infected with scrapie via scarified skin, showing an effect at 2 weeks but not at 6 weeks after exposure.[55] In summary, these studies show that FDCs are critical after scrapie exposure by different peripheral routes, but the length of time they remain critical differs according to the route. Therefore, if FDCs are to be regarded as a target for postexposure prophylactic treatment, the treatment window is likely to differ according to the route of exposure.

## Mechanism of FDC Infection

The consensus of the above studies, which used a range of approaches in several different rodent TSE models, is that FDCs are likely to be a major site of TSE agent replication and accumulation in the lymphoid tissues. This conclusion raises the question of how these cells may become infected. The normal function of FDCs is to trap and retain intact circulating antigens and to present them to B lymphocytes in the course of the maturation of antibody responses. Antigens, in the form of immune complexes with antibody and/or complement, are trapped on the FDC surface via complement or antibody receptors.[56] Scrapie infection of spleen has been found to be impaired in transgenic mice lacking complement components or their receptors, an observation which suggests that it is the complement-dependent antigen-trapping mechanism that facilitates infection of FDCs.[57,58] On the other hand, deficiencies in antibodies or their receptors had no effect on scrapie pathogenesis.[57]

It therefore appears that TSE agents may exploit a normal function of FDCs to target infectivity to a cell surface environment that is rich in normal PrP. Interaction between an infective agent and normal PrP on the FDC cell surface may be the critical event in the infection of these cells. Indeed, electron microscopy studies showed that pathologic PrP accumulates extracellularly between FDC processes, within the complex glomerular structures that are formed when these cells are activated.[35] This is exactly the site of long-term retention of antigens. Moreover, as the glomerular structures of FDCs appear to be hyperplastic in mice with end-stage scrapie, long-term infection of lymphoid tissues may have some pathologic effects on FDC function.[35,59] Despite the intimate association of pathologic PrP accumulation with cells that support antibody responses, no specific immune response to an ongoing TSE infection has ever been detected.

## Uptake and Transport of Infectivity

The involvement of FDCs in pathogenesis appears to be reasonably well understood, but far less is known about how infection is taken up at a body surface and transported to the lymphoid tissues. Because TSEs are often transmitted by a dietary route, interest has focused on the early events after experimental oral challenge. Evidence for infection is seen first in the lymphoid tissues associated with the gut (the Peyer's patches and draining mesenteric lymph nodes) and later throughout the lymphoid system.[10,60,61] There are a number of mechanisms by which macromolecules are taken into the body from the gut lumen. M cells reside in the gut epithelium overlying the Peyer's patches and are specialized to sample and transport antigens from the gut lumen across the epithelium, although they may also take up enteric pathogens.[62] There is evidence from a cell culture model that M cells are able to transport TSE agent, and that is certainly a potential mechanism for uptake in vivo.[63] Indeed, pathologic PrP has been observed within M cells in hamsters after oral scrapie infection.[60] However, antigens may also be taken up directly by gut dendritic cells or in a cell-free manner, and these mechanisms might also be relevant for TSE uptake.

Once infectivity has crossed the gut epithelium, it is most likely that it is transported to the Peyer's patches and to the draining lymph nodes by dendritic cells, because other ingested antigens are transported by these cells. Unlike FDCs, which are stroma-derived nonmigratory cells, dendritic cells are derived from the marrow and are highly mobile. They circulate through the tissues and fluids, sampling antigens and delivering them to the lymphoid tissues.[63] It has been shown that a subset of migratory dendritic cells in the lymph can transport disease-specific PrP from the intestine to the draining lymph nodes,[65] but there is no definitive evidence yet that this capability is relevant for disease progression.

The role of dendritic cells in the uptake of infectivity through the skin has also been investigated. Langerhans cells are a subset of dendritic cells in the epidermis that take up antigen and transport it to the draining lymph node.[64] The application of a drop of scrapie brain homogenate on lightly scarified skin is surprisingly effective in transmitting infection to mice, and it has been shown that transmission by this route depends on a functional immune system.[66,67] Infection becomes established in the draining lymph node before spreading throughout the lymphoid system.[68] To test whether Langerhans cells are involved in the uptake and transport of scrapie to the lymph node, mice with an impaired migration of Langerhans cells from the epidermis were exposed to scrapie by this route. These models involved either permanent inhibition of migration in CD40 ligand knockout mice[69] or temporary impairment by treatment with a caspase-1 inhibitor.[70] Surprisingly, there was no reduction in either scrapie susceptibility or accumulation of infectivity in the draining lymph node in these models.[68] Even more surprisingly, the incubation period of the disease was significantly shorter in CD40 ligand-deficient mice than in wild-type mice. These results suggest that Langerhans cells are not involved in the transport of infectivity to the lymph nodes, but that, instead, they may reduce the effectiveness of infection via the skin by degrading infectivity or by clearing infectivity from the epidermis. However, it remains possible that other dendritic cell subtypes transport infectivity or that transport occurs by a cell-free mechanism.

The effectiveness of a peripheral exposure in establishing infection in an animal is likely to depend on a balance between the degradation or sequestration of infective agent from the inoculum and its effective delivery to initial replication sites. As indicated above, there is in-vivo evidence that certain types of dendritic cells participate in the degradation of infectivity. This is supported by cell culture studies, which showed that a cell line isolated from mouse epidermis and having the characteristics of mature Langerhans cells can take up and degrade scrapie infectivity in vitro.[68,71] Similar in-vitro studies have shown that macrophages can also gradually inactivate scrapie agent.[72] Moreover, evidence for a role for macrophages in the clearance of infectivity in vivo has come from studies using a treatment that depletes macrophages (dichloromethylene diphosphonate). When treated and untreated mice were peripherally injected with scrapie, more of the inoculum was initially detected in the spleens of the treated mice and replication was accelerated.[73] Macrophages also appear to take up and sequester pathologic PrP (and possibly associated infectivity) later in the disease process, because accumulations of this protein in infected spleens are seen within the lysosomes of tingible body macrophages, as well as on FDC networks.[35] This interplay between the degradation of infectivity and the transport to replication sites could well account for the differences in efficiency observed between the various peripheral routes.

## Spread of Infectivity Between Lymphoid Organs

The transition from a localized infection of the Peyer's patches or draining lymph nodes to a generalized infection of the lymphoid tissues is likely to involve spread via the bloodstream, merely because this is the most plausible explanation for such a rapid dissemination of infectivity. Indeed, low levels of infectivity have been detected in buffy coat and plasma in rodent TSE models, both preclinically and at the end stage of the disease.[74-76] Infection has also been transmitted to sheep by transfusion of whole blood or buffy coat from clinically or preclinically infected sheep with experimental BSE or natural scrapie.[77,78] The source of infectivity in blood is not known, but it is likely to be infected lymphoid tissues, at least in the early stages of the disease. FDCs themselves are fixed in the lymphoid tissues but may release infectivity to be taken up by other lymphoid cells, such as lymphocytes and dendritic cells, that circulate in the bloodstream. There is also the possibility that infectivity is released into the bloodstream in a cell-free form, directly from infected cells or from cells that are passively transporting the infection.

Various cell types, including dendritic cells and B lymphocytes, release membranous vesicles called exosomes, which are derived from endosomes and which carry cell-specific proteins.[79] Recently, it was shown that both pathologic PrP and infectivity are associated with exosomes released by a scrapie-infected cell line,[80] suggesting a potential mechanism for the in-vivo spread of infection between cells. As FDCs can bind exosomes released from other cell types on their surface,[81] an attractive speculation is that TSE infection spreads to the FDC surface in these membrane-associated forms. FDCs themselves are not thought to produce exosomes, but it has been suggested that they shed parts of their cell membranes that carry immune complexes (called iccosomes), which are then taken up by B cells.[82] Again, this may be a mechanism by which infectivity spreads to mobile cells within the lymphoid tissues, which are able to export infectivity into the bloodstream. Similarly, the release and uptake of membrane-associated infectivity could be relevant to the infection of the peripheral nervous system (PNS).

## Spread of Infectivity to the Nervous System

Although the spread of infectivity between lymphoid tissues is likely to occur via the bloodstream, there is no evidence that blood-borne infection is directly involved in the spread to the CNS. In fact, there is convincing evidence that invasion of the CNS from the lymphoid tissues occurs mainly, if not entirely, via the PNS. Early work using a mouse scrapie model indicated that infectivity spreads from the spleen and other viscera via the sympathetic fibers of the splanchnic nerve to the thoracic spinal cord and then to the brain.[83] Confirmation that sympathetic neural pathways are involved came from studies in which chemical or immunologic sympathectomy, conducted in mice before peripheral scrapie infection, prevented or delayed neuroinvasion.[84] Conversely, neuroinvasion was accelerated in transgenic mice in which the lymphoid organs were hyperinnervated.[84] Further work in orally infected hamsters, using the accumulation of pathologic PrP as a marker for infection, also confirmed that the splanchnic route is important but showed that TSE infection can gain access to the CNS via other nerves, such as the vagus.[85,86] Furthermore, tracking PrP accumulation in these neural pathways at intervals through the incubation period showed that spread was most likely to occur via the efferent fibers.[87] A similar pattern of spread has been observed in time-course studies of natural scrapie in sheep, suggesting a pathogenesis similar to that in the rodent models.[61] Pathologic PrP has been detected in the peripheral nerve ganglia of patients with vCJD[88] and of patients with sporadic, iatrogenic, and familial forms of human TSEs.[89] However, the presence of pathologic PrP in the PNS at the end stage of disease is not necessarily indicative of neural spread from the periphery. Late in the disease process, it is possible that infection spreads centrifugally from the CNS to the PNS, as has been suggested in a mouse scrapie model.[90]

The above observations raise the question of how infection spreads to the peripheral nerves. The immediate environment of FDCs in the lymphoid follicles of the spleen and lymph nodes is not well innervated, so there is a missing link between the lymphoid and peripheral nervous elements of pathogenesis. A recent study showed that scrapie neuroinvasion was accelerated in transgenic mice with an abnormal spleen architecture, in which the FDCs and nerves were closer together than those in normal mice.[91] This finding suggests that infection does indeed spread from the FDC surface to the nerves and may also offer an explanation for the apparently rapid spread of infection to the nervous system after oral scrapie challenge (see above). The gut is extremely well innervated, and the enteric ganglia and nerve fibers lie in close apposition to the FDCs of the Peyer's patches, perhaps providing a shortcut for TSE neuroinvasion.[60] This suggestion is supported by the early accumulation of pathologic PrP in the enteric nervous system of hamsters orally infected with scrapie.[60] It is not clear whether the transfer of infectivity from FDCs to nerves involves simple cell-free diffusion or whether other cell types such as lymphocytes or dendritic cells are involved. A study in mice lacking FDCs showed scrapie transmission by peripheral injection of isolated spleen dendritic cells from an infected donor, suggesting that dendritic cells might be able to transfer infectivity to the nervous system.[92] Transmission to mice lacking FDCs can also be achieved by peripheral injection of high doses of infectious agent (generally much higher doses than would usually be encountered in a "natural" exposure).[39,45] Under these circumstances, the need for a lymphoid replication phase appears to be bypassed, possibly because there is direct infection of nerve endings.

## Implications for Iatrogenic Spread and Prophylactic Treatments

An outline of TSE pathogenesis after peripheral exposure is given above, but, in reality, there are deviations from this general scheme. As already noted, there is no prominent lymphoid involvement in BSE or in sporadic CJD and associated iatrogenic cases, although restricted BSE infectivity has been detected in a small number of lymphoid tissues in experimentally infected cattle.[93,94] Even within the mouse models, there are differences between scrapie strains in the degrees of lymphotropism and neurotropism and, possibly, of cell targeting within the lymphoid tissues. Furthermore, infectivity and/or pathologic PrP can sometimes be detected in a range of peripheral sites other than the major lymphoid organs and peripheral nerve ganglia. It has been shown experimentally in mice that a generalized lymphoid TSE infection can spread to ectopic lymphoid follicles that are associated with chronic inflammation in tissues such as kidney, pancreas, and liver.[95] Moreover, pathologic PrP accumulation has been observed in the mammary glands of scrapie-infected sheep with mastitis.[96] It is also possible that, in the later stages of the disease, TSE infection can spread centrifugally from the CNS via peripheral nerves to peripheral tissues. Indeed, in rodent TSE models, pathologic PrP and low levels of infectivity have been detected in skeletal muscle and tongue—the pattern of PrP deposition that was seen suggests the spread of infection to these tissues via their innervation.[97-99] Pathologic PrP has also been detected in the muscles of patients with sCJD in the absence of widespread infection of the lymphoid tissues[100] and in the muscles of sheep with natural scrapie at a preclinical stage of the disease.[101] Therefore, although the major risks of iatrogenic spread of vCJD are likely to be associated with nervous and lymphoid tissues and blood, under some circumstances, other tissues may present a low but significant risk.

An understanding of the role of lymphoid tissues in pathogenesis also highlights possible risk factors in exposed people. The fact that immune system manipulations in experimental models can profoundly influence susceptibility to infection and the progression of the disease suggests that similar effects could operate in the naturally occurring diseases. It has been known for many years that nonspecific immune stimulation by mitogens, such as phytohemagglutinin, which is extracted from beans, can increase susceptibility to an experimental peripheral TSE challenge.[102] Conversely, some other compounds of plant origin, such as pentosan polysulphate and carrageenan, have been shown to reduce susceptibility.[103,104] It is therefore possible that components of the diet might influence whether a person becomes infected when exposed to low levels of TSE agents. It is striking that vCJD has occurred predominantly in young adults, and one possible explanation is that an age-related decline in immune function leads to a reduced susceptibility in older people.[105] It is already known that developmental factors in the lymphoid tissues influence scrapie susceptibility in mice; thus, newborn mice are approximately one-tenth as susceptible to peripheral infection as are adults.[106,107] The increase in susceptibility over the first 10 days of life correlates with the maturation of FDCs and the first appearance of normal PrP in the lymphoid tissues.[106] However, it remains to be seen whether the senescence of FDCs is associated with a decline in susceptibility in experimentally challenged old animals.

The early stages of pathogenesis after peripheral TSE exposure present a series of potential targets for postexposure prophylactic treatment. Treatments that specifically ablate FDCs or alter their function have been shown to reduce disease incidence in rodent models when administered up to a few weeks after a peripheral TSE infection.[51,53,57,58] However, the window of effectiveness can be very narrow after TSE exposure by some routes (see above). Several other compounds have been shown to reduce the disease incidence and/or to slow disease progression,[108] but specific FDC-targeted interventions are generally most effective when applied shortly before or after TSE exposure. Once infection has spread to the CNS, the disease becomes much more intractable. An effective treatment may block TSE replication directly at the molecular level, or it may target cells or body systems involved in the replication, degradation, or transport of infectivity. Whatever the mechanism of action, an appreciation of the details of pathogenesis underpins the development of new approaches to treatment and informs the most effective application (timing, delivery, etc) of known potential treatments.

## Conclusion

In recent years, great progress has been made in understanding the details of TSE pathogenesis. Studies using a range of experimental approaches, mostly in rodent models, have implicated FDCs of the lymphoid follicles as key cells in pathogenesis. These cells have a number of features in common with neurons, in that they are long-lived, highly structured cells that are associated with high levels of normal PrP in uninfected animals. The FDC, as part of its function, also has the ability to trap foreign antigens and even intact viruses on its surface. Therefore, it is likely to provide an environment in which relatively low levels of TSE infectivity, acquired by a peripheral route, can be concentrated in a PrP-rich setting to trigger an active infection of the animal. Once this has happened, the normal mechanisms of antigen exchange between FDCs and other lymphoid cell types are likely to facilitate the spread of infection throughout the lymphoid system, most probably via the bloodstream. Although hematogenous spread to the nervous system cannot be ruled out, it is most likely that infection spreads to the CNS via the peripheral innervation of the lymphoid tissues. Many steps in this sequence, in particular the mechanisms of cell-to-cell transfer, are not yet understood. An understanding of the whole series of events will help us to assess the risks of iatrogenic and food-borne transmission, provide potential targets for intervention, and reveal the possibilities and limitations of diagnostic approaches.

# References

1. Wilesmith JW. An epidemiologist's view of bovine spongiform encephalopathy. Phil Trans R Soc Lond B 1994;343:357-61.
2. Nathanson N, Wilesmith J, Wells GA, Griot C. Bovine spongiform encephalopathy and related diseases. In: Prusiner SB, ed. Prion biology and diseases. Woodbury, NY: Cold Spring Harbor Laboratory Press, 1999:431-63.
3. Will RG, Ironside JW, Zeidler M, et al. A new variant of Creutzfeldt-Jakob disease in the UK. Lancet 1996;347:921-5.
4. Llewelyn CA, Hewitt PE, Knight RSG, et al. Possible transmission of variant Creutzfeldt-Jakob disease by blood transfusion. Lancet 2004; 363:417-21.
5. Peden AH, Head MW, Ritchie DL, et al. Preclinical vCJD after blood transfusion in a PRNP codon 129 heterozygous patient. Lancet 2004; 364:527-9.
6. Health Protection Agency. New case of transfusion-associated variant CJD. Communicable Disease Report Weekly 2006;16:2.

7. Will RG, Alpers MP, Dormont D, et al. Infectious and sporadic prion diseases. In: Prusiner SB, ed. Prion biology and diseases. Woodbury, NY: Cold Spring Harbor Laboratory Press, 1999:465-507.

8. Hadlow WJ, Kennedy RC, Race RE. Natural infection of Suffolk sheep with scrapie virus. J Infect Dis 1982;146:657-64.

9. van Keulen LJM, Schreuder BEC, Meloen RH, et al. Immunohisto-chemical detection of prion protein in lymphoid tissues of sheep with natural scrapie. J Clin Microbiol 1996;34:1228-31.

10. Sigurdson CJ, Barillas-Mury C, Miller MW, et al. PrP$^{CWD}$ lymphoid cell targets in early and advanced chronic wasting disease of mule deer. J Gen Virol 2002;83:2617-28.

11. Bruce ME, McConnell I, Will RG, Ironside JW. Detection of variant Creutzfeldt-Jakob disease infectivity in extraneural tissues. Lancet 2001;358:208-9.

12. Head MW, Ritchie DL, Smith N, et al. Peripheral tissue involvement in sporadic, iatrogenic, and variant Creutzfeldt-Jakob disease: An immunohistochemical, quantitative, and biochemical study. Am J Pathol 2004;164:143-53.

13. Fraser H, Foster J. Transmision to mice, sheep and goats and bioassay of bovine tissues. In: Bradley R, Marchant B, eds. Transmissible spongiform encephalopathies. Brussels, Belgium: Commission of the European Communities, 1994:145-59.

14. Kimberlin RH, Walker CA. Pathogenesis of mouse scrapie: Dynamics of agent replication in spleen, spinal cord and brain after infection by different routes. J Comp Pathol 1979;89:551-62.

15. Foster JD, Bruce M, McConnell I, et al. Detection of BSE infectivity in brain and spleen of experimentally infected sheep. Vet Rec 1996;138: 546-8.

16. Foster JD, Parnham DW, Hunter N, Bruce M. Distribution of the prion protein in sheep terminally affected with BSE following experimental oral challenge. J Gen Virol 2001;82:2319-26.

17. Kimberlin RH, Walker CA. Pathogenesis of mouse scrapie: Effect of route of inoculation on infectivity titres and dose-response curves. J Comp Pathol 1978;88:39-47.

18. Bruce ME, McConnell I, Fraser H, Dickinson AG. The disease charac-teristics of different strains of scrapie in Sinc congenic mouse lines: Implications for the nature of the agent and host control of patho-genesis. J Gen Virol 1991;72:595-603.

19. Dickinson AG, Fraser H, Outram GW. Scrapie incubation period can exceed natural lifespan. Nature 1975;256:732-3.

20. Farquhar CF, Dornan J, Somerville RA, et al. Effect of Sinc genotype, agent isolate and route of infection on the accumulation of prote-ase-resistant PrP in non-central nervous system tissues during the de-velopment of murine scrapie. J Gen Virol 1994;75:495-504.

21. Wadsworth JDF, Joiner S, Hill A, et al. Tissue distribution of protease resistant prion protein in variant Creutzfeldt-Jakob disease using a highly sensitive immunoblotting assay. Lancet 2001;358:171-80.

22. Hilton DA, Fathers E, Edwards P, et al. Prion immunoreactivity in appendix before clinical onset of variant Creutzfeldt-Jakob disease. Lancet 1998;352:703-4.
23. Hilton DA, Ghani AC, Conyers L, et al. Accumulation of prion protein in tonsil and appendix: Review of tissue samples. Br Med J 2002; 325:633-4.
24. Hilton DA, Ghani AC, Conyers L, et al. Prevalence of lymphoreticular prion protein accumulation in UK tissue samples. J Pathol 2004;203: 733-9.
25. Fraser H, Dickinson AG. Studies of the lymphoreticular system in the pathogenesis of scrapie: The role of spleen and thymus. J Comp Pathol 1978;88:563-73.
26. Fraser H, Farquhar CF. Ionising radiation has no influence on scrapie incubation period in mice. Vet Microbiol 1987;13:211-23.
27. Kitamoto T, Muramoto T, Mohri S, et al. Abnormal isoform of prion protein accumulates in follicular dendritic cells in mice with Creutzfeldt-Jakob disease. J Virol 1991;65:6292-5.
28. McBride PA, Eikelenboom P, Kraal G, et al. PrP protein is associated with follicular dendritic cells of spleens and lymph nodes in uninfected and scrapie-infected mice. J Pathol 1992;168:413-8.
29. Andreoletti O, Berthon P, Levavasseur E, et al. Phenotyping of protein-prion (PrPsc)-accumulating cells in lymphoid and neural tissues of naturally scrapie-affected sheep by double labeling immunohistochemistry. J Histochem Cytochem 2002;50:1357-70.
30. Brown KL, Stewart K, Ritchie DL, et al. Scrapie replication in lymphoid tissues depends on prion protein-expressing follicular dendritic cells. Nat Med 1999;5:1308-12.
31. Bueler H, Aguzzi A, Sailer A, et al. Mice devoid of PrP are resistant to scrapie. Cell 1993;73:1339-47.
32. Burthem J, Urban B, Pain A, Roberts DJ. The normal cellular prion protein is strongly expressed by myeloid dendritic cells. Blood 2001; 98:3733-8.
33. Cashman NR, Loertscher R, Nalbantoglu J, et al. Cellular isoform of the scrapie agent protein participates in lymphocyte activation. Cell 1990;61:185-92.
34. Mabbott NA, Brown KL, Manson J, Bruce ME. T-lymphocyte activation and the cellular form of the prion protein. Immunology 1997;92: 161-5.
35. Jeffrey M, McGovern G, Goodsir CM, et al. Sites of prion protein accumulation in scrapie-infected mouse spleen revealed by immuno-electron microscopy. J Pathol 2000;190:323-32.
36. Kapasi ZF, Qin D, Kerr WG, et al. Follicular dendritic cell (FDC) precursors in primary lymphoid tissues. J Immunol 1998;160:1078-84.
37. Chaplin DD, Fu Y-X. Cytokine regulation of secondary lymphoid development. Curr Opin Immunol 1998;10:289-97.
38. Bosma GC, Custer RP, Bosma MJ. A severe combined immunodeficiency mutation in the mouse. Nature 1983;301:527-30.

39. Fraser H, Brown KL, Stewart K, et al. Replication of scrapie in spleens of SCID mice follows reconstitution with wild-type mouse bone marrow. J Gen Virol 1996;77:1935-40.

40. Lasmezas CI, Cesbron JY, Deslys JP, et al. Immune system-dependent and -independent replication of the scrapie agent. J Virol 1996;70:1292-5.

41. O'Rourke KI, Huff TP, Leathers CW, et al. SCID mouse spleen does not support scrapie agent replication. J Gen Virol 1994;75:1511-4.

42. Klein MA, Frigg R, Flechsig E, et al. A crucial role for B cells in neuroinvasive scrapie. Nature 1997;390:687-90.

43. Endres R, Alimzhanov MB, Pliz T, et al. Mature follicular dendritic cell networks depend on expression of lymphotoxin beta receptor by radioresistant stromal cells and of lymphotoxin beta and tumor necrosis factor by B cells. J Exp Med 1999;189:159-68.

44. Tkachuk M, Bolliger S, Ryffel B, et al. Crucial role of tumor necrosis factor receptor 1 expression on nonhematopoietic cells for B cell localization within the splenic white pulp. J Exp Med 1998;187:469-77.

45. Mabbott NA, Williams A, Farquhar CF, et al. Tumor necrosis factor alpha-deficient, but not interleukin-6-deficient, mice resist peripheral infection with scrapie. J Virol 2000;74:3338-44.

46. Prinz M, Montrasio F, Klein MA, et al. Lymph nodal prion replication and neuroinvasion in mice devoid of follicular dendritic cells. Proc Natl Acad Sci U S A 2002;99:919-24.

47. Shlomchik MJ, Radebold K, Duclos N, Manuelidis L. Neuroinvasion by a Creutzfeldt-Jakob disease agent in the absence of B cells and follicular dendritic cells. Proc Natl Acad Sci U S A 2001;98:9289-94.

48. Oldstone MBA, Race R, Thomas D, et al. Lymphotoxin-alpha- and lynphotoxin-beta-deficient mice differ in susceptibility to scrapie: Evidence against dendritic cell involvement in neuroinvasion. J Virol 2002;76:4357-63.

49. Mackay F, Browning JL. Turning off follicular dendritic cells. Nature 1998;395:26-7.

50. Mohler KM, Torrance DS, Smith CA, et al. Soluble tumour necrosis factor (TNF) receptors are effective therapeutic agents in lethal endotoxemia and function simultaneously as both carriers and TNF antagonists. J Immunol 1993;151:1584-61.

51. Mabbott NA, Mackay F, Minns F, Bruce ME. Temporary inactivation of follicular dendritic cells delays neuroinvasion of scrapie. Nat Med 2000;6:719-20.

52. Mabbott NA, McGovern G, Jeffrey M, Bruce ME. Temporary blockade of the tumor necrosis factor receptor signaling pathway impedes the spread of scrapie to the brain. J Virol 2002;76:5131-9.

53. Montrasio F, Frigg R, Glatzel M, et al. Impaired prion replication in spleens of mice lacking functional follicular dendritic cells. Science 2000;288:1257-9.

54. Mabbott NA, Young J, McConnell I, Bruce ME. Follicular dendritic cell dedifferentiation by treatment with an inhibitor of the lympho-

toxin pathway dramatically reduces scrapie susceptibility. J Virol 2003;77:6845-54.

55. Mohan J, Bruce ME, Mabbott NA. Follicular dendritic cell dedifferentiation reduces scrapie susceptibility following inoculation via the skin. Immunology 2005;114:225-34.

56. van den Berg TK, Yoshida K, Dijkstra CD. Mechanism of immune complex trapping by follicular dendritic cells. Curr Top Microbiol Immunol 1995;201:49-67.

57. Klein MA, Kaeser PS, Schwarz P, et al. Complement facilitates early prion pathogenesis. Nat Med 2001;7:488-92.

58. Mabbott NA, Bruce ME, Botto M, et al. Temporary depletion of complement component C3 or genetic deficiency of C1q significantly delays onset of scrapie. Nat Med 2001;7:485-7.

59. McGovern G, Brown KL, Bruce ME, Jeffrey M. Murine scrapie infection causes an abnormal germinal centre reaction in spleen. J Comp Pathol 2004;130:181-94.

60. Beekes M, McBride PA. Early accumulation of pathological PrP in the enteric nervous system and gut-associated lymphoid tissue of hamsters orally infected with scrapie. Neurosci Lett 2000;278:181-4.

61. van Keulen LJ, Vromans ME, van Zijderveld FG. Early and late pathogenesis of natural scrapie infection in sheep. APMIS 2002; 110:23-32.

62. Neutra MR, Frey A. Epithelial M cells: Gateways for mucosal infection and immunization. Cell 1996;86:345-8.

63. Heppner FL, Christ AD, Klein MA, et al. Transepithelial prion transport by M cells. Nat Med 2001;7:976-7.

64. Banchereau J, Briere F, Caux C, et al. Immunobiology of dendritic cells. Annu Rev Immunol 2000;18:767-811.

65. Huang FP, Farquhar CF, Mabbott NA, et al. Migrating intestinal dendritic cells transport PrP(Sc) from the gut. J Gen Virol 2002;83:267-71.

66. Taylor DM, McConnell I, Fraser H. Scrapie infection can be established readily through skin scarification in immunocompetent but not immunodeficient mice. J Gen Virol 1996;77:1595-9.

67. Mohan J, Brown KL, Farquhar CF, et al. Scrapie transmission following exposure through the skin is dependent on follicular dendritic cells in lymphoid tissues. J Dermatol Sci 2004;35:101-11.

68. Mohan J, Bruce ME, Mabbott NA. Neuroinvasion by scrapie following inoculation via the skin is independent of migratory Langerhans cells. J Virol 2005;79:1888-97.

69. Moodycliffe AM, Shreedhar V, Ullrich SE, et al. CD40-CD40 ligand interactions in vivo regulate migration of antigen-bearing dendritic cells from the skin to draining lymph nodes. J Exp Med 2000;191: 2011-20.

70. Antonopoulos C, Cumberbatch M, Dearman RJ, et al. Functional caspase-1 is required for Langerhans cell migration and optimal contact sensitization in mice. J Immunol 2001;166:3672-7.

71. Mohan J, Hopkins J, Mabbott NA. Skin-derived dendritic cells acquire and degrade the scrapie agent following in vitro exposure. Immunology 2005;116:122-33.
72. Carp RI, Callahan SM. Effect of mouse peritoneal macrophages on scrapie infectivity during extended in vitro incubation. Intervirology 1982;17:201-7.
73. Beringue V, Demoy M, Lasmezas CI, et al. Role of spleen macrophages in the clearance of scrapie agent early in pathogenesis. J Pathol 2000;190:495-502.
74. Brown P, Rohwer RG, Dunstan BC, et al. The distribution of infectivity in blood components and plasma derivatives in experimental models of transmissible spongiform encephalopathy. Transfusion 1998;38:810-6.
75. Cervenakova L, Yakovleva O, McKenzie C, et al. Similar levels of infectivity in the blood of mice infected with human-derived vCJD and GSS strains of transmissible spongiform encephalopathy. Transfusion 2003;43:1687-94.
76. Taylor DM, Fernie K, Reichl HE, Somerville RA. Infectivity in the blood of mice with a BSE-derived agent. J Hosp Infect 2000;46:78-9.
77. Houston F, Foster JD, Chong A, et al. Transmission of BSE by blood transfusion in sheep. Lancet 2000;356:999-1000.
78. Hunter N, Foster J, Chong A, et al. Transmission of prion diseases by blood transfusion. J Gen Virol 2002;83:2897-905.
79. Denzer K, Kleijmeer MJ, Heijnen HF, et al. Exosome: From internal vesicle of the multivesicular body to intercellular signaling device. J Cell Sci 2000;113:3365-74.
80. Fevrier B, Vilette D, Archer F, et al. Cells release prions in association with exosomes. Proc Natl Acad Sci U S A 2004;101:9683-8.
81. Denzer K, van Eijk M, Kleijmeer MJ, et al. Follicular dendritic cells carry MHC class II-expressing microvesicles at their surface. J Immunol 2000;165:1259-65.
82. Wu J, Qin D, Burton GF, et al. Follicular dendritic cell-derived antigen and accessory activity in initiation of memory IgG responses in vitro. J Immunol 1996;157:3404-11.
83. Kimberlin RH, Walker CA. Pathogenesis of mouse scrapie: Evidence for neural spread of infection to the CNS. J Gen Virol 1980;51:183-7.
84. Glatzel M, Heppner FL, Albers KM, Aguzzi A. Sympathetic innervation of lymphoreticular organs is rate limiting for prion neuroinvasion. Neuron 2001;31:25-34.
85. Beekes M, McBride PA, Baldauf E. Cerebral targeting indicates vagal spread of infection in hamsters fed with scrapie. J Gen Virol 1998;79:601-7.
86. McBride PA, Beekes M. Pathological PrP is abundant in sympathetic and sensory ganglia of hamsters fed with scrapie. Neurosci Lett 1999;265:135-8.
87. McBride PA, Schulz-Schaeffer WJ, Donaldson M, et al. Early spread of scrapie from the gastrointestinal tract to the central nervous system

involves autonomic fibers of the splanchnic and vagus nerves. J Virol 2001;75:9320-7.

88. Haik S, Faucheux BA, Sazdovitch V, et al. The sympathetic nervous system is involved in variant Creutzfeldt-Jakob disease. Nat Med 2003;9:1121-3.

89. Lee CC, Kuo LT, Wang CH, et al. Accumulation of prion protein in the peripheral nervous system in human prion diseases. J Neuropathol Exp Neurol 2005;64:716-21.

90. Kimberlin RH, Field HJ, Walker CA. Pathogenesis of mouse scrapie: Evidence for spread of infection from central to peripheral nervous system. J Gen Virol 1983;64:713-6.

91. Prinz M, Heikenwalder M, Junt T, et al. Positioning of follicular dendritic cells within the spleen controls prion neuroinvasion. Nature 2003;425:957-62.

92. Aucouturier P, Geissmann F, Damotte D, et al. Infected splenic dendritic cells are sufficient for prion transmission to the CNS in mouse scrapie. J Clin Invest 2001;108:703-8.

93. Wells GA, Spiropoulos J, Hawkins SA, Ryder SJ. Pathogenesis of experimental bovine spongiform encephalopathy: Preclinical infectivity in tonsil and observations on the distribution of lingual tonsil in slaughtered cattle. Vet Rec 2005;156:401-7.

94. Wells GAH, Hawkins SAC, Green RB, et al. Preliminary observations on the pathogenesis of experimental bovine spongiform encephalopathy (BSE): An update. Vet Rec 1998;142:103-6.

95. Heikenwalder M, Zeller N, Seeger H, et al. Chronic lymphocytic inflammation specifies the organ tropism of prions. Science 2005;307: 1107-10.

96. Ligios C, Sigurdson CJ, Santucciu C, et al. PrP(Sc) in mammary glands of sheep affected by scrapie and mastitis. Nat Med 2005;11: 1137-8.

97. Bosque PJ, Ryou C, Telling G, et al. Prions in skeletal muscle. Proc Natl Acad Sci U S A 2002;99:3812-7.

98. Mulcahy ER, Bartz JC, Kincaid AE, Bessen RA. Prion infection of skeletal muscle cells and papillae in the tongue. J Virol 2004;78:6792-8.

99. Thomzig A, Schulz-Schaeffer W, Kratzel C, et al. Preclinical deposition of pathological prion protein PrPSc in muscles of hamsters orally exposed to scrapie. J Clin Invest 2004;113:1465-72.

100. Glatzel M, Abela E, Maissen M, Aguzzi A. Extraneural pathologic prion protein in sporadic Creutzfeldt-Jakob disease. N Engl J Med 2003;349:1812-20.

101. Andreoletti O, Simon S, Lacroux C, et al. PrPSc accumulation in myocytes from sheep incubating natural scrapie. Nat Med 2004;10: 591-3.

102. Dickinson AG, Fraser H, McConnell I, Outram GW. Mitogenic stimulation of the host enhances susceptibility to scrapie. Nature 1978; 272:54-5.

103. Farquhar C, Dickinson A, Bruce M. Prophylactic potential of pentosan polysulphate in transmissible spongiform encephalopathies (letter). Lancet 1999;353:117.
104. Kimberlin RH, Walker CA. Suppression of scrapie infection in mice by heteropolyanion 23, dextran sulfate, and some other polyanions. Antimicrob Agents Chemother 1986;30:409-13.
105. Ghani A, Ferguson NM, Donnelly CA, Anderson RM. Factors determining the pattern of the variant Creutzfeldt-Jakob disease (vCJD) epidemic in the UK. Proc R Soc Lond B 2003;270:689-98.
106. Ierna M, Farquhar CF, Outram GW, Bruce ME. Resistance of neonatal mice to scrapie is associated with inefficient infection of the immature spleen. J Virol 2006;80:474-82.
107. Outram GW, Dickinson AG, Fraser H. Developmental maturation of susceptibility to scrapie in mice. Nature 1973;241:536-7.
108. Head MW, Farquhar CF, Mabbott NA, Fraser H. The transmissible spongiform encephalopathies: Pathogenic mechanisms and strategies for therapeutic intervention. Expert Opin Ther Targets 2001;5:569-85.

In: Turner ML, ed.
*Creutzfeldt-Jakob Disease: Managing the Risk of
Transmission by Blood, Plasma, and Tissues*
Bethesda, MD: AABB Press, 2006

# 3

# Clinical and Pathologic Features of Human Prion Diseases

JAMES W. IRONSIDE, BMSc(HONS), MBCHB,
FRCPATH, FRCP(ED), FMEDSCI

PRION DISEASES OR transmissible spongiform encephalopathies are characterized by progressive neurologic dysfunction, which reflects the damage and loss of neurons occurring in multiple sites within the central nervous system.[1] There is little evidence for functional impairment or pathologic conditions in any other system in the body, although occasional cases have been reported in which the peripheral nervous system also appears to be involved.[2] As tools for the pathologic diagnosis of prion dis-

*James W. Ironside, BMSc(hons), MBChB, FRCPath, FRCP(Ed), FMedSci; Professor of Clinical Neuropathology, National Creutzfeldt-Jakob Disease Surveillance Unit, Division of Pathology, School of Molecular and Clinical Medicine, University of Edinburgh and The National Health Service Lothian University, Hospitals Division and Tayside, University Hospitals Division, Edinburgh, United Kingdom*

*[This work forms part of the EU NeuroPrion network of excellence (FOOD-CT-2004-506579) subproject PRIOGEN.]*

eases have become more sensitive and specific,[3-5] a widening spectrum of human prion diseases, including idiopathic, familial, and acquired disorders, has been identified (Table 3-1).[6] This diversity is accompanied by a correspondingly broad range of clinical features, which are discussed in more detail under the individual disease entities below.

Since the identification of bovine spongiform encephalopathy (BSE) in 1987,[7] many countries have undertaken surveillance for human prion diseases, which led to the identification in the United Kingdom (UK) in 1996 of a new disorder, now known as variant Creutzfeldt-Jakob disease (vCJD).[8] Through these activities, criteria for the clinical diagnosis of human prion diseases have been formulated and modified as the results of new investigative techniques have emerged (Table 3-2).[9] These criteria have been validated in prospective studies with neuropathologic confirmation of the diagnosis after death; thus, they represent important tools that allow a clinical diagnosis to be achieved with a high degree of certainty. However, it should be noted that the success of these criteria is dependent upon the context in which they are employed, and it

### Table 3-1. Classification of Human Prion Diseases*

| | |
|---|---|
| Idiopathic | Sporadic Creutzfeldt-Jakob Disease |
| | Sporadic fatal insomnia |
| Familial | Gerstmann-Sträussler-Scheinker syndrome |
| | Familial Creuzfeldt-Jakob disease |
| | Fatal familial insomnia |
| Acquired | Bovine source: variant Creutzfeldt-Jakob disease |
| | Human source: iatrogenic Creutzfeldt-Jakob disease |
| | Kuru |

*Modified from Ironside.[6]

## Table 3-2. Clinical Diagnostic Criteria for Sporadic and Variant Creutzfeldt-Jakob Disease (CJD)[9]

### Sporadic CJD

Definite: Neuropathologically/immunocytochemically confirmed
Probable: I + 2 of II + III, or possible + positive 14.3.3 in
  cerebrospinal fluid
Possible: I + 2 of II + duration of illness less than 2 years

|      |                                          |
|------|------------------------------------------|
| I.   | Rapidly progressive dementia             |
| II.  | A. Myoclonus                             |
|      | B. Visual or cerebellar problems         |
|      | C. Pyramidal or extrapyramidal features  |
|      | D. Akinetic mutism                       |
| III. | Typical electroencephalogram (EEG)       |

### Variant CJD

Definite: IA + neuropathologic confirmation of variant CJD
Probable: I + 4/5 of II and IIIA + IIIB, or I + IVA
Possible: I + 4/5 of II + IIIA

|      |    |                                                       |
|------|----|-------------------------------------------------------|
| I.   | A. | Progressive neuropsychiatric disorder                 |
|      | B. | Duration of illness greater than 6 months             |
|      | C. | No history of potential iatrogenic exposure           |
|      | D. | No evidence of a familial form of prion disease       |
| II.  | A. | Early psychiatric symptoms                            |
|      | B. | Persistent painful sensory symptoms                   |
|      | C. | Ataxia                                                |
|      | D. | Myoclonus or chorea or dystonia                       |
|      | E. | Dementia                                              |
| III. | A. | EEG does not show a typical appearance of sporadic CJD, or no EEG performed |
|      | B. | Bilateral pulvinar high signal                        |
| IV.  |    | A positive tonsil biopsy                              |

is particularly important, before these criteria are applied, to exclude by appropriate methods other potential causes for the neurologic features found on clinical examination.

In addition to the results of neurologic examination, a range of investigative techniques is employed to aid diagnosis. These include electroencephalography (EEG), neuroradiologic studies, particularly magnetic resonance imaging (MRI), and measurement of S100 and 14.3.3 proteins in the cerebrospinal fluid (CSF).[10] Brain biopsy now is seldom employed for diagnosis but is usually reserved for cases in which the possibility of an underlying treatable disorder (such as cerebral vasculitis) has not been excluded or for cases with atypical clinical features or an unusual duration of illness.

## Neuropathology of Prion Diseases

Neuropathologic examination of the brain is required for a definitive diagnosis of a prion disease.[11,12] In addition to classical morphologic assessment, ancillary techniques to detect the disease-associated form of the prion protein ($PrP^{TSE}$), including immunohistochemistry and Western blotting techniques,[5,12] are now widely used to aid diagnosis. Western blotting techniques require unfixed tissue, which places a high priority on obtaining frozen brain tissue samples at autopsy. In addition, sequence analysis of the prion protein gene (*PRNP*) from a frozen tissue sample or blood sample allows the detection of pathogenic mutations and insertions in familial prion diseases and establishes the status of the polymorphism at codon 129, which has a major influence on the phenotype in idiopathic, acquired, and familial prion disorders.[13]

The neuropathologic features of human prion diseases include spongiform change, neuronal loss, reactive proliferation of glial cells, and amyloid plaque formation (although the latter occurs in only a minority of cases).[6,14] Although these features are the mainstay of morphologic diagnosis, they are not in themselves specific for human prion disease. A more specific finding is the accumulation in the brain of the disease-associated isoform of the prion protein, PrP$^{TSE}$, which can be detected by immunohistochemistry or Western blot examination (see below).[5,12] Certain human prion diseases, such as fatal familial insomnia, show very little spongiform change,[15,16] so the use of immunohistochemistry and Western blotting for PrP$^{TSE}$ and *PRNP* sequencing is essential for diagnosis. Spongiform change is characterized by multiple rounded vacuoles in the neuropil that vary from about 2 to 20 microns in diameter, often referred to as microvacuolar spongiform change (Fig 3-1A). In some forms of human prion disease, spongiform change can become confluent, which results in the formation of larger cyst-like spaces (Fig 3-1B). The location and type of spongiform change can vary considerably from one region of the brain to another in the same case and also from case to case in the same disease type.[6,14] This phenomenon is sometimes referred to as neuropathologic targeting, but the mechanisms underlying its occurrence are poorly understood.

Neuronal loss and gliosis usually occur in brain regions that exhibit spongiform change, but there is not always a consistent relationship between these histologic features. Some regions of the brain, such as the pulvinar in vCJD, exhibit severe neuronal loss and gliosis in the virtual absence of spongiform change.[8] The amyloid plaques that form in human prion diseases are composed of aggregated PrP$^{TSE}$ and bear no relationship to the plaques of Alzheimer's disease (see below). Amyloid plaque formation tends to occur only in well-defined human prion disease subgroups. The first type to be identified was the rounded fibrillary plaques occurring in kuru, but a range of other plaque morphologies has been identified, inluding multicentric plaques in the Gerstmann-Sträussler-Scheinker syndrome (GSS) and florid plaques that are characteristic of vCJD.[17] Human prion diseases may occur in association with other neurodegenerative disorders, of which the most frequent is Alzheimer's disease. However, this appears to be an unrelated coincidence, because there is no evidence to indicate any pathogenic relationship between these disorders.

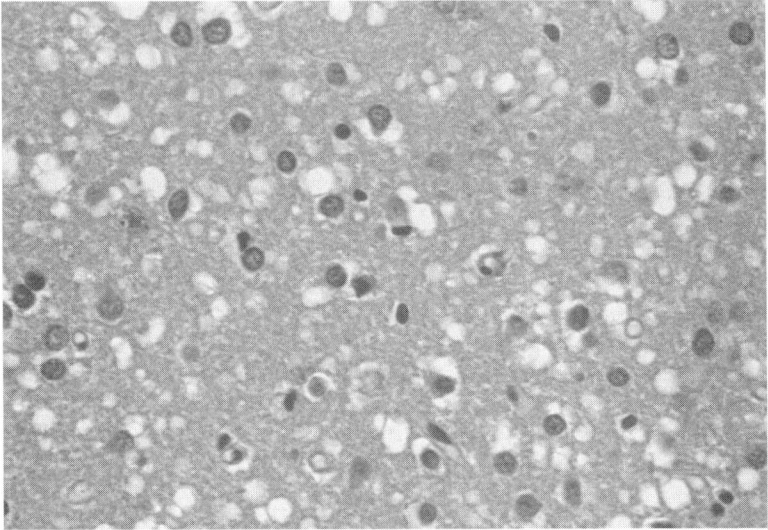

(A)

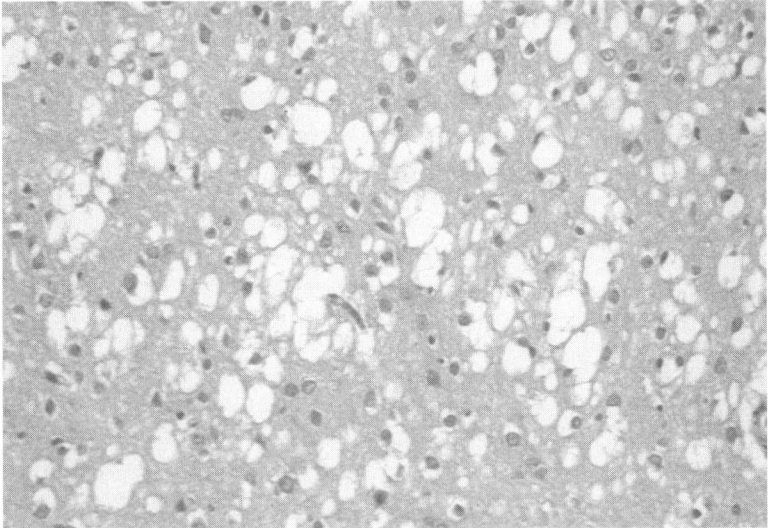

(B)

Figure 3-1. Different patterns of spongiform change in the cerebral cortex in sporadic Creutzfeldt-Jakob disease (sCJD). (A) Microvacuolar spongiform change in the MM1 subtype; (B) confluent spongiform change in the MM2 subtype. Hematoxylin and eosin stains, original magnifications × 200.

# PrP$^{TSE}$ Biochemistry

According to the prion hypothesis,[18] the disease-associated form of the prion protein, PrP$^{TSE}$, exists in several different conformations that may encode the strain characteristics of the transmissible agent.[19] PrP$^{TSE}$ is relatively insoluble and has a high beta-sheet content, which allows it to aggregate as amyloid plaques. This structure also confers relative resistance to proteolytic digestion, distinguishing PrP$^{TSE}$ from its normal cellular counterpart, PrP$^{C}$, which is expressed at high levels in the brain.[20] Because there are few readily available antibodies that are specific for PrP$^{TSE}$, and because most PrP antibodies react with both isoforms of the protein, proteolytic digestion is employed in Western blot preparations to distinguish PrP$^{TSE}$ from PrP$^{C}$. The protease-resistant core of PrP$^{TSE}$ is thought to exist in two major conformational variants, termed type 1 and type 2.[4] Type 1 has a molecular weight of ~21 kDa, with an $N$-terminus at glycine 82. Type 2 has a molecular weight of ~19 kDa with an $N$-terminus at serine 97.[21] In addition to the differentiating molecular size, Western blots also allow the identification of three possible glycoforms of PrP (di-, mono-, and nonglycosylated). PrP$^{TSE}$ typing studies may include data on the ratio of these three glycoforms[22]; in other studies, the suffix B is used to denote PrP$^{TSE}$ types in which the diglycosylated band predominates, and the suffix A is used for PrP$^{TSE}$ types in which the mono- or nonglycosylated forms predominate.[23] Examples of type 1, type 2A, and type 2B PrP$^{TSE}$ are shown in Western blots in Fig 3-2. Additional details on PrP$^{TSE}$ typing in human prion diseases are discussed in the following sections.

# Sporadic CJD

## Clinical Features

Most cases of CJD occur as a sporadic disorder in which the underlying cause is not apparent. Sporadic CJD (sCJD) has a worldwide distribution, with a relatively uniform incidence of around 1 to 1.5 cases per million per year, and it occurs with

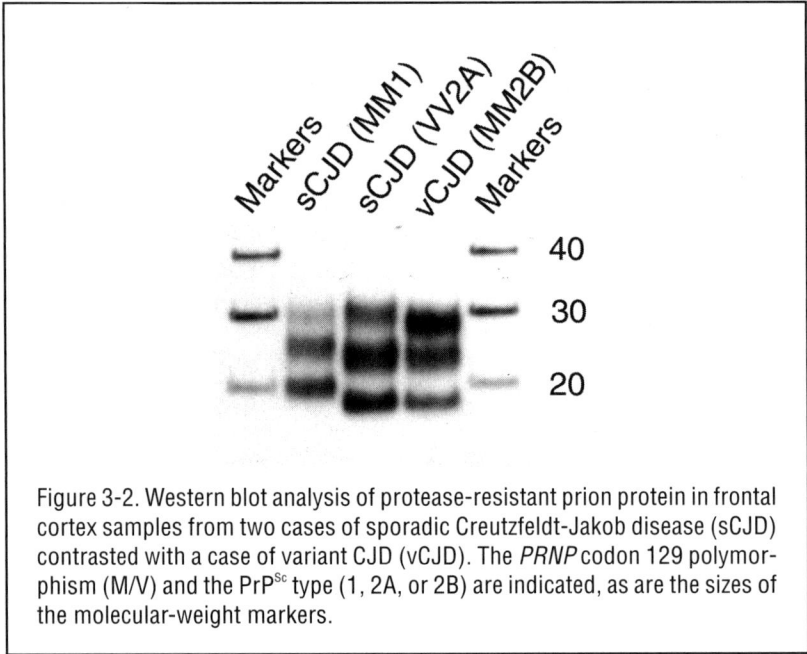

Figure 3-2. Western blot analysis of protease-resistant prion protein in frontal cortex samples from two cases of sporadic Creutzfeldt-Jakob disease (sCJD) contrasted with a case of variant CJD (vCJD). The PRNP codon 129 polymorphism (M/V) and the PrP$^{Sc}$ type (1, 2A, or 2B) are indicated, as are the sizes of the molecular-weight markers.

equal frequency in males and females, with a peak incidence in the 7th decade of life (Fig 3-3).[13,24] However, persons in a wide age range can be affected, and there have been a small number of cases in teenagers. Most patients with sCJD present with a rapidly progressive dementia accompanied by other neurologic signs, of which myoclonus, ataxia, pyramidal and extrapyramidal features, and visual abnormalities are the most frequent. However, it has been recognized for many years that there is a considerable degree of phenotypic variability in sCJD[25]; some cases present with ataxia, whereas others have severe and early visual abnormalities that result in cortical blindness. Most patients die within 4 months of onset of the disease, but cases with survival of more than 3 years have been recorded (Fig 3-4).

The differential diagnosis of sCJD includes other neurodegenerative disorders, particularly Alzheimer's disease and Lewy body dementia, and a range of other conditions producing progressive multifocal pathologic conditions in the brain,

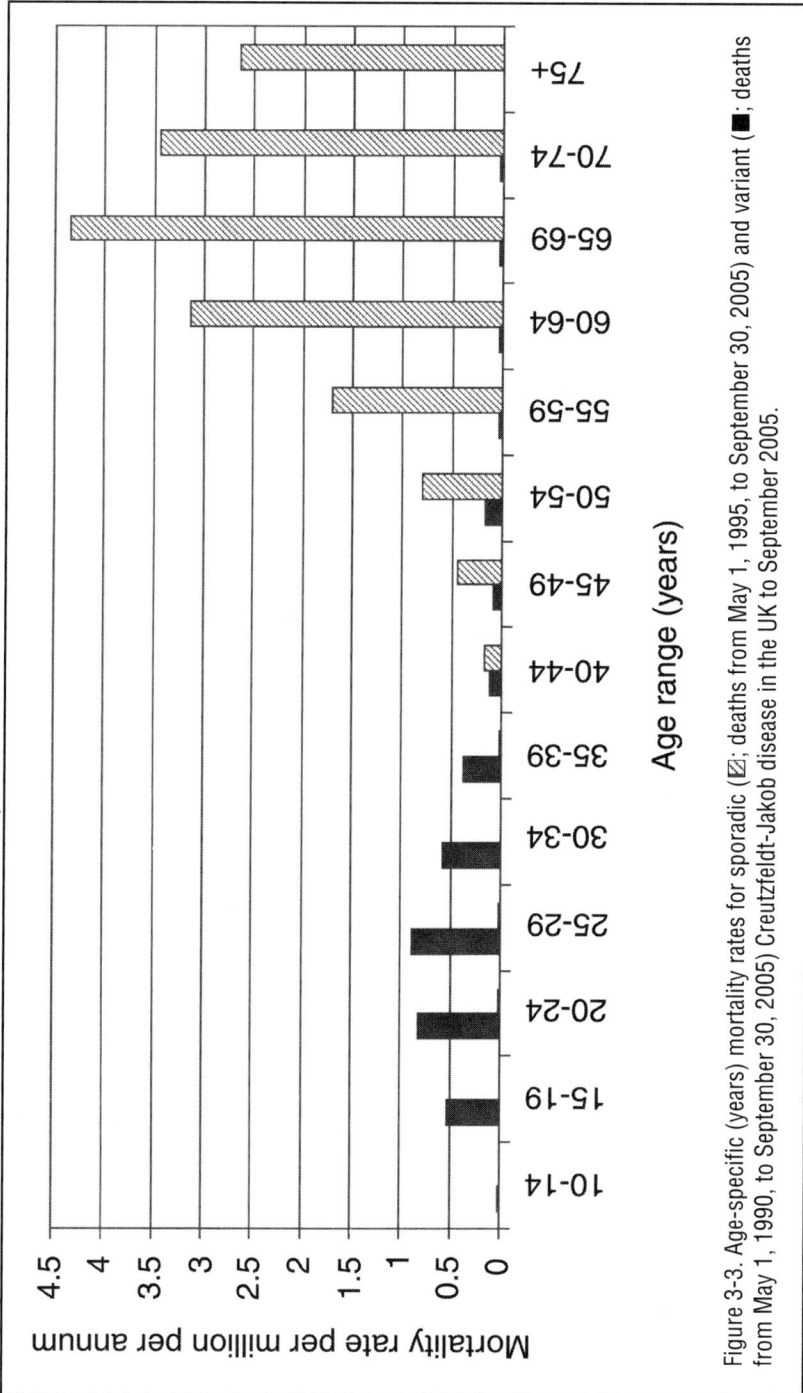

Figure 3-3. Age-specific (years) mortality rates for sporadic (▨; deaths from May 1, 1995, to September 30, 2005) and variant (■; deaths from May 1, 1990, to September 30, 2005) Creutzfeldt-Jakob disease in the UK to September 2005.

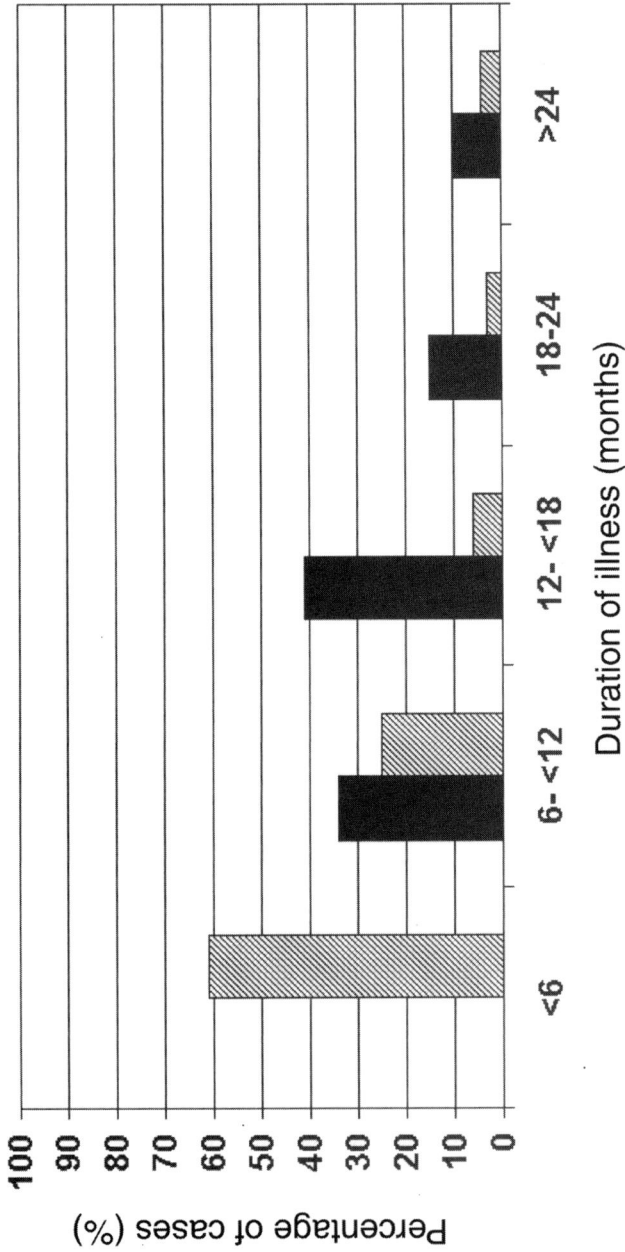

Figure 3-4. Median duration of illness (months) in sporadic (▨) and variant (■) Creutzfeldt-Jakob disease cases in the UK to September 2005.

such as cerebral vasculitis and intravascular B-cell lymphoma. A diagnosis of sCJD is aided by the results of additional clinical investigations. Approximately 65% of patients have a "typical" EEG, in which generalized periodic sharp wave complexes occur with a frequency of up to 1 Hz (Fig 3-5). MRI studies of the brain have recently reported areas of increased signal in the basal ganglia in T2-weighted and fluid-attenuated inversion recovery (FLAIR) sequences (Fig 3-6), but the sensitivity and specificity of this particular finding are still under investigation, and it has not yet been included in the diagnostic criteria for sCJD.[26] Measurement of the protein 14.3.3 in the CSF is very helpful for diagnosis, because the levels are elevated in most cases, and this finding can have a positive predictive value of 97% in an appropriate clinical setting.[10] Ge-

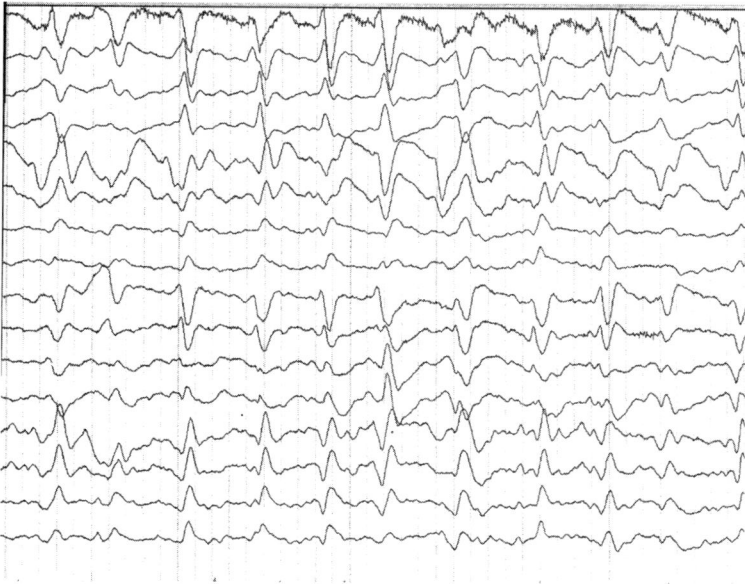

Figure 3-5. A typical electroencephalogram in a person with sporadic Creutzfeldt-Jakob disease, showing periodic triphasic sharp wave complexes in most leads.

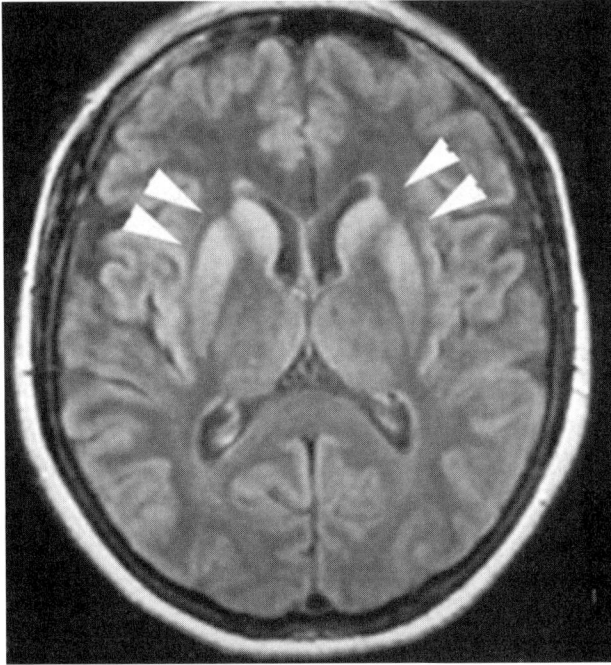

Figure 3-6. Transverse fluid-attenuated inversion recovery (FLAIR) magnetic resonance imaging (MRI) scan showing bilateral anterior basal ganglia high signal (arrowheads) in a patient with sporadic Creutzfeldt-Jakob disease.

netic investigations have revealed that the naturally occurring polymorphism at codon 129 in *PRNP* influences susceptibility to sCJD.[27] This polymorphism can encode either valine or methionine; in the normal Caucasian population, the heterozygote genotype is most common, but the frequency of homozygotes is increased in sCJD, particularly for methionine homozygotes (Table 3-3).

## Neuropathology

Macroscopic examination of the brain in sCJD often shows no significant abnormality. There may be a variable degree of cerebral cortical atrophy or cerebellar cortical atrophy, with the

## Table 3-3. *PRNP* Codon 129 Genotype Distributions in Human Prion Diseases

|  | Codon 129 Genotype (%) | | |
| --- | --- | --- | --- |
|  | MM | VV | MV |
| Normal population | 39 | 11 | 50 |
| Sporadic CJD | 61 | 18 | 21 |
| Variant CJD | 100 | — | — |

CJD = Creutzfeldt-Jakob disease; M = methionine; V = valine.

latter particularly involving the vermis. The hippocampus is normally spared in CJD, unlike in Alzheimer's disease.[6,14] In occasional cases of sCJD, there is widespread atrophy of the cerebral cortex and cerebellum, which is accompanied by secondary degenerative changes in the white matter. Such cases are often referred to as the panencephalopathic variant of sCJD, which appears to occur with highest frequency in Japan.[28]

Adequate histologic sampling of the brain in sCJD should include the frontal, temporal, and occipital lobes; the basal ganglia; thalamus; and cerebellum, because the distribution and severity of the histologic features vary greatly from one area of the brain to another.[11] Spongiform change (see above) is not entirely specific for sCJD, because similar changes have been described in other neurodegenerative disorders, such as Lewy body dementia, but the distribution of spongiform change in the brain in these disorders is often restricted to certain anatomic locations, particularly the temporal cortex.[6,14] The severity of spongiform change in sCJD varies greatly from one case to another and between different brain regions within the same case.[25] Studies of the nature and severity of the neuropathologic lesions in the brain in sporadic CJD have allowed the identification of distinct disease subtypes (see below).[4,29]

### Phenotypic Variability

It is possible to subclassify sCJD according to the codon 129 polymorphism and the two major PrP[TSE] isotypes.[4,29] This allows for at least six possible combinations, each of which has been proposed to possess particular clinical and neuropathologic manifestations.[4] These subtypes also exhibit some different clinical and investigative findings. For example, the MM1 and MV1 subtypes are associated with a "typical" EEG, high levels of 14.3.3 in the CSF, and a relatively short clinical history; the MM2, VV2, and MV2 subtypes tend to have a longer clinical history and an abnormal but not "typical" EEG; and the MV2 subtypes also have low or negative 14.3.3 levels in the CSF.[10] Table 3-4 summarizes the distinguishing clinical and neuropathologic features of sCJD according to combinations of codon 129 status and PrP[TSE] types 1 and 2. The MM2 subtype has 2 possible forms of phenotypic expression, the more common cortical subtype and the rarer thalamic subtype, which now is often referred to as sporadic fatal insomnia.[4,16]

Apart from these major subtypes, there are occasional cases of sCJD that exhibit "atypical" clinical and/or neuropathologic features.[25,30] In some of these cases, detailed Western blot examination of the brain has found more than one type of PrP[TSE] to be present.[12,30] Whether this finding relates to the biologic properties of the infectious agent requires further investigation.

# Familial Prion Diseases

Familial disorders account for approximately 10% of all human prion diseases, although their incidence varies considerably from one country to another.[24] All forms of familial prion disease occur as autosomal dominant disorders with a high rate of penetrance; they are associated with more than 30 point

## Table 3-4. Subtypes of Sporadic Creutzfeldt-Jakob Disease (CJD): Main Clinical and Pathologic Features*

| Subtype | Frequency (%) | Age at Onset of Illness | Duration | Major Feature |
|---|---|---|---|---|
| MM1 | 65 | 65 years | 4 months | Typical sporadic CJD |
| MM2 cortical | 3 | 65 years | 16 months | Long duration of illness |
| MM2 thalamic | 2 | 52 years | 24 months | Sporadic fatal insomnia |
| VV1 | 1 | 39 years | 15 months | Early onset |
| VV2 | 16 | 60 years | 6 months | Ataxic onset |
| MV1 | 4 | 65 years | 4 months | Typical sporadic CJD |
| MV2 | 9 | 60 years | 17 months | Kuru plaques in cerebellum |

*Modified from Gambetti et al.[13]

mutations and a range of deletion and insertion mutations in the *PRNP*.[13,31] The clinical features of familial prion diseases range from conditions resembling sCJD to other distinct clinical syndromes, including fatal familial insomnia and GSS.[16,31] The neuropathologic features of these conditions also exhibit considerable variability,[32] which will be considered below in four major subgroups according to the genetic abnormality and the associated disease phenotype.

## Familial CJD

The E200K mutation is the most common *PRNP* mutation, and it has been reported in several large clusters across the world.[33] Most cases have clinical features comparable to the MM1 subtype of sCJD, with an average age of onset of 60 years, a mean duration of illness of approximately 6 months, and a "typical" EEG.[13,34] The neuropathology of these cases also resembles the sCJD MM1 subgroup, with spongiform degeneration predominantly of the microvacuolar type, neuronal loss, and astrocytosis in the absence of amyloid plaques.[32] A type 1 PrP$^{TSE}$ is present in the brain on Western blot examination. Other mutations associated with a sCJD-like phenotype include D178N-129V, V180I-129M, T183A-129M, and M232R-129M.[13,32]

## Fatal Familial Insomnia

The D178N mutation, when accompanied by methionine at codon 129 in the mutant allele, results in a distinctive disorder known as fatal familial insomnia (FFI). Onset of the disease can take place between 32 and 62 years of age, with a duration of illness of approximately 12 to 21 months. This disease is characterized clinically by abnormalities of sleep and autonomic and motor disturbances, usually in the absence of dementia.[16] Myoclonus is common, and a "typical" EEG may appear late in the illness in some patients. Polysomnography is helpful in distinguishing FFI from other forms of sleep disturbance.[13] The neuropathology of this disorder is strikingly different from other forms of inherited prion diseases: thalamic atrophy is accompanied by severe neuronal loss and marked gliosis in the anterior ventral, dorsomedial, and pulvinar nuclei of the thalamus.[35] Spongiform change is usually difficult to detect, but it may occur in the entorhinal cortex in patients with a short disease duration and can be observed in other regions of the cerebral cortex and in the cerebellum in patients with a longer disease duration.[13] Immunohistochemistry for PrP$^{TSE}$ is often negative in FFI, but positive staining has been reported in the cerebellum and brain stem in cases with a lengthy disease duration.[15] Western blot examination has found the highest levels of PrP$^{TSE}$ in the thalamus and lower levels in the brain stem and limbic structures, with a type 2 isoform.[35]

## Familial CJD with PRNP Insertional Mutations

Four octapeptide repeat sequences occur in the region of the *PRNP* between positions 51 and 91. Insertions of extra repeats (1, 2, or 4 to 9) at this site have been associated with familial CJD, but deletion of a single repeat is not pathogenic.[13] The disease phenotype in this form of inherited human prion disease is variable and appears to be influenced by the number of the octapeptide repeat insertions. Patients with no more than 4 octapeptide repeat insertions have an illness similar to the MM1 subtype of sCJD (see above), whereas patients with 5 to 7 repeats show a similar clinical phenotype but have a slower disease progression. Patients with 8 or 9 octapeptide inserts show a clinical phenotype similar to GSS (see below).[13,32] However, there is marked phenotypic variability within affected families,[36] some of which is influenced by the codon 129 polymorphism in the mutant allele.

Neuropathologic examination shows features resembling the MM1 subtype of sCJD in patients with 1 to 7 octapeptide repeats.[13] However, there is a distinctive pattern of PrP$^{TSE}$ accumulation in the cerebellum, which takes the form of linear aggregates on immunohistochemistry within the molecular layer that often run in a vertical pattern.[37] These aggregates provide a useful pathologic marker that can raise suspicion of an underlying genetic disorder in cases that occur without any obvious family history.

## GSS

GSS is an inherited neurologic disorder characterized by ataxia, tremor, difficulty in walking and sitting, dysarthria, pyramidal signs, and pseudobulbar signs; personality change and impaired intellectual function appear late in the illness. Onset of the disease usually occurs in the 4th to 6th decade of life, and the duration of illness varies from several months to approximately 6 years. Some patients in an affected family can exhibit clinical features that more closely resemble the MM1 subtype of sCJD, but the reasons for this phenotypic variability are not fully understood.[31]

The neuropathology of GSS involves cerebellar atrophy; multiple multicentric amyloid plaques in the cerebellum (Fig 3-7A), cerebral cortex, basal ganglia, and thalamus; and neuronal loss and gliosis, particularly in the cerebellar cortex.[31,32] Spongiform change is not a common feature in most cases, but it can be detected in some patients who have a clinical illness similar to sCJD.[38]

The first *PRNP* mutation to be found in a GSS family was the P102L mutation; since that case, an increasing number of mutations associated with a similar phenotype have been identified.[31,39] Some of these mutations have characteristic additional neuropathologic features, such as tau-positive neurofibrillary tangles and neuropil threads in the F198S and Q217R mutations.[31] In one unique mutation, Y145STOP, a PrP-amyloid angiopathy occurs, involving small and medium-sized vessels in the meninges and the brain.[40]

## Iatrogenic CJD

The first case of iatrogenic CJD was reported after a corneal transplant from a donor who had died of CJD in 1974,[41] and ret-

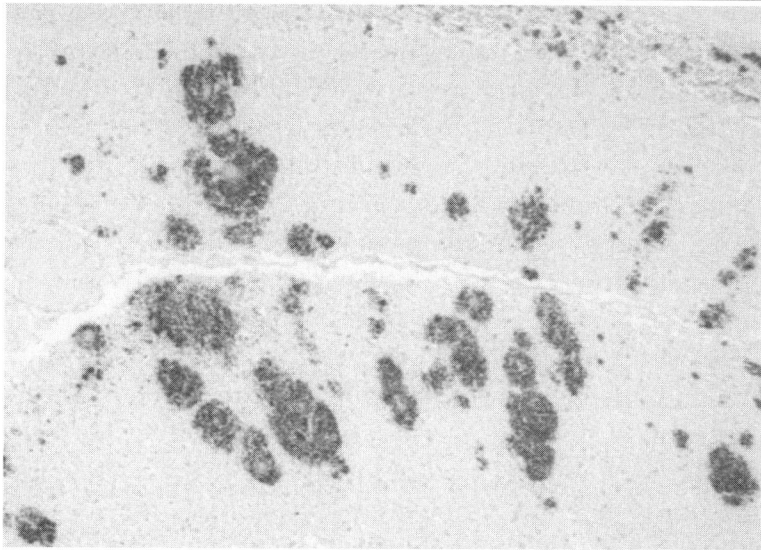

(A)

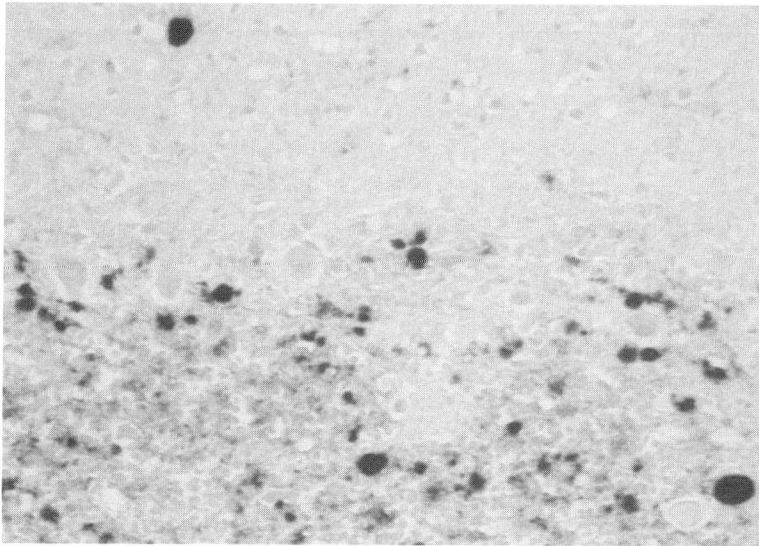

(B)

Figure 3-7. Immunohistochemistry for prion protein (PrP) amyloid deposits in the cerebellum shows (A) large multicentric plaques in a case of Gerstmann-Sträussler-Scheinker syndrome with the P102L mutation, original magnification × 100; (B) small rounded kuru-type plaques in a case of iatrogenic Creutzfeldt-Jakob disease in a human growth hormone recipient, original magnification × 200. KG9 anti-PrP antibody with a hematoxylin counterstain.

rospective studies identified earlier cases that were transmitted by contaminated neurosurgical instruments.[42] At present, more than 250 cases of iatrogenic CJD have been identified worldwide, most of which have occurred in recipients of human pituitary growth hormone and dura mater grafts. Cases of human-to-human transmission of CJD have been also described after exposure to contaminated intracerebral electrodes and corneal grafts.[43] Three recent cases of probable vCJD transmission by red cell transfusion are described below.

The incubation period in iatrogenic CJD varies according to the site of infection. Intracerebral exposure via neurosurgical instruments and electrodes is associated with the shortest incubation periods, whereas peripheral routes of inoculation, particularly those involving human growth hormone, have resulted in prolonged incubation periods of more than 30 years in some cases.[43] The clinical features of iatrogenic CJD are correspondingly varied; cases after neurosurgical exposure have features similar to those of the MM1 subtype of sCJD. However, the site of implantation of dura mater grafts in some patients has been found to correlate with the clinical presentation, as in cerebellar ataxia after a posterior fossa dura mater graft. In general, the clinical illness in recipients of human pituitary hormones is characterized by cerebellar ataxia, with dysarthria, myoclonus, and relative intellectual preservation until late in the illness. The duration of the clinical illness is also variable, but, in human growth hormone recipients, it tends to be approximately 12 months. Iatrogenic CJD in growth hormone recipients and dura mater graft recipients occurs most frequently in those who are homozygotes at codon 129 in the *PRNP*.[44,45] Homozygosity at codon 129 also appears to influence the incubation period, and heterozygotes have the longest incubation periods.[44]

The neuropathologic findings in iatrogenic CJD are similar to those in sCJD, but focally severe pathologic conditions in the region of the brain over which the dura mater graft was applied have been identified, including cases with selective cerebellar atrophy or parietal and occipital lobe atrophy.[45] A subset

of iatrogenic CJD cases occurring after dura mater graft procedures shows florid plaques in the cerebral cortex.[46] These are
less numerous and not as widespread as the florid plaques in
vCJD. Iatrogenic CJD in human pituitary hormone recipients
often shows cerebellar cortical atrophy, with extensive
neuronal loss and gliosis in addition to spongiform change
and occasional kuru-type amyloid plaques (Fig 3-7B).[47] Analysis of the PrP isotypes in the brain in iatrogenic CJD cases has
shown a type 1 $PrP^{TSE}$ isoform in cases associated with dura
mater grafts, but a predominantly type 2 $PrP^{TSE}$ is found in human pituitary hormone cases.[45,48]

# Kuru

Kuru occurred as an epidemic in the Fore tribe and their near
neighbors in the eastern highlands of New Guinea and was
first reported in 1957 by Gajdusek and Zigas.[49] They described
a progressive neurologic syndrome commencing with pos-
tural instability and loss of coordination and progressing to
ataxia, dysarthria, and "shivering tremors." The disease was
transmitted through the practice of cannibalistic feasting; this
practice was ended around 1956, which indicates that the most
recent cases represent incubation periods of more than 40
years.[50] Cerebellar atrophy was a common finding in kuru;
spongiform change was present in the cerebral cortex, the
caudate nucleus, and putamen, and patchy vacuolation occurred in the thalamus and hypothalamus. The molecular
layer in the cerebellum also showed prominent spongiform
change with loss of Purkinje cells and gliosis. The cerebellum
in many cases contained small, rounded, fibrillary amyloid
plaques in the granular layer,[51] which have become known as
"kuru-type" plaques. Similar plaques are identified in cases of
sCJD in the MV2 subgroup[4] and have also occurred in some
cases of iatrogenic CJD in growth hormone recipients (Fig
3-7B).

# Variant CJD

vCJD is the only acquired human prion disease to occur as a zoonosis, in which BSE infection occurs across a species barrier from bovines to humans. vCJD was first described in 1996 in the UK,[8] and additional cases have been identified subsequently in 10 other countries. France has the second largest total (17 cases) after the UK (161 cases at time of writing). The link between BSE and vCJD was made initially on the basis of epidemiology; however, subsequent experimental transmission studies showed that the infectious agent responsible for vCJD is identical to the BSE agent.[52] Epidemiologic studies of vCJD in the UK have indicated that the most likely route of infection in humans is through the consumption of BSE-contaminated meat products. There has been one significant cluster of vCJD cases in the UK, in a rural area of Leicestershire, and it was associated with a single potential source of infected meat products. vCJD occurs with a higher incidence in the northern part of the UK than in the southern part, but the reasons for this distribution remain unclear.[53]

## Clinical Features

The clinical features of vCJD are relatively uniform, and they differ in several important respects from those of sCJD and other human prion diseases.[8] The clinical course can be divided into three phases, the first of which is the early or psychiatric phase, in which depression, anxiety, and withdrawal are the main symptoms. This phase lasts for approximately 6 months, during which a diagnosis may be impossible until the first neurologic symptoms and signs appear.[54] Sensory abnormalities may occur in the early phase, with dysesthesia or paresthesia involving the face, arms, back, or legs. The next neurologic signs to appear are those of cerebellar dysfunction, usually commencing with gait ataxia. These are accompanied by a range of other neurologic abnormalities, including involuntary movements (chorea, dystonia, and myoclonus), progressive cognitive deficit, and other multifocal signs, such as dysphasia and pyramidal tract signs.[54] The final phase of the illness is one of akinetic mutism, which may last from several months to a few years.

The median duration of illness in vCJD is 14 months, and the range is 6 to 42 months; the median age at onset is 28 years, and the range is 12 to 74 years.[54] The disease occurs with equal frequency in males and females. The main differential diagnosis of vCJD is sCJD and other multifocal neurologic disorders such as Wilson's disease and cerebral vasculitis. A diagnosis of vCJD is aided by several clinical investigations. The EEG is abnormal, but a "typical" EEG of the type occurring in sCJD (see above) has not been identified in the early phase of the illness. Elevated levels of S100 and 14.3.3 proteins in the CSF occur only in approximately 50% of cases, so the results of these investigations are not included in the clinical diagnostic criteria (Table 3-2). MRI scans show a characteristic abnormality in T2-weighted and FLAIR sequences in more than 80% of cases and a bilateral area of high intensity in the pulvinar region of the thalamus, which may extend medially (Fig 3-8).[55] Brain biopsy was performed in several of the early cases of vCJD, but this procedure is now used seldom, if ever. However, the identification of PrP$^{TSE}$ in lymphoid tissues in vCJD (see below) has allowed the use of tonsil biopsy for diagnosis, with a type 2B PrP$^{TSE}$ isoform present on Western blotting[56] that is similar to that seen in the brain (Fig 3-2). Tonsil biopsy is an invasive procedure best reserved for patients with atypical clinical features or in whom the MRI scan does not show the characteristic abnormality in the pulvinar.

## Neuropathology

The neuropathologic features of vCJD are relatively uniform, in contrast to those of sCJD.[8] In most cases, the brain is macroscopically normal, but cerebellar and cerebral cortical atrophy may occur in cases with a prolonged disease duration.[17,57] The diagnostic neuropathologic features of vCJD are summarized in Table 3-5. Histologically, the most striking feature is the

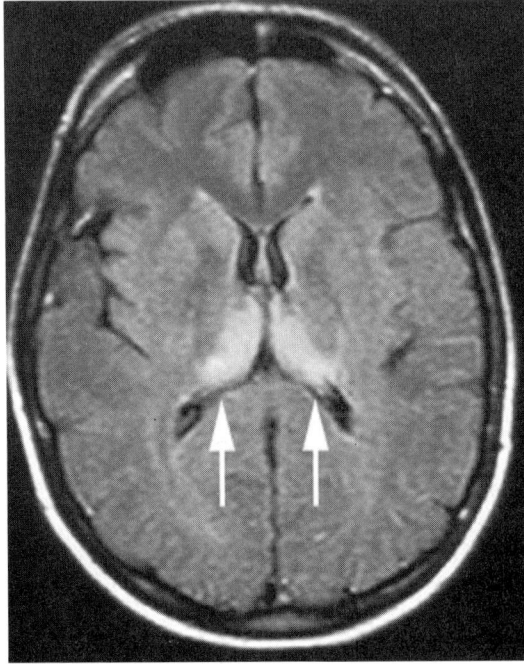

Figure 3-8. Transverse FLAIR MRI Scan showing bilateral and symmetrical high signal in the pulvinar nuclei of the thalamus—the "pulvinar sign" in a patient with variant Creutzfeldt-Jakob disease.

presence of florid plaques in the cerebral and cerebellar cortex. These comprise fibrillary amyloid plaques surrounded by a corona or halo of spongiform change, which are most numerous in the occipital cortex (Fig 3-9A). Smaller fibrillary plaques without surrounding spongiform change can be found in the basal ganglia and thalamus. Spongiform change is present in a widespread distribution in the brain, but it is most severe in the putamen and caudate nucleus. Neuronal loss in most brain regions accompanies the spongiform change, but severe neuronal loss is present in the posterior thalamic nuclei, particularly the pulvinar, often with minimal spongiform change.[57] Severe astrocytosis accompanies this marked neuronal loss, the distribution of which correlates with the ar-

## Table 3-5. Neuropathologic Diagnostic Criteria for Variant Creutzfeldt-Jakob Disease*

1.   Cerebral cortex and cerebellum

     Multiple florid plaques in routine stained sections

     Numerous small cluster plaques in prion protein (PrP)-stained sections

     Amorphous and pericapillary PrP accumulation

2.   Basal ganglia

     Severe spongiform change in caudate nucleus and putamen

     Perineuronal and periaxonal PrP accumulation

     Few florid plaques

3.   Thalamus

     Marked neuronal loss and gliosis in posterior thalamic nuclei (particularly the pulvinar)

     Patchy spongiform change in thalamic nuclei

     Few florid plaques

4.   Hypothalamus, brainstem, and spinal cord

     Perineuronal and synaptic PrP accumulation

     Little evidence of spongiform change or florid plaques

5.   Brain biochemistry

     Western blot analysis reveals a type 2B $PrP^{Sc}$ isoform in all brain regions

6.   Peripheral tissues

     Accumulation of PrP in germinal centers in all lymphoid tissues

     Western blot analysis reveals a type 2B $PrP^{Sc}$ isoform

*Modified from Will et al[8] and Ironside et al.[17]

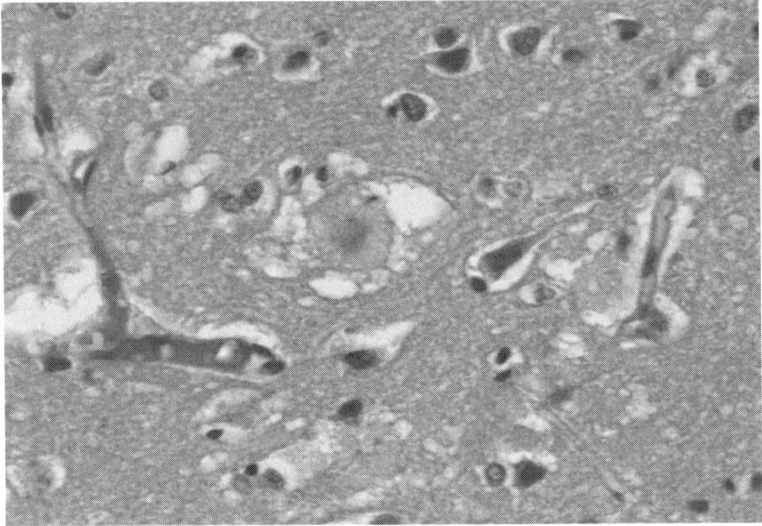

(A)

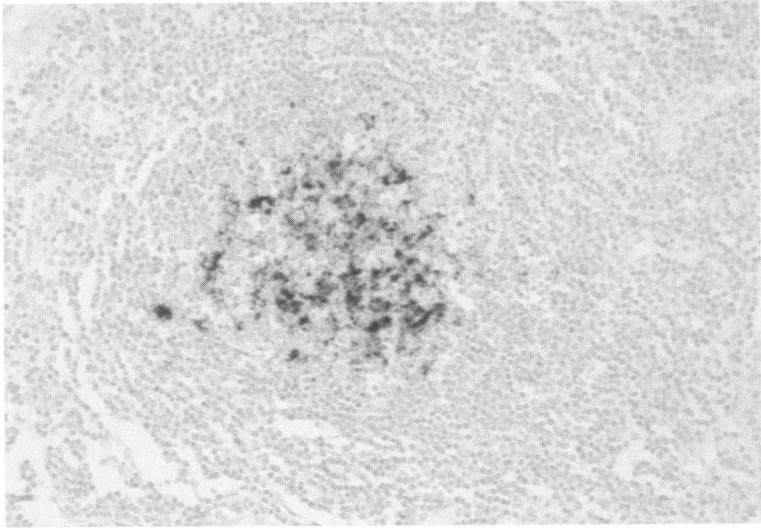

(B)

Figure 3-9. Brain and peripheral pathology in variant Creutzfeldt-Jakob disease. (A) A florid plaque (center) with a fibrillary amyloid core in the occipital cortex. Hematoxylin and eosin stain, original magnification × 400; (B) immunohistochemistry for prion protein in the tonsil shows a positive reaction in follicular dendritic cells and macrophages within a germinal center. KG9 anti-PrP antibody with hematoxylin counterstain, original magnification × 200.

eas of hyperintensity seen on T2-weighted and FLAIR sequence MRI scans of the thalamus in the clinical stage of variant CJD.[55]

Immunohistochemistry for PrP shows widespread positivity in vCJD, not only in the florid plaques but also in large numbers of smaller plaque-like lesions that are not evident on routine stains.[57] A widespread pericellular accumulation of PrP occurs in an amorphous or feathery distribution around small neurons and astrocytes. Perivascular accumulation of PrP is also noted around capillaries in the cerebral and cerebellar cortex, but there is no evidence of an amyloid angiopathy. In the basal ganglia, there is a combined perineuronal and periaxonal pattern of PrP positivity, often in a linear distribution.[17] In other brain regions, PrP accumulation occurs in a plaque-like and synaptic pattern. The neuropathologic findings in brain biopsies are similar to those in the cerebral cortex in autopsy cases, but the extent and severity of the lesions are less pronounced.

## Peripheral Pathology

Unlike other human prion diseases, $PrP^{TSE}$ accumulation and infectivity can be readily detected outside the central nervous system in vCJD.[48,58] There is intense positivity for PrP on immunohistochemistry of lymphoid tissues (spleen, tonsil, lymph nodes, and gut-associated lymphoid tissues) within germinal centers, involving follicular dendritic cells and macrophages.[48,56] PrP positivity in lymphoid follicles during the clinical disease has also allowed the use of tonsil biopsy as an aid to diagnosis (Fig 3-9B). A review of appendixes removed before the onset of clinical disease in vCJD patients found PrP positivity in lymphoid follicles up to 2 years before the onset of disease.[59] This finding has been exploited in a large retrospective study of anonymized tonsil and appendix tissues, which found that the UK may have had more vCJD infection than the number of clinical cases to date would suggest.[60]

The widespread distribution of PrP[TSE] in vCJD raises the possibility that the disease could be transmitted accidentally by medical or surgical procedures.[48,58] There have been three cases of probable transmission of vCJD infectivity by transfusion of nonleukocyte-reduced red cells from asymptomatic persons who developed vCJD after blood donation. The first and third recipients developed vCJD 6.5 years and around 8 years, respectively after transfusion,[61] but the second recipient died about 5 years after the transfusion without developing any clinical features of this illness. However, PrP[TSE] accumulation was detected by Western blotting and by immunohistochemistry in some lymphoid tissues (spleen and lymph nodes) of that patient, but not in the tonsil, appendix, or central nervous system, and those findings indicate an asymptomatic or preclinical infection.[62] The involvement of the spleen and lymph nodes, but not the tonsil and appendix, in this case might relate to an intravenous route of infection, rather than the oral route that is likely for primary cases of vCJD.

To date, all persons developing vCJD in the UK and other countries have been methionine homozygotes at codon 129 in the *PRNP* and have had type 2B PrP[TSE] in the brain.[12,48] However, the second transfusion-associated vCJD infection occurred in a person who was a heterozygote at codon 129 in the *PRNP*, which confirms that other *PRNP* genotypes are susceptible to infection.[62] It remains to be seen whether BSE infection in other human *PRNP* genotypes will result in a clinical illness and, if so, whether the clinical and neuropathologic features will be similar to those of the cases of vCJD that have occurred in *PRNP* codon 129 methionine homozygotes. Continuing surveillance for human prion diseases is required to address this important issue.

## Conclusion

Human prion diseases are a group of neurodegenerative disorders that occur as sporadic, familial, or acquired diseases. Most human prion diseases are transmitted experimentally, but the precise nature of the infectious agent remains unclear. There is an increasing body of evidence to support the prion hypothesis, which proposes that the agent is composed entirely of the modified host protein PrP$^{TSE}$. The emergence of BSE and the identification of vCJD have renewed interest in this group of otherwise rare diseases, which has resulted in improved clinical and laboratory-based diagnostic techniques. The continuing uncertainties over vCJD in the UK have led to the introduction of a number of measures designed to prevent secondary spread of the disease by blood and blood products or by surgical instruments. Neuropathologic examination is essential for a definitive diagnosis of prion disease, and it has a key role to play in establishing the range of phenotypic variation in this group of disorders, which considerably surpasses the range in other neurodegenerative diseases. Continuing surveillance for human prion diseases is required to study these variables and to monitor the incidence and spread of vCJD across the world.

## Acknowledgments

The author thanks Mark Head for providing Fig 3-2, Jan Mackenzie for providing Figs 3-3 and 3-4, Kirsteen Forrest for assistance in the preparation of this manuscript, Diane Ritchie for photographic assistance, and Linda McCardle, Suzanne Lowry, Margaret LeGrice, and Chris-Anne McKenzie for technical support. The UK National Creutzfeldt-Jakob Disease Surveillance Unit is funded by the Department of Health and the Scottish Executive. We are indebted to neurologists and neuropathologists across the UK for their continuing support.

## References

1.  Prusiner SB. An introduction to prion biology and diseases. In: Crotty D, Schaefer S, eds. Prion biology and diseases. 2nd ed. Woodbury, NY: Cold Spring Harbor Laboratory Press, 2004:1-87.

2.  Neufeld MY, Josiphov J, Korczyn AD. Demyelinating peripheral neuropathy in Creutzfeldt-Jakob disease. Muscle Nerve 1992;15:1234-9.
3.  Bell JE, Gentleman SM, Ironside JW, et al. Prion protein immunocytochemistry—UK Five Centre Consensus Report. Neuropathol Appl Neurobiol 1997;23:26-35.
4.  Parchi P, Giese A, Capellari S, et al. Classification of sporadic Creutzfeldt-Jakob disease based on molecular and phenotypic analysis of 300 subjects. Ann Neurol 1999;46:224-33.
5.  Kovacs GG, Head MW, Hegyi I, et al. Immunohistochemistry for the prion protein: Comparison of different monoclonal antibodies in human prion disease subtypes. Brain Pathol 2002;12:1-11.
6.  Ironside JW. Creutzfeldt-Jakob disease. Brain Pathol 1996;6:379-88.
7.  Wells GA, Scott AC, Johnson CT, et al. A novel progressive spongiform encephalopathy in cattle. Vet Rec 1987;121:419-20.
8.  Will RG, Ironside JW, Zeidler M, et al. A new variant of Creutzfeldt-Jakob disease in the UK. Lancet 1996;347:921-5.
9.  Clinical diagnostic criteria for CJD. Edinburgh, UK: National Creutzfeldt-Jakob Disease Surveillance Unit, University of Edinburgh, 2005. [Available at http://cjd.ed.ac.uk/criteria.htm (accessed February 3, 2006).]
10. Zerr I, Schulz-Schaeffer WJ, Giese A, et al. Current clinical diagnosis in Creutzfeldt-Jakob disease: Identification of uncommon variants. Ann Neurol 2000;48:323-9.
11. Budka H, Aguzzi A, Brown P, et al. Neuropathological diagnostic criteria for Creutzfeldt-Jakob disease (CJD) and other human spongiform encephalopathies. Brain Pathol 1995;4:459-66.
12. Head MW, Bunn TJR, Bishop MT, et al. Prion protein heterogeneity in sporadic but not variant Creutzfeldt-Jakob disease: UK cases 1991-2002. Ann Neurol 2004;55:851-9.
13. Gambetti P, Kong Q, Zou W, et al. Sporadic and familial CJD: Classification and characterisation (review). Br Med Bull 2003;66:213-39.
14. Budka H. Neuropathology of prion disease (review). Br Med Bull 2003;66:121-30.
15. Almer G, Hainfellner JA, Brucke T, et al. Fatal familial insomnia: A new Austrian family. Brain 1999;122:5-16.
16. Montagna P, Gambetti P, Cortelli P, et al. Familial and sporadic fatal insomnia. Lancet Neurol 2003;2:167-76.
17. Ironside JW, McCardle L, Horsburgh A, et al. Pathological diagnosis of variant Creutzfeldt-Jakob disease. APMIS 2002;11:79-87.
18. Prusiner SB. Development of the prion concept. In: Crotty D, Schaefer S, eds. Prion biology and diseases. 2nd ed. Woodbury, NY: Cold Spring Harbor Laboratory Press, 2004:89-141.
19. Bessen RA, Marsh RF. Distinct PrP properties suggest the molecular basis of strain variation in transmissible mink encephalopathy. J Virol 1994;68:7859-68.
20. Aguzzi A, Polymenidou M. Mammalian prion biology: One century of evolving concepts. Cell 2004;116:313-27.

21. Parchi P, Zou W, Wang W, et al. Genetic influence on the structural variations of the abnormal prion protein. Proc Natl Acad Sci U S A 2000;97:10168-72.
22. Collinge J, Sidle KCL, Meads J, et al. Molecular analysis of prion strain variation and the aetiology of 'new variant' CJD. Nature 1996;383: 685-90.
23. Parchi P, Capellari S, Chen SG, et al. Typing prion isoforms. Nature 1997;386:232-4.
24. Ladogana A, Puopolo M, Croes EA, et al. Mortality from Creutzfeldt-Jakob disease and related disorders in Europe, Australia and Canada. Neurology 2005;64:1586-91.
25. Ironside JW, Ritchie DL, Head MW. Phenotypic variability in human prion diseases. Neuropathol Appl Neurobiol 2005;31:565-79.
26. Tschampa HJ, Kallenberg K, Urbach H, et al. MRI in the diagnosis of sporadic Creutzfeldt-Jakob disease: A study on inter-observer variability. Brain 2005;128:2026-33.
27. Alperovitch A, Zerr I, Pocchiari M, et al. Codon 129 prion protein genotype and sporadic Creutzfeldt-Jakob disease. Lancet 1999;353:1673-4.
28. Mizutani T. Neuropathology of Creutzfeldt-Jakob disease in Japan. With special reference to the panencephalopathic type. Acta Pathol Jpn 1981;31:903-22.
29. Hill AF, Joiner S, Wadsworth JDF, et al. Molecular classification of sporadic Creutzfeldt-Jakob disease. Brain 2003;126:1333-46.
30. Head MW, Tissingh G, Uitdehaag BM, et al. Sporadic Creutzfeldt-Jakob disease in a young Dutch valine homozygote: Atypical molecular phenotype. Ann Neurol 2001;50:258-61.
31. Ghetti B, Tagliavini F, Takao M, et al. Hereditary prion protein amyloidoses. Clin Lab Med 2003;23:65-85.
32. Kovacs GG, Trabattoni G, Hainfellner JA, et al. Mutations of the prion protein gene phenotypic spectrum. J Neurol 2002;249:1567-82.
33. Lee HS, Sambuughin N, Cervenakova L, et al. Ancestral origins and worldwide distribution of the PRNP 200K mutation causing familial Creutzfeldt-Jakob disease. Am J Hum Genet 1999;64:1063-70.
34. Puoti G, Rossi G, Giaccone G, et al. Polymorphism at codon 129 of PRNP affects the phenotypic expression of Creutzfeldt-Jakob disease linked to E200K mutation. Ann Neurol 2000;48:269-70.
35. Parchi P, Petersen RB, Chen SG, et al. Molecular pathology of fatal familial insomnia. Brain Pathol 1998;8:539-48.
36. King A, Doey L, Rossor M, et al. Phenotypic variability in the brains of a family with a prion disease characterized by a 144-base pair insertion in the prion protein gene. Neuropathol Appl Neurobiol 2003; 29:98-105.
37. Vital C, Gray F, Vital A, et al. Prion encephalopathy with insertion of octapeptide repeats: The number of repeats determines the type of cerebellar deposits. Neuropathol Appl Neurobiol 1998;24:125-30.
38. Hainfellner J, Brantner-Inhaler S, Cervenakova L, et al. The original Gerstmann-Sträussler-Scheinker family of Austria: Divergent clinico-

pathological phenotypes but constant PrP genotype. Brain Pathol 1995;5:201-13.

39.  Hsiao K, Baker HF, Crow TJ, et al. Linkage of a prion protein missense variant to Gerstmann-Sträussler syndrome. Nature 1989;338:342-5.

40.  Kitamoto T, Iizuka R, Tateishi J. An amber mutation of prion protein in Gerstmann-Sträussler syndrome with mutant PrP plaques. Biochem Biophys Res Commun 1993;192:525-31.

41.  Duffy P, Wolf J, Collins G, et al. Possible person-to-person transmission of Creutzfeldt-Jakob disease. N Engl J Med 1974;290:692-3.

42.  Nevin S, McMenemey WH, Behrman S, et al. Subacute spongiform encephalopathy—a subacute form of encephalopathy attributable to vascular dysfunction (spongiform cerebral atrophy). Brain 1960;83: 519-63.

43.  Brown P, Preece M, Brandel JP, et al. Iatrogenic Creutzfeldt-Jakob disease at the millennium. Neurology 2000;55:1075-81.

44.  Brandel JP, Preece M, Brown P, et al. Distribution of codon 129 genotype in human growth hormone-treated CJD patients in France and the UK. Lancet 2003;62:128-30.

45.  Heath CA, Barker RA, Esmonde TFG, et al. Dura mater-associated Creutzfeldt-Jakob disease—experience from UK Surveillance. J Neurol Neurosurg Psych 2006 (in press).

46.  Shimizu S, Hoshi T, Homma M, et al. Creutzfeldt-Jakob disease with florid-type plaques after cadaveric dura mater grafting. Arch Neurol 1999;56:357-63.

47.  Swerdlow AJ, Higgins CD, Adlard P, et al. Creutzfeldt-Jakob disease in United Kingdom patients treated with human pituitary growth hormone. Neurology 2003;61:783-91.

48.  Head MW, Ritchie D, Smith N, et al. Peripheral tissue involvement in sporadic, iatrogenic and variant Creutzfeldt-Jakob disease: An immunohistochemical, quantitative and biochemical study. Am J Pathol 2004; 164:143-53.

49.  Gajdusek DC, Zigas V. Degenerative disease of the central nervous system in New Guinea. The endemic occurrence of "kuru" in the native population. N Engl J Med 1957;257:974-8.

50.  Goldfarb LG, Cervenakova L, Gajdusek DC. Genetic studies in relation to kuru: An overview. Curr Mol Med 2004;4:375-84.

51.  McLean CA, Ironside JW, Alpers MP, et al. Comparative neuropathology of kuru with the new variant of Creutzfeldt-Jakob disease: Evidence for strain of agent predominating over genotype of host. Brain Pathol 1998;8:428-37.

52.  Bruce E, Will RG, Ironside JW, et al. Transmissions to mice indicate that "new variant" CJD is caused by the BSE agent. Nature 1997;389: 498-501.

53.  Cousens S, Smith PG, Ward H, et al. Geographic distribution of variant Creutzfeldt-Jakob disease in Great Britain 1994-2000. Lancet 2001; 357:1002-7.

54. Ward HJT, Head MW, Will RG, et al. Variant Creutzfeldt-Jakob disease. Clin Lab Med 2003;23:87-108.

55. Collie DA, Summers DM, Sellar RJ, et al. Diagnosing variant Creutz-feldt-Jakob disease with the pulvinar sign: MR imaging findings in 86 neuropathologically confirmed cases. Am J Neuroradiol 2003;24:1560-9.

56. Hill AF, Butterworth RJ, Joiner S, et al. Investigation of variant Creutz-feldt-Jakob disease and other human prion diseases with tonsil biopsy samples. Lancet 1999;353:183-9.

57. Ironside JW, Head MW, Bell JE, et al. Laboratory diagnosis of variant Creutzfeldt-Jakob disease. Histopathology 2000;37:1-9.

58. Bruce ME, McConnell I, Will RG, et al. Detection of variant Creutz-feldt-Jakob disease infectivity in extraneural tissues. Lancet 2001;358: 208-9.

59. Hilton DA, Fathers E, Edwards P, et al. Prion immunoreactivity in ap-pendix before clinical onset of variant Creutzfeldt-Jakob disease. Lan-cet 1998;352:703-4.

60. Hilton DA, Ghani AC, Conyers L, et al. Prevalence of lymphoreticular prion protein accumulation in UK tissue samples. J Pathol 2004;203: 733-9.

61. Llewelyn CA, Hewitt PE, Knight RS, et al. Possible transmission of variant Creutzfeldt-Jakob disease by blood transfusion. Lancet 2004; 363:417-21.

62. Peden AH, Head MW, Ritchie DL, et al. Preclinical vCJD after blood transfusion in a PRNP codon 129 heterozygous patient. Lancet 2004; 364:477-9.

In: Turner ML, ed.
*Creutzfeldt-Jakob Disease: Managing the Risk of
Transmission by Blood, Plasma, and Tissues*
Bethesda, MD: AABB Press, 2006

4

# Blood Infectivity in the Transmissible Spongiform Encephalopathies

## PAUL BROWN, MD

ATTEMPTS TO SHOW BLOOD infectivity in transmissible spongiform encephalopathy (TSE) span nearly half a century, from the early days of research on naturally-occurring and experimentally-induced scrapie in sheep[1-33] (Tables 4-1 and 4-2). Among the many early failures were some scattered successes that met with little enthusiasm in light of the uniformly negative results reported in the magisterial pathogenesis studies by Hadlow et al[1,2,15] and Eklund et al.[18] However, during the next 20 years, a continuing record of successes and failures accumulated enough successes to dispel any doubts about at least the occasional occurrence of blood infectivity in several different experimental models of TSE. The debut of systematic time-course studies carried out during both the preclinical and clinical phases of disease led to the realization that, with due attention to opti-

*Paul Brown, MD, Bethesda, Maryland*

mal bioassay methods, blood infectivity might even be shown to be a general phenomenon.

Transmissibility of disease via blood has now been established in several experimental models: bovine spongiform encephalopathy (BSE), Gerstmann-Sträussler-Scheinker disease (GSS), and variant Creutzfeldt-Jakob disease (vCJD) in mice[25,29-31,33]; sporadic Creutzfeldt-Jakob disease (sCJD) in guinea pigs[32]; scrapie in hamsters[19-21]; BSE in sheep[28]; and GSS in chimpanzees.[10] Blood has also been shown to be infectious in naturally occurring scrapie in sheep[3] and in human vCJD.[34,35] Whether infectivity is (or can be) present in the blood of nonvariant cases of Creutzfeldt-Jakob disease (CJD) remains an open question, and, although all epidemiologic evidence to date suggests that it is not present, the pathologically misfolded prion protein (PrP$^{TSE}$) associated with infectivity has recently been detected in the blood of at least some patients with both variant and nonvariant forms of disease.[36,37]

## Issues of Interpretation

An even casual inspection of the data summarized in Tables 4-1 and 4-2 reveals a disconcerting lack of consistency from study to study that calls for an explanation. The problem stems largely from the comparatively low concentration of infectivity in blood, which makes detection more difficult than in central nervous system or lymphoreticular tissues, which contain much higher levels of the infectious agents.

At least three conditions or issues must be appreciated to understand and interpret the results. The first issue is that of a "species barrier" between the blood donor and the recipient used for the infectivity bioassay. Susceptibility to infection is an obvious requirement (hamsters, for example, are not susceptible to infection by the agent of BSE and would be useless for bioassay). More important, even if the recipient species is susceptible, the pathogen must adapt to the new host, which can require at least one or two serial passages in the new species to achieve its full potential. Thus, if tissue from a scra-

## Table 4-1. Attempts to Transmit Transmissible Spongiform Encephalopathy from Blood or Blood Components of Naturally Infected Animals and Humans

| Species Donor | Species Recipient | Inoculum | Route of Inoculation* | Positive/ Total Donors | Reference |
|---|---|---|---|---|---|
| **Scrapie** | | | | | |
| Goat | Mouse | Blood clot | IC | 0/3 | Hadlow, 1980[1] |
| | | Serum | IC | 0/3 | |
| Sheep | Mouse | Blood clot | IC | 0/17 | Hadlow, 1982[2] |
| | | Serum | IC | 0/8 | |
| Sheep | Sheep | Whole blood | IV | 4/10 | Hunter, 2002[3] and unpublished data |
| | | Buffy coat | IV | 5/11 | |
| **BSE** | | | | | |
| Cow | Mouse | Blood clot | IC + IP | 0/1 | Fraser, 1993[4] |
| | | Buffy coat | IC + IP | 0/1 | |
| | | Serum | IC + IP | 0/1 | |
| **sCJD** | | | | | |
| Human | Guinea pig | Buffy coat | IC | 2/2 | Manuelidis, 1985[5] |
| Human | Mouse | Buffy coat | IC | 1/1 | Tateishi, 1985[6] |
| Human | Mouse | Buffy coat | IC | 1/1 | Tamai, 1992[7] |
| Human | Hamster | Buffy coat | IC | 1/1 | Deslys, 1994[8] |
| Human | Chimpanzee | Whole blood | IV | 0/3 | Gibbs and Gajdusek |
| | Monkey | Whole blood | IC, IV, IP, IM | 0/2 | (cited in Brown, 1995[9]) |

**(continued)**

## Table 4-1. Attempts to Transmit Transmissible Spongiform Encephalopathy from Blood or Blood Components of Naturally Infected Animals and Humans (Continued)

| Donor | Recipient | Inoculum | Route of Inoculation* | Positive/Total Donors | Reference |
|---|---|---|---|---|---|
| | | Buffy coat | IC + IV | 0/4 | |
| | Guinea pig | Whole blood | IC + IP | 0/1 | |
| Human | Monkey[†] | Buffy coat | IC + IV | 0/2 (pools) | Brown, 2004[10] (Unpublished data) |
| | | Plasma | IC + IV | 0/2 (pools) | |
| **vCJD** | | | | | |
| Human | Mouse | Buffy coat | IC | 0/4 | Bruce, 2001[11] |
| Human | Monkey[†] | Buffy coat | IC + IV | 0/3 | Brown, 2004[10] (Unpublished data) |
| | | Plasma | IC + IV | 0/3 | |
| Human | Monkey[†] | Whole blood | IV | 0/2 | Lasmézas, 2005[12] (Unpublished data) |
| | | Buffy coat | IC | 0/2 | |

*"+" indicates inocula given by multiple routes to the same assay animals.
[†]Ongoing experiment (unpublished data provided by N Hunter, C Lasmézas, and GAH Wells).
BSE = bovine spongiform encephalopathy; sCJD = sporadic Creutzfeldt-Jakob disease; vCJD = variant CJD; IC = intracerebral; IM = intramuscular; IV = intravenous; IP = intraperitoneal.

## Table 4-2. Attempts to Transmit Transmissible Spongiform Encephalopathy from Blood or Blood Components of Experimentally Infected Animals

| Species | | | | | |
|---|---|---|---|---|---|
| Donor | Recipient | Inoculum | Route of Inoculation* | Positive/Total Donors | Reference |
| **Scrapie** | | | | | |
| Goat | Goat | Whole blood | IC | 0/14 | Pattison, 1962[13] |
| Sheep | Mouse | Serum | IC | 1/1 | Gibbs, 1965[14] |
| Mouse | Mouse | Blood clot/serum | IC | 0/13 (pools) | Eklund, 1967[18] |
| | | Serum | IC | 0/13 (pools) | |
| Mouse | Mouse | Serum | IC | 1/1 (pool) | Clarke, 1967[16] |
| | Rat | Serum | IC | 1/1 (pool) | |
| Mouse | Mouse | Whole blood | IC | 4/12 | Dickinson, 1969[17] |
| Goat | Mouse | Blood clot | IC | 0/17 | Hadlow, 1974[15] |
| | | | SC | 0/3 | |
| Hamster | Hamster | Whole blood | IC | 0/9 | Diringer, 1984[19] |
| | | Blood concentrate | IC | 5/5 (pools) | |
| Hamster | Hamster | Blood concentrate | IC | 10/11 (pools) | Casaccia, 1989[20] |
| Hamster | Hamster | Whole blood | IC | 31/124 | Rohwer, 2002[21] (Unpublished data) |
| | | | IV | 3/112 | |

(continued)

**Table 4-2. Attempts to Transmit Transmissible Spongiform Encephalopathy from Blood or Blood Components of Experimentally Infected Animals (Continued)**

| Species | | | | Posi- | |
| --- | --- | --- | --- | --- | --- |
| Donor | Reci- pient | Inoculum | Route of Inocula- tion* | tive/ Total Donors | Reference |
| **TME** | | | | | |
| Mink | Mink | Serum | IC | 0/2 | Marsh, 1969[22] |
| Mink | Mink | Whole blood and blood compo- nents | IC | 0/8 | Marsh, 1973[23] |
| **BSE** | | | | | |
| Cow | Mouse | Buffy coat | IC + IP | 0/8 (pools) | Wells, 1998[24] and unpublished data |
| Mouse | Mouse | Plasma | IC | 4/48 | Taylor, 2000[25] |
| Microcebe | Micro- cebe | Buffy coat | IC | 1/1 | Bons, 2002[26] |
| Cow | Cow[†] | Buffy coat | IC | 0/4 (pools) | Wells, 2005[27] |
| Sheep | Sheep[†] | Whole blood | IV | 5/16 | Houston, 2000[28] and unpublished data |
| | | Buffy coat | IV | 1/7 | |
| Monkey | Monkey[†] | Whole blood | IV | 0/2 | Lasmézas, 2005[12] (Unpublished data) |
| | | Buffy coat | IC | 0/1 | |
| | | Plasma | IC | 0/1 | |

## Table 4-2. Attempts to Transmit Transmissible Spongiform Encephalopathy from Blood or Blood Components of Experimentally Infected Animals (Continued)

| Species | | | | | |
|---|---|---|---|---|---|
| Donor | Recipient | Inoculum | Route of Inoculation* | Positive/Total Donors | Reference |
| **GSS** | | | | | |
| Mouse | Mouse | Buffy coat | IP | 4/7 (pools) | Kuroda, 1983[29] |
| Mouse | Mouse | Buffy coat | IC | 5/5 (pools) | Brown, 1998[30], 1999[31] |
| | | Plasma | IC | 5/5 (pools) | |
| | | Buffy coat | IV | 2/2 (pools) | |
| | | Plasma | IV | 2/2 (pools) | |
| Chimpanzee | Monkey | Leukocytes | IC + IV | 1/1 | Brown, 2004[10] (Unpublished data) |
| | | Plasma | IC + IV | 0/1 | |
| | | Platelets | IC + IV | 0/1 | |
| | | Red cells | IC + IV | 0/1 | |
| **sCJD** | | | | | |
| Guinea pig | Guinea pig | Buffy coat | IC, SC, IM, IP | 10/28 | Manuelidis, 1978[32] |
| Monkey† | Monkey | Whole blood | IV | 0/4 | Brown, 2004[10] (Unpublished data) |

**(continued)**

### Table 4-2. Attempts to Transmit Transmissible Spongiform Encephalopathy from Blood or Blood Components of Experimentally Infected Animals (Continued)

| Species | | | | Posi- | |
| Donor | Reci- pient | Inoculum | Route of Inocula- tion* | tive/ Total Donors | Reference |
|---|---|---|---|---|---|
| Chimpan- zee | Monkey | Leukocytes | IC + IV | 0/2 | |
| | | Plasma | IC + IV | 0/2 | |
| | | Platelets | IC + IV | 0/2 | |
| | | Red cells | IC + IV | 0/3 | |
| **vCJD** | | | | | |
| Mouse | Mouse | Buffy coat | IC | 2/2 (pools) | Cervenakova, 2003[33] |
| | | | IV | 2/2 (pools) | |
| | | Plasma | IC | 2/2 (pools) | |
| | | | IV | 2/2 (pools) | |
| Monkey | Monkey[†] | Whole blood | IV | 0/4 | Brown, 2004[10] and unpub- lished data |
| Monkey | Monkey | Whole blood | IV | 0/1 | Lasmézas, 2005[12] (Unpublished data) |
| | | Buffy coat | IC | 0/2 | |

*"+" indicates inocula given by multiple routes to the same assay animals.
[†]Ongoing experiment (unpublished data provided by N Hunter, C Lasmézas, and GAH Wells).
BSE = bovine spongiform encephalopathy; TME = transmissible mink encephalopathy; GSS = Gerstmann-Sträussler-Scheinker syndrome; sCJD = sporadic Creutzfeldt-Jakob disease; vCJD = variant CJD; IC = intracerebral; IM = intramuscular; IV = intravenous; IP = intraperitoneal; SC = subcutaneous.

pie-infected sheep is bioassayed in a mouse, low levels of infectivity may not be detectable until after one or more subsequent mouse-to-mouse passages. Because of time, space, and financial constraints, none of the bioassays performed in a species different from that of the donor used this more sensitive method of serial passage detection.

The second issue is also related to the sensitivity of detection. Until the late 1980s, evaluation of the positive status of bioassayed animals depended solely on clinical observation and neuropathologic verification. Since then, a more sensitive method—Western Blot or immunohistochemical detection of the pathognomonic misfolded protein (PrP$^{TSE}$)—has made it possible to reveal infection in some bioassay animals with either ambiguous or absent clinical and neuropathologic signs, ie, animals in a prolonged preclinical (or subclinical) phase of disease.

The third issue is that of dose and route of infection that are used for the bioassay. Intracerebral inoculation is the optimal route for transmitting infection, but the volumes that can be inoculated are small—0.03 to 0.05 mL in rodents and not more than 0.25 mL in primates and ruminants. Two strategies can be used to increase the dose of inoculated material: the use of peripheral (intravenous or intraperitoneal) routes that permit much larger inoculation volumes, and the use of much larger numbers of intracerebrally inoculated animals than are customarily used for bioassays. This approach is more expensive but also much more sensitive when the aim is to distinguish between little or no infectivity rather than to measure the difference between two high levels of infectivity.

Technical issues aside, we must also be wary of accepting the results from experimental animal models of disease as directly applicable to naturally occurring human disease. TSE strains that have been adapted to animals (usually rodents) often show a greater degree of what may be called "virulence"— higher concentrations of infectivity in a more widespread organ distribution—than is seen in naturally occurring infections. Still, animal studies can be evaluated for clues to answer the following four questions: 1) how frequently does infectivity occur? 2) how soon during the course of disease does it occur? 3) in which components does it occur? and 4) at what concentrations does it occur?

# Animal Studies

## Frequency and Timing

From a superficial inspection of the studies shown in Tables 4-1 and 4-2, it would appear to be impossible to judge the frequency with which infectivity occurs in blood, ranging as it does over the full scale from 0% to 100% (42% on average). Attention to the methods used in the various studies can help us understand and interpret this apparent inconsistency: scrapie, the most thoroughly studied of the listed TSEs, is a good illustrative example. Most of the earlier investigations, including the meticulous studies of Hadlow and Eklund and their colleagues,[1,2,15,18] failed to transmit disease from the blood of either naturally occurring or experimentally induced scrapie infections, but more recent studies have consistently succeeded in transmitting disease. The explanation can be found in the fact that the earlier studies were all conducted by using very small volumes of blood (≤0.05 mL) that were inoculated into comparatively small numbers of bioassay animals. When much larger volumes of blood were administered, either by intravenous administration or by using large numbers of inoculated animals by the intracerebral route, the dose was high enough to exceed the threshold of detection for the low levels of infectivity that are now known to be present in blood. Similar considerations apply to the other categories of TSE listed in the Tables—most importantly to the negative studies so far conducted on BSE in cattle—and to most studies of CJD in primates that have so far failed to transmit disease during observation periods of up to 5 years. It seems likely that further studies using optimal bioassay methods may well succeed and that infectivity may be present in the blood of a significant proportion of animals during the symptomatic phase of all forms of TSE.

The more important question is that of timing—how long before the onset of symptoms infectivity may be present in blood—because it is during this preclinical period that silently infected persons would still be healthy active blood donors. Here again, there is much inconsistency in the results from experimental infection of animals. In the earliest time-course study in which infectivity was demonstrable, whole blood from scrapie-infected mice was shown to begin to be infectious approximately two-thirds of the way through the incubation period.[17] Other studies found blood to be infectious throughout the incubation period, only in the last two-thirds of the incubation period, or only in the last one-third of the incubation period (Table 4-3). From these results, it is possible to conclude that blood from a proportion of animals with both natural and experimentally induced TSE can transmit disease during the preclinical phase of disease, but it is not possible to stipulate the length of time before symptoms appear, which seems to depend on both the type of TSE and the species of infected animal.

## Distribution and Concentration

It is somewhat easier to evaluate the distribution and levels of infectivity in blood and its components from animals with TSE (Table 4-4). Studies of experimental scrapie,[21,38] BSE,[25] GSS,[29-31] and vCJD[33] have all tended to the conclusion that the highest levels of infectivity in blood are associated with leukocytes. Plasma contains lower levels of infectivity, some of which is not cell associated, and the infectivity present in red cell and platelet fractions is most likely due to contamination by leukocytes (although one study of highly purified red cells has not yet been completed[10]). It is important to note that the much larger proportional volume of plasma than of buffy coat in

## Table 4-3. Time-Course Studies of Blood Infectivity in Transmissible Spongiform Encephalopathy

| Species | | | Infectivity During Incubation Period (by thirds) | | | |
|---|---|---|---|---|---|---|
| Donor | Reci-pient | Inoculum | 1st | 2nd | 3rd | Reference |
| **Scrapie** | | | | | | |
| Mouse | Mouse | Whole blood | – | – | – | Eklund, 1967[15] |
| Mouse | Mouse | Whole blood | – | + | + | Dickinson, 1969[17] |
| Goat | Mouse | Blood clot | – | – | – | Hadlow, 1974[18] |
| Hamster | Hamster | Blood con-centrate | + | NT | NT | Diringer, 1984[19] |
| Hamster | Hamster | Blood con-centrate | + | + | + | Casaccia, 1989[20] |
| Hamster | Hamster | Whole blood | – | + | + | Rohwer, 2002[21] |
| Sheep | Sheep | Whole blood | NT | + | + | Hunter, 2002[3] and unpub-lished data |
| | | Buffy coat | NT | + | + | |
| **TME** | | | | | | |
| Mink | Mink | Lympho-cytes | – | – | – | Marsh, 1973[23] |
| **BSE** | | | | | | |
| Cattle | Mouse | Blood clot, serum, and buffy coat | – | – | – | Wells, 1998[24] and un-published data |

## Table 4-3. Time-Course Studies of Blood Infectivity in Transmissible Spongiform Encephalopathy (Continued)

| Species | | | Infectivity During Incubation Period (by thirds) | | | |
|---------|---------|---------|-----|-----|-----|-----------|
| Donor | Recipient | Inoculum | 1st | 2nd | 3rd | Reference |
| Cattle* | Cattle | Buffy coat | – | – | – | Wells, 2005[27] |
| Sheep* | Sheep | Whole blood | NT | + | + | Houston, 2000[28] and unpublished data |
| | | Buffy coat | NT | – | + | |
| **GSS** | | | | | | |
| Mouse | Mouse | Buffy coat | – | + | + | Kuroda, 1983[29] |
| Mouse | Mouse | Buffy coat/ plasma | – | – | + | Brown, 1999[31] |
| **sCJD** | | | | | | |
| Guinea pig | Guinea pig | Buffy coat | + | + | + | Manuelidis, 1978[32] |
| **vCJD** | | | | | | |
| Mouse | Mouse | Buffy coat/ plasma | NT | NT | + | Cervenakova, 2003[33] |

*Ongoing experiment. NT = not tested; TME = transmissible mink encephalopathy; BSE = bovine spongiform encephalopathy; GSS = Gerstmann-Sträussler-Scheinker syndrome; sCJD = sporadic Creutzfeldt-Jakob disease; vCJD = variant CJD.

**Table 4-4. Blood Infectivity Titers in Experimental Models of Transmissible Spongiform Encephalopathy**

| TSE | Agent Strain | Species | Blood Component | Titer Range (ID/mL) | Reference |
|-----|-----|-----|-----|-----|-----|
| Scrapie | 263K | Hamster | Whole blood | ≈40-60* | Casaccia, 1989[20] |
| Scrapie | 263K | Hamster | Whole blood | 9-24 | Rohwer, 2002[21] (Unpublished data) |
| | | | Buffy coat | 26-35 | |
| | | | Whole blood | 13 | Gregori, 2004[38] |
| BSE | 301V | Mouse | Plasma | 4-5 | Taylor, 2000[25] |
| GSS | Fukuoka-1 | Mouse | Buffy coat | ≈60* | Kuroda, 1983[29] |
| | | | Buffy coat | 44-106 | Brown, 1998,[30] 1999[31] |
| | | | Plasma | 10-34 | |
| vCJD | ND | Mouse | Buffy coat | 18 | Cervenakova, 2003[33] |
| | | | Plasma | 21 | |

*Estimated from incubation periods. TSE = transmissible sponiforn encepholopathy; ID = infectious doses; BSE = bovine spongiform encephalopathy; GSS = Gerstmann-Sträussler-Scheinker syndrome; vCJD = variant Creutzfeldt-Jakob disease; ND = not designated (human isolate of vCJD passaged in RIII mice).

whole blood means that the total amount of infectivity in plasma may equal or exceed the total amount of infectivity in buffy coat.

In four studies, infectivity levels have been measured during the course of the incubation period. In one study of the hamster scrapie model, infectivity progressively decreased during the course of the incubation period[20]; in another study of the same model and in two studies of the mouse-adapted GSS model, very low levels of infectivity began to appear about halfway through the incubation period, and they steadily increased through the clinical phase of the disease,[29,31] as shown in Figs 4-1 and 4-2. No infectivity titration studies have been conducted in any nonrodent model of TSE.

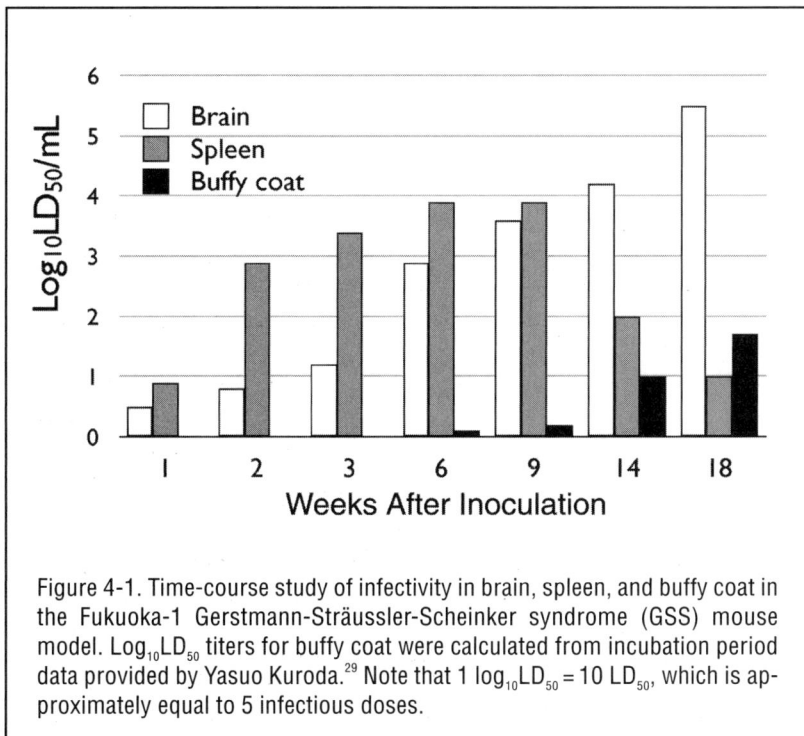

Figure 4-1. Time-course study of infectivity in brain, spleen, and buffy coat in the Fukuoka-1 Gerstmann-Sträussler-Scheinker syndrome (GSS) mouse model. $Log_{10}LD_{50}$ titers for buffy coat were calculated from incubation period data provided by Yasuo Kuroda.[29] Note that 1 $log_{10}LD_{50} = 10$ $LD_{50}$, which is approximately equal to 5 infectious doses.

Figure 4-2. Time-course study of infectivity in whole blood in the 263K scrapie hamster model. Data presented by Robert Rohwer at the 2002 Cambridge Healthtech meeting.[21] ID = infectious dose.

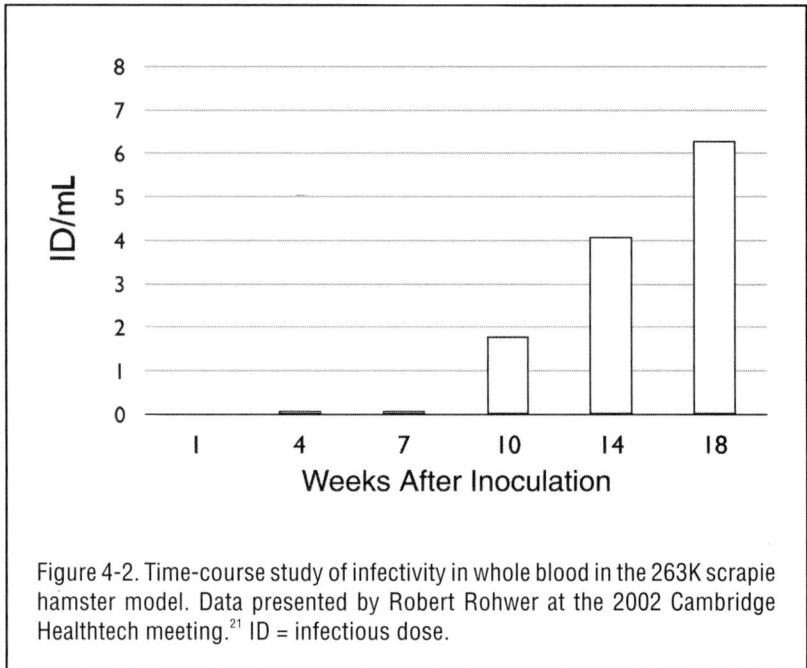

## Observations in Humans

Early reports of transmission of CJD to rodents from the blood of human patients were viewed with some caution because of a variety of technical issues that have been described elsewhere,[9] and all the transmission studies conducted in primates (three are still ongoing) have so far been negative. Epidemiologic evidence indicates that blood from patients with vCJD has transmitted disease and that blood from patients with other forms of CJD has (probably) not transmitted disease.

### vCJD

The recognition of vCJD blood transmissions came about only because of the intensive and systematic epidemiologic surveillance initiated in the early 1990s by the UK National CJD Surveillance Unit in Edinburgh and extended throughout the

European Community in anticipation of the possibilities that CJD may result from exposure to BSE and may lead to secondary iatrogenic transmissions (see Fig 4-3). The first case occurred in a codon 129 MM recipient who became ill 7 years after having received a nonleukocyte-reduced red cell transfusion from a 24-year-old donor who did not begin to show signs of vCJD until 3 years after the donation.[34] The second transmission occurred in a codon 129 MV recipient who died of an unrelated illness 5 years after having received a similar transfusion from a young adult who did not become ill until 18 months after donating the blood.[35] This transmission was identified only by the postmortem discovery of PrP$^{TSE}$ in a lymph node and spleen (the brain was normal), and it will never be known whether the infection would have persisted in a silent carrier state or whether it would have evolved into clinical disease. The third transmission, also caused by nonleukocyte-reduced red cells, occurred in a codon 129 MM recipi-

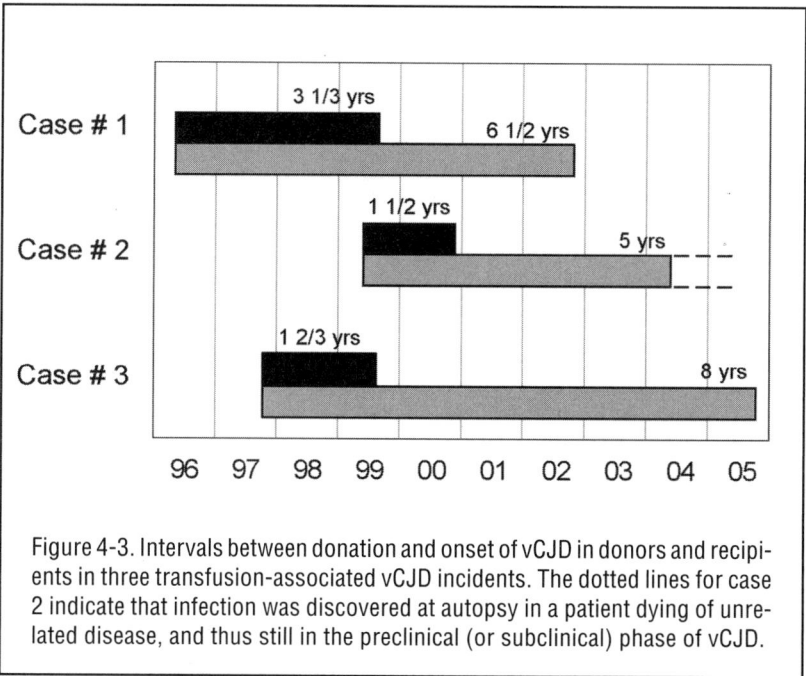

Figure 4-3. Intervals between donation and onset of vCJD in donors and recipients in three transfusion-associated vCJD incidents. The dotted lines for case 2 indicate that infection was discovered at autopsy in a patient dying of unrelated disease, and thus still in the preclinical (or subclinical) phase of vCJD.

ent approximately 8 years after transfusion from a donor who developed vCJD 20 months after the donation (RG Will, personal communication).

Two aspects of these cases merit particular attention: first, genetic susceptibility to vCJD is not limited to codon 129 MM homozygous individuals, and, second, blood in human vCJD can be infectious during the preclinical phase of disease, which may extend at least 3 years before the onset of symptomatic disease. Because the 24-year-old who made this donation had most likely been exposed to BSE about 10 years earlier, it is reasonable to imagine that his or her blood may have been infectious during much of the last third of the preclinical phase of disease.

These three secondary vCJD transmissions have occurred in a group of 64 recipients of whole blood or labile blood components donated by 22 persons who later died of vCJD. Thirty-eight of the recipients have died of unrelated illnesses, of whom six lived at least 5 years after receiving the donation; 26 recipients are still alive, of whom 14 have lived at least 5 years after receiving the donation (RG Will, personal communication). An additional 41 persons, in France, are known to have received blood from three vCJD patients, of whom at least 12 are still alive or died of non-CJD illnesses 5 or more years after receiving the donation (JPH Trouvin, personal communication).

Will more transfusion-associated infections occur? The proportion of patients dying of primary vCJD who had been blood donors is similar to that in the general population, and the incidence of new cases of primary vCJD is diminishing. These observations suggest that new cases of secondary transfusion-associated infections will most likely be restricted to recipients of blood from donors now already identified as vCJD cases, unless it turns out that the prevalence of inapparent infections has been accurately predicted by the retrospective search for PrP[TSE] in appendixes removed from healthy young people during the past decade (3 positives among 12,600 examined samples).[39] The question remains under investigation.

## sCJD

Although animal studies have not suggested any major difference between the risks of blood transmission from humans with vCJD or sCJD, all of the epidemiologic evidence to date concerning human sCJD blood transmission is negative. As long ago as the late 1960s (shortly after the discovery that CJD is a transmissible disease), it was known that, occasionally, sCJD patients had been blood donors, including one or two patients who were still donating blood after the onset of symptomatic disease. However, serious attention to the possibility of iatrogenic transmission via blood did not begin until the 1980s, when an individual donor–recipient study failed to uncover any recipient cases of CJD.[40] Since then, a much larger (and ongoing) study in the United States has brought to 368 the current tally of known recipients of labile blood components from persons who later died of sCJD; of this group, 125 have been followed for at least 5 years after donation.[41] None have died of sCJD. As-yet-unpublished results of other ongoing studies in Europe will further increase the tally of recipients and, in the continued absence of any cases, should provide an ever greater assurance of the comparative safety of blood during at least the preclinical (donating) phase of sCJD.

Several statistical studies have also been undertaken, either with a specific focus on blood or as part of larger analyses of risk factors for sCJD.[42-45] None has shown any increased risk of disease associated with prior therapy with blood or blood components; however, it must be understood that these analyses do not have sufficient sensitivity to exclude the occurrence of cases at a frequency too low to achieve a statistically significant difference from the baseline occurrence of sCJD in the general population.

## Plasma Protein Derivatives

When plasma is subjected to the Cohn fractionation protocol, infectivity progressively decreases through the sequence of fractions. When these fractions are further processed to therapeutic proteins through the use of precipitation, depth filtration, or chromatography steps, a further reduction of infectivity occurs (on average, approximately 500 $ID_{50}$/mL), which makes it extremely unlikely that any infectivity present in the original plasma could carry through to the final protein products. A wealth of information about processing reductions of both $PrP^{TSE}$ and infectivity has accumulated during the past decade and is the subject of several recent and current reviews[46-49] (see Chapter 7).

The most convincing evidence of freedom from risk of transmitting disease through the administration of therapeutic plasma protein products comes from the fact that no case of CJD has occurred among more than 20,000 hemophilia patients who have been repeatedly treated with coagulation factors during the past 10 years.[49,50] Similarly, no case has been identified in any of the smaller patient populations requiring repeated administration of other coagulation factors or of immunoglobulin. The absence of cases among these populations undergoing chronic therapy with plasma protein products is especially significant in light of a recent study in mice showing that a single parenteral injection of scrapie agent at a concentration too low to transmit disease did transmit disease when given on a daily or even weekly basis over a period of many weeks.[51]

## Conclusion

A large and still expanding body of experimental studies has explored the subject of blood infectivity in different TSEs in various animal species and (with due regard for the different methods used) has not yielded any substantial differences in the frequency, distribution, or concentration of infectivity among the different forms of disease. In view of the fact that epidemiologic studies have affirmed the presence of blood infectivity in vCJD and suggested the absence of blood infectivity in sCJD, it may be asked what purpose the experimental studies have served.

As predictive clues to the relative risk of human cases of transfusion-related sCJD and vCJD, they would not seem to have been particularly useful. On the other hand, the ensemble of positive results gave notice that blood from human TSE patients might be infectious during both the preclinical and clinical stages of disease, that leukocytes are the most infectious blood component, and that processing steps in the production of therapeutic proteins greatly reduce any infectivity that may be present in plasma. These considerations led both to the initiation of an array of precautionary measures that minimize the risk of iatrogenic CJD via labile blood components, and to the realization that therapeutic plasma protein products are almost certainly risk-free. In a sense, these precautions have already been validated by the cases of transfusion-associated vCJD in humans that occurred before the precautions were put into operation. Epidemiologic evidence to the contrary, animal studies have also highlighted the possibility that blood from sporadic cases of CJD may occasionally also be capable of transmitting disease, a possibility that only time and continuing surveillance will resolve.

# References

1. Hadlow WJ, Kennedy RC, Race RE, Ecklund CM. Virologic and neurohistologic findings in dairy goats affected with natural scrapie. Vet Pathol 1980;17:187-99.
2. Hadlow WJ, Kennedy RC, Race RE. Natural infection of Suffolk sheep with scrapie virus. J Infect Dis 1982;146:657-64.
3. Hunter N, Foster J, Chong A, et al. Transmission of prion diseases by blood transfusion. J Gen Virol 2002;83:2897-905.
4. Fraser H, Foster J. Transmission to mice, sheep and goats and bioassay of bovine tissues. In: Bradley R, Marchant B, eds. Transmissible spongiform encephalopathies: Consultation on BSE with the Scientific Veterinary Committee of the Commission of the European Communities, Brussels, Belgium, 14-15 September 1993. Document VI/4131/94-EN. Brussels: European Commission Agriculture, 1993:145-59.
5. Manuelidis EE, Kim JH, Mericangas JR, Manuelidis L. Transmission to animals of Creutzfeldt-Jakob disease from human blood. Lancet 1985;ii:896-7.

6. Tateishi J. Transmission of Creutzfeldt-Jakob disease from human blood and urine into mice (letter). Lancet 1985;ii:1074.

7. Tamai Y, Kojima H, Kitajima R, et al. Demonstration of the transmissible agent in tissue from a pregnant woman with Creutzfeldt-Jakob disease (letter). N Engl J Med 1992;327:649.

8. Deslys J-P, Lasmézas C, Dormont D. Selection of specific strains in iatrogenic Creutzfeldt-Jakob disease. Lancet 1994;343:848-9.

9. Brown P. Can Creutzfeldt-Jakob disease be transmitted by transfusion? (review) Curr Opin Hematol 1995;2:472-7.

10. Brown P. Update on Baxter monkey TSE research. Presented at the 8th Annual Cambridge Healthtech Institute Conference on Transmissible Spongiform Encephalopathies, Washington, DC, February 23-24, 2004.

11. Bruce ME, McConnell I, Will RG, Ironside JW. Detection of variant Creutzfeldt-Jakob disease infectivity in extraneural tissues. Lancet 2001;358:208-9.

12. Lasmézas CI. Pathogenesis of vCJD in non-human primates. Presented at the 9th Annual Cambridge Healthtech Institute Conference on Transmissible Spongiform Encephalopathies, McLean, VA, February 14-15, 2005.

13. Pattison IH, Millson GC. Distribution of the scrapie agent in the tissue of experimentally inoculated goats. J Comp Pathol 1962;72:233-44.

14. Gibbs CJ Jr, Gajdusek DC, Morris A. Viral characteristics of the scrapie agent in mice. In: Gajdusek DC, Gibbs CJ Jr, Alpers M, eds. Slow, latent, and temperate virus infections. NINDB Monograph no. 2. PHS Publication no. 1378. Washington, DC: US Government Printing Office, 1965:195-202.

15. Hadlow WJ, Eklund CM, Kennedy RC, et al. Course of experimental scrapie virus infection in the goat. J Infect Dis 1974;129:559-67.

16. Clarke MC, Haig DA. Presence of the transmissible agent of scrapie in the serum of affected mice and rats. Vet Rec 1967;80:504.

17. Dickinson AB, Meikle VMH. Genetic control of the concentration of ME7 scrapie agent in the brain of mice. J Comp Pathol 1969;79:15-22.

18. Eklund CM, Kennedy RC, Hadlow WJ. Pathogenesis of scrapie virus infection in the mouse. J Infect Dis 1967;117:15-22.

19. Diringer H. Sustained viremia in experimental hamster scrapie. Arch Virol 1984;82:105-9.

20. Casaccia P, Ladogana A, Xi YG, Pocchiari M. Levels of infectivity in the blood throughout the incubation period of hamsters peripherally injected with scrapie. Arch Virol 1989;108:145-9.

21. Rohwer RG. New data on blood-borne TSE infectivity. Presented at the 6th Annual Cambridge Healthtech Institute Conference on Transmissible Spongiform Encephalopathies, Washington, DC, February 6-7, 2002.

22. Marsh RF, Burger D, Hanson RP. Transmissible mink encephalopathy: Behavior of the disease agent in mink. Am J Vet Res 1969;30: 1637-42.

23. Marsh RF, Miller JM, Hanson RP. Transmissible mink encephalopathy: Studies on the peripheral lymphocyte. Infect Immun 1973;7: 352-5.
24. Wells GAH, Hawkins SAC, Green RB, et al. Limited detection of sternal bone marrow infectivity in the clinical phase of experimental bovine spongiform encephalopathy (BSE): An update. Vet Rec 1998;144: 292-4.
25. Taylor DM, Fernie K, Reichel HE, Somerville RA. Infectivity in the blood of mice with a BSE-derived agent (letter). J Hosp Infect 2000; 46:78-9.
26. Bons N, Lehmann S, Mestre-Frances N, et al. Brain and buffy coat transmission of bovine spongiform encephalopathy to the primate *Microcebus murinus*. Transfusion 2002;42:513-6.
27. Wells GAH, Spiropoulos J, Hawkins SAC, Ryder SJ. Pathogenesis of experimental bovine spongiform encephalopathy: Preclinical infectivity in tonsil and observations on the distribution of lingual tonsil in slaughtered cattle. Vet Rec 2005;156:401-7.
28. Houston F, Foster JD, Chong A, et al. Transmission of BSE by blood transfusion in sheep. Lancet 2000;356:999-1000.
29. Kuroda Y, Gibbs CJ Jr, Amyx H, et al. Creutzfeldt-Jakob disease in mice: Persistent viremia and preferential replication of virus in low-density lymphocytes. Infect Immun 1983;41:154-61.
30. Brown P, Rohwer RG, Dunstan BC, et al. The distribution of infectivity in blood components and plasma derivatives in experimental models of transmissible spongiform encephalopathy. Transfusion 1998;38: 810-6.
31. Brown P, Cervenakova L, McShane LM, et al. Further studies of blood infectivity in an experimental model of transmissible spongiform encephalopathy, with an explanation of why blood products do not transmit Creutzfeldt-Jakob disease in humans. Transfusion 1999;39: 1169-78.
32. Manuelidis EE, Gorgacz EJ, Manuelidis L. Viremia in experimental Creutzfeldt-Jakob disease. Science 1978;200:1069-71.
33. Cervenakova L, Yakovleva O, McKenzie C, et al. Similar levels of infectivity in the blood of mice infected with human-derived vCJD and GSS strains of transmissible spongiform encephalopathy. Transfusion 2003;43:1687-94.
34. Llewelyn CA, Hewitt RE, Knight RSE, et al. Possible transmission of variant Creutzfeldt-Jakob disease by blood transfusion. Lancet 2004; 363:417-21.
35. Peden AH, Head MW, Ritchie DE, et al. Autopsy detection of pre-clinical vCJD transmission following blood transfusion from a PRNP codon 129 heterozygote. Lancet 2004;364:527-9.
36. Orser C, Pan T, Sethi J, et al. A new TSE diagnostic blood test. Presented at Prion 2005: Between Fundamentals and Society's Needs, Düsseldorf, Germany, October 19-21, 2005.
37. Perron H, Dupin M, Cecillon S, et al. A novel immunoassay for the detection of resistant prion protein (PrPres) in human plasma. Presented

at Prion 2005: Between Fundamentals and Society's Needs, Düsseldorf, Germany, October 19-21, 2005.

38. Gregori L, McCombie N, Palmer D, et al. Effectiveness of leucoreduction for removal of infectivity of transmissible spongiform encephalopathies from blood. Lancet 2004;364:529-31.

39. Hilton DA, Ghani AC, Conyers L, et al. Prevalence of lymphoreticular prion protein accumulation in UK tissue samples. J Pathol 2004;203: 733-9.

40. Heye N, Hensen S, Müller N. Creutzfeldt-Jakob disease and blood transfusion. Lancet 1994;343:298-9.

41. Zou S, Notari IV, Fuji K, et al. An update on the Creutzfeldt-Jakob disease look-back study. Presented at the AABB Annual Meeting and TXPO, Seattle, WA, October 15-18, 2005.

42. Esmonde TFG, Will RG, Slattery JM, et al. Creutzfeldt-Jakob disease and blood transfusion. Lancet 1993;341:205-7.

43. Holman RC, Khan AS, Belay ED, et al. Creutzfeldt-Jakob disease in the United States, 1974-1994: Using national mortality data to assess the possible occurrence of variant cases. Emerg Infect Dis 1996;2:333-7.

44. van Duijn CM, Delasnerie-Lauprêtre N, Masullo C, et al. Case-control study of risk factors of Creutzfeldt-Jakob disease in Europe during 1993-95. Lancet 1998;351:1081-5.

45. Wilson K, Code C, Ricketts M. Risk of acquiring Creutzfeldt-Jakob disease from blood transfusions: Systematic review of case-control studies. Br Med J 2000;321:17-19.

46. Foster PR. Removal of TSE agents from blood products. Vox Sang 2004;87(Suppl 2):8-10.

47. Brown P. Blood infectivity, processing, and screening tests in transmissible spongiform encephalopathy. Vox Sang 2005;89:63-70.

48. Flan B, Aubin J-T. Evaluation de l'efficacité des procédés de purification des protéines plasmatiques à éliminer les agents transmissibles nonconventionnels. Virologie 2005;9:S45-56.

49. Souci JM, Jackson D, Evatt B. The occurrence of hemophilia in the United States. Am J Hematol 1998;59:288-94.

50. Evatt B, Austin E, Barnhart L, et al. Surveillance for Creutzfeldt-Jakob disease among persons with hemophilia. Transfusion 1998;38:817-20.

51. Jacquemot C, Cuche C, Dormont D, Lazarini F. High incidence of scrapie induced by repeated injections of subinfectious prion doses. J Virol 2005;79:8904-8.

In: Turner ML, ed.
*Creutzfeldt-Jakob Disease: Managing the Risk of Transmission by Blood, Plasma, and Tissues*
Bethesda, MD: AABB Press, 2006

# 5

# Diagnostic Tests for Antemortem Screening of Creutzfeldt-Jakob Disease

PHILIP MINOR, BA, PhD, AND PAUL BROWN, MD

THE TRANSMISSIBLE SPONGIFORM encephalopathies (TSEs) are currently undetectable by any easily applied noninvasive method until clinical signs develop. The distribution of infectivity in the tissues of an infected person, the number of infected persons, and the efficiency of the various possible routes of transmission are not fully defined, and the possible risk of secondary transmission of disease between human subjects (eg, from blood transfusion or surgical cross-contamination) during the presymptomatic phase of disease is difficult to judge. Therefore, the position of regulatory authorities with respect to TSEs has been extremely conservative, and public concern has been very high.

*Philip Minor, BA, PhD, Head, Division of Virology, National Institute for Biological Standards and Control, South Mimms, Hertfordshire, United Kingdom, and Paul Brown, MD, Bethesda, Maryland*

A diminishing annual number of bovine spongiform encephalopathy (BSE) cases still occurs in the United Kingdom (UK). Whereas the incidence of new cases of variant Creutzfeldt-Jakob disease (vCJD) in humans in the UK is also declining, there are many unknowns. The clinical cases so far have all been homozygous for methionine at codon 129 in the *PRNP* gene, although there is evidence for infection without disease in a methionine/valine heterozygote[1]; more cases may appear in the other genotypes, or there may be asymptomatic carriers who for many years could pass the disease to others. The age of those infected has remained constant over the past 10 years, which suggests that they were exposed at different times and that there is an age-related sensitivity the nature of which is not understood, but which has implications for the future course of the disease.

The number of infected persons is not known, but estimates from the number of clinical cases so far suggest that it may be at most a few hundred; however, a survey of appendix tissue for the presence of the pathognomonic misfolded form of prion protein ($PrP^{TSE}$) in lymphoid follicles implies that the number of infected persons may be 10 to 100 times as high.[2] This discrepancy might be explained by a high proportion of asymptomatic carriers who will either never develop the disease or only do so after a very long incubation period, or by a substantial second wave of disease in codon 129 heterozygotes. Different measures would be required to deal with these alternatives.

Studies in animals have documented the presence of infectivity in the blood of rodents,[3] lemurs,[4] and sheep infected with BSE or naturally infected with scrapie[5,6] (see Chapter 4). In rodent experiments, there are approximately 10 IU/mL of blood. Data from the sheep transfusion experiments show similarly low levels in infected sheep blood, in that transmission occurred when large amounts of blood were given by transfusion, but not in previous experiments in which smaller volumes were inoculated into the brain.[7] It is therefore reasonable to assume that blood transfusion may be an effective route of secondary transmission of vCJD in humans but also that the level of infectivity is likely to be low and difficult to detect. Nonetheless, transmission of infectivity by blood transfusion has been identified in three instances in the UK in which recipients of blood from donors later diagnosed with vCJD became infected; two of the three developed the disease.[1,8]

A premortem diagnostic method for infection that could be readily applied and minimally invasive would make it technically possible to estimate the size of the vCJD epidemic and prevent or reduce secondary transmission by blood transfusion or other medical procedures. Also, preclinical diagnostic methods would help in the development of therapies, because any eventual treatment would be more effective in preventing or ameliorating disease if it were given in the presymptomatic phase after a known or suspected exposure, and any positive effects of the treatment on the infectious load could be monitored.

## Types of Tests

The only practical material for the application of a screening test is blood. Moreover, there is evidence that infectivity may be present in blood, and it is precisely the presence of infectivity that is of concern. In contrast, other easily obtained fluids such as saliva or urine are highly variable in composition, may be difficult to obtain in the setting of a donor session, and have not been reliably shown to contain infectivity.[9-11] Other tissue samples, including lymph node, spleen, or tonsil, may be usable in other circumstances, such as the assessment of cadaveric tissue donors (see Chapter 8).

A highly sensitive, rapid infectivity assay would be the most appropriate test either for screening or for confirmation of a positive result from another test. However, infectivity bioassays in animals are expensive and laborious and (most important) require far too much time for completion than could ever be practical in the clinical donor setting. Cell culture infectivity bioassays for certain TSE agents have been described and may in time extend to vCJD. Although they are unlikely ever to be used as a screening method because of their technically elaborate nature, they could be well suited as a confirmatory test that is based on an entirely different principle than the more practical screening assay methods under development (see Table 5-1).

Surrogate assays include measurement of erythroid differentiation-related factor (EDRF),[12] antibodies claimed to be specific for the diseased state (although not against the agent itself), circulating nucleic acids,[13] and proteomics. Some of these assays may eventually prove to be of value, but most attention has focused on the detection of $PrP^{TSE}$, and this chapter is concerned only with the methods used in its detection.

# $PrP^{TSE}$

$PrP^{TSE}$ is an abnormal isoform of the glycosylphosphatidylinositol (GPI)-anchored cellular PrP, $PrP^{C}$, a protein of approximately 230 amino acids with two potential glycosylation sites that is widely distributed in mammalian tissues. It was originally defined in terms of its relative resistance to proteolytic treatments, notably proteinase K (PK); therefore, it is sometimes designated as $PrP^{Res}$. However, it can be digested with higher levels of proteinase and longer incubation periods, and there is accumulating evidence for one or more forms of protease-sensitive but abnormal PrP.[14] $PrP^{TSE}$ has more β-sheet and less α-helical content than does $PrP^{C}$, forms amyloid aggregates, and is believed by many to be the infectious agent itself, which acts as a template for the formation of more $PrP^{TSE}$ from $PrP^{C}$. It is accepted as a marker of the disease state, although the amount and site of deposition of the amyloid in relation to infectivity depend on the infected species and the strain of TSE concerned.

There is no known humoral immune response to $PrP^{TSE}$ in the infected or diseased human or animal, which indicates that the structure is not recognized as foreign. The relationship between $PrP^{TSE}$ and infectivity is not simple, even if it is ac-

# Table 5-1. Stages in the Development of Different Premortem Blood Tests for TSEs*

| Laboratory | Test Method | rPrP | Brain PrP$^{TSE}$ | Animal Blood Sx | Animal Blood Pre-Sx | Human Blood Sx | Human Blood Pre-Sx |
|---|---|---|---|---|---|---|---|
| University of Maryland | Immuno-PCR | + | + | ? | ? | | |
| Veterans Affairs Medical Center, Baltimore | Capture Ab + label Ab | + | + | ? | ? | | |
| People Bio | Single Ab capture/label | + | + | ? | ? | | |
| University of California, San Francisco | CDI + Ab | + | + | (+) | ? | | |
| Iowa State University | CE + Ab | + | + | + | (+) | | |
| Prionics | Anti-PrP$^{TSE}$ Ab | NA | + | + | (+) | | |
| ACGT Pro Genomics | PrP fibril seed (FACS) | + | + | (+) | ? | | |
| University of Texas | PMCA | + | + | + | + | | |
| Microsens | Polyanion ligand + Ab | NA | + | + | (+) | (+) | |
| bioMérieux | Strep ppt, then C-6-A capture + Ab | NA | + | + | (+) | (+) | |
| Adlyfe | Polypeptide ligand | NA | + | + | + | (+) | |

*None of the tests have been independently verified, and the data are mostly unpublished. rPrP = recombinant PrP; Sx and Pre-Sx = symptomatic and presymptomatic phases of disease; Ab = antibody; CDI = conformation-dependent immunoassay; CE = capillary electrophoresis; FACS = fluorescence-activated cell sorting; PMCA = protein misfolding cyclic amplification; Strep ppt = streptomycin precipitation; C-6-A = calyx-(6)-arene; NA = not applicable; ? = not attempted; (+) = small number of samples.

cepted that $PrP^{TSE}$ is the infectious agent. Early studies of infected hamster brain concluded that there were about $10^5$ molecules of $PrP^{TSE}$ for every infectious unit, based on the concentration of infectivity in a known weight of proteinase-resistant $PrP^{TSE}$ and the molecular weight of the protein. These studies did not allow for the possibility that an infectious unit could consist of polymeric aggregates or for the possibility that proteinase-sensitive forms of the protein may also be infectious. If the correlation were correct, the level of infectivity in blood would correspond to about $10^6$ molecules per mL, an amount that would be very difficult to detect.

Recent studies indicated that the infectivity associated with $PrP^{Res}$ is principally found in a particle size range of 300 to 600 kDa, or about 14 to 28 molecules of $PrP^{TSE}$ [15]; thus, 1 mL of blood containing 10 infectious doses could contain only about 140 to 280 molecules of $PrP^{TSE}$, an amount three or four orders of magnitude less than the previous estimate and correspondingly even more difficult to detect. In view of this low concentration of infectious particles, the success reported in the development of assays based on detection of $PrP^{TSE}$ is perhaps surprising. However, because it is not yet known whether abnormal but proteinase-sensitive forms of PrP are infectious, and because there is a great deal of $PrP^{TSE}$ in large aggregates of lower specific infectivity, calculation of the number of molecules of $PrP^{TSE}$ in a unit of infectivity may seriously underestimate the actual number of molecules correlated with a single infectious unit.

Methods for the detection of $PrP^{TSE}$ will now be described. Some have been developed sufficiently to be considered as candidate diagnostic approaches, and a few are reported to detect infectivity in the blood of human patients. However, we emphasize three important qualifications: 1) much of the test detection data presented at recent scientific meetings has not included blind testing or yet been subjected to peer review in scientific journals; 2) the path from a validated detection test under laboratory conditions to a practical screening test for use in blood donor facilities can be long and arduous; and 3) even assuming a practical validated test that has 100% sensitivity and specificity, the interpretation of a positive result both for the blood and the donor will require correlative bioassay studies to ascertain what, if any, relationship it bears to infectivity and transmissibility.

## Immunoblotting

For many years, immunoblotting after a proteinase digestion step was the only method by which $PrP^{TSE}$ could be detected, and it remains the standard against which other methods of detection of $PrP^{TSE}$ in solid tissues are measured. Exposure of tissue to proteinase totally digests $PrP^C$ but removes only the first 70 to 90 amino acids of $PrP^{TSE}$, which yields a truncated protein that on gel electrophoresis shows three bands corresponding to its three different glycosylation states. The migration rates of the bands may vary from strain to strain, and mixed types may be found in certain cases (Fig 5-1). Technical variations include the use of different digestion conditions, different antibodies for detection, and different dilution matrices, including normal tissue homogenate, with or without concentration methods to improve sensitivity.[16]

Wadsworth et al[17] described a sensitive assay that included the use of enhanced detection of reacting antibody by chemiluminescence and specific and quantitative concentration of $PrP^{TSE}$ from large sample volumes by using sodium phosphotungstic acid (PTA). It was calculated that the enhanced method would reliably detect $PrP^{TSE}$ at a concentration 10,000-fold less than that found in brain. Opinions on the sensitivity required for a blood test remain divided, but this sensitivity is probably about one-tenth that required without concentration, depending on the assumptions made about the infectious titers in brain and blood. However, buffy coat prepared from 15 mL of blood from a vCJD patient was negative.

The World Health Organization (WHO) Working Group on International Reference Materials for the Diagnosis and Study of Transmissible Spongiform Encephalopathies has overseen

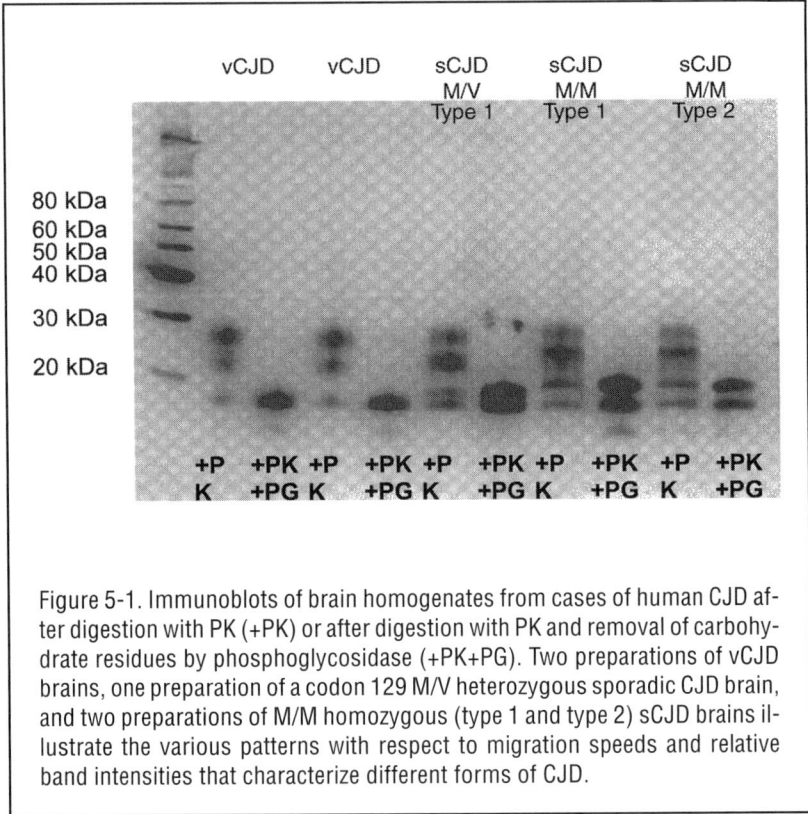

Figure 5-1. Immunoblots of brain homogenates from cases of human CJD after digestion with PK (+PK) or after digestion with PK and removal of carbohydrate residues by phosphoglycosidase (+PK+PG). Two preparations of vCJD brains, one preparation of a codon 129 M/V heterozygous sporadic CJD brain, and two preparations of M/M homozygous (type 1 and type 2) sCJD brains illustrate the various patterns with respect to migration speeds and relative band intensities that characterize different forms of CJD.

the preparation of materials from cases of both sporadic Creutzfeldt-Jakob disease (sCJD) and vCJD for the purpose of providing reagents by the use of which the amount of infectious material present can be expressed and assays can be compared by their limits of sensitivity. A collaborative study was reported involving four preparations of brain, two from sCJD, one from vCJD, and one from a non-CJD case.[16] Six laboratories used a version of an immunoblot, with different sample sizes and treatments and varying in other technical details. When the results were expressed in terms of the minimum detectable equivalent volume of homogenate, all methods were of very similar sensitivity. For the vCJD preparation, this sensitivity corresponded to about 0.2 µL or 200 nL, about 4- to

40-fold lower sensitivity than that reported by Wadsworth et al[17] for their most sensitive format using different brain preparations. The materials were established as reference reagents by the WHO Expert Committee of Biological Standardization in 2003, and they provide a direct means of comparing assay sensitivity. The study found that most methods based on immunoblot after proteinase K digestion are of similar sensitivity, and the data of Wadsworth et al suggested that immunoblot assays alone are not of sufficient sensitivity to detect PrP$^{TSE}$ in blood.

## Immunocapillary Electrophoresis

Immunocapillary electrophoresis was one of the first methods for detecting PrP$^{TSE}$ in blood. Buffy coat was used as the starting material for extraction of PrP$^{TSE}$, which was then treated with proteinase and prepared for capillary electrophoresis.[18,19] PrP$^{TSE}$ was recognized by a competitive antibody inhibition test involving the specimen, a labeled peptide, and a monoclonal antibody reactive with both PrP$^{TSE}$ and the peptide. Initial reports indicated that the abnormal protein could be detected in the blood of a variety of animals infected with TSE; however, the technique is complex, and there are many variables, including the protease treatment of the concentrates, the balance of the antibody and peptide required, and the resolution of the complexes from the free peptide by capillary electrophoresis. Its results have proved difficult to reproduce, and when challenged with blinded blood samples from humans or chimpanzees infected with CJD, it failed to differentiate between infected and uninfected samples.[20]

## Conformation-Dependent Immunoassay

The conformation-dependent immunoassay (CDI) is based upon differences in antibody-binding of PrP$^{C}$ and PrP$^{TSE}$: an antibody-binding site exists that is fully accessible in the normal protein but largely inaccessible in its pathologic conformation unless first unfolded by denaturation.[21] Signal intensity produced by a mixture of labeled antibody and either native or denatured protein is measured by using time-resolved fluorescence spectroscopy. $PrP^C$ gives a similar signal intensity whether in its native or denatured state, whereas the signal from $PrP^{TSE}$ increases after denaturation. The results are expressed as a ratio of denatured to native protein signal intensity.[22]

Safar et al[23] described CDIs that were specific for bovine and cervid TSE. The background signal was reduced and the sensitivity thus increased by using an antibody to attach the protein to the plate and treating the preparation with proteinase to reduce the signal from $PrP^C$. The authors claimed that the sensitivity achieved in an endpoint dilution assay approximated that of an infectivity assay in appropriate transgenic mice.

The CDI without the proteinase treatment step has been applied to an analysis of brain from cases of CJD in humans, and the results have been compared to the findings of immunohistochemistry.[14] $PrP^{TSE}$ was detected in regions found negative by immunohistochemistry after standard procedures to detect $PrP^{TSE}$ (which included hydrolytic autoclaving). It was concluded that the CDI, unlike the other methods, was detecting forms of $PrP^{TSE}$ that were susceptible to degradation. The infectivity of these forms has not been shown. As for the bovine and cervid studies, the sensitivity of the CDI in human disease was reported to be comparable to infectivity assays in transgenic mice carrying the human PrP gene.

Bellon et al[24] used the WHO working reagents in a comparative study of CDIs and immunoblotting. In its modified format (replacing glutaraldehyde capture with a specific antibody and reducing $PrP^C$ content by proteinase treatment), the CDI had a sensitivity 2 orders of magnitude greater than that of the immunoblot assays for the same samples, as expressed in terms of the minimum amount of the reference brain homogenate that could be detected.[16] The signal from normal preparations treated with proteinase was essentially undetectable. In

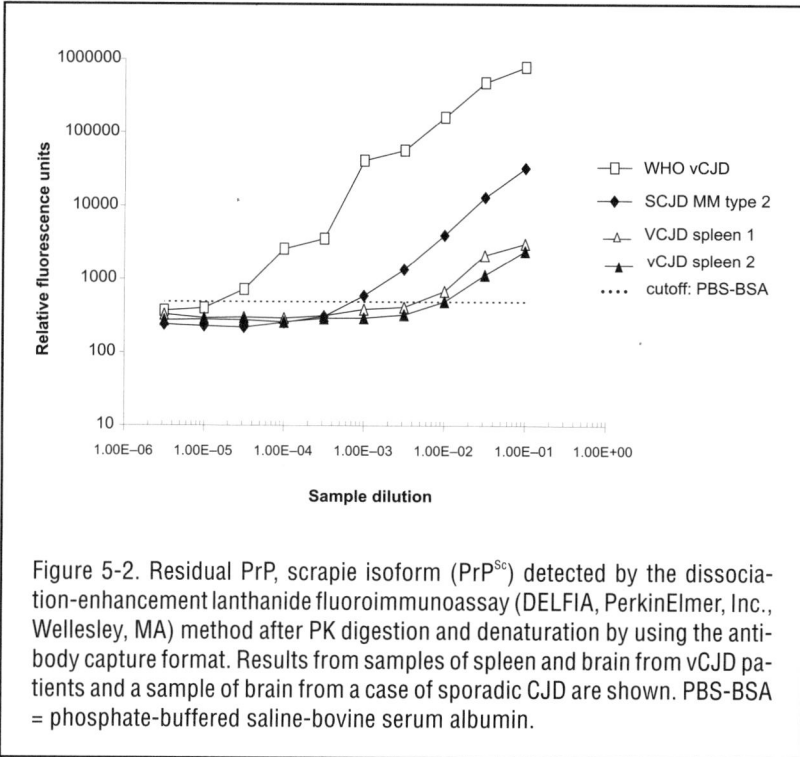

Figure 5-2. Residual PrP, scrapie isoform (PrP$^{Sc}$) detected by the dissociation-enhancement lanthanide fluoroimmunoassay (DELFIA, PerkinElmer, Inc., Wellesley, MA) method after PK digestion and denaturation by using the antibody capture format. Results from samples of spleen and brain from vCJD patients and a sample of brain from a case of sporadic CJD are shown. PBS-BSA = phosphate-buffered saline-bovine serum albumin.

separate studies (P Minor, unpublished observations; Fig 5-2), the difference in potency between the spleen and brain preparations in the CDI format including proteinase treatment is about 2.5 $\log_{10}$, which is similar to the difference between the tissues seen in infectivity assays.[25]

The CDI therefore appears to be a highly sensitive assay that may approximate the sensitivity of infectivity bioassays in transgenic mice. In one format,[14] which may not be the most sensitive,[24] it is able to detect abnormal forms of PrP that are proteinase sensitive, but their significance to infection is not yet known. At the time of this writing, there are no published reports of its application to blood samples. The method depends on the capture of PrP$^{TSE}$ by specific antibody, which for general use would have to be broadly reactive across species.

# PrP$^{TSE}$-Specific Antibodies

The structural difference between the normal and abnormal forms of PrP has led to a search for antibodies specific for the abnormal form, despite the lack of a detectable immune response in infected animals. Korth et al[26] described a monoclonal antibody prepared by immunizing null mice (transgenic mice in which the prion gene had been deleted) with recombinant PrP. The antibody, designated 15B3, was shown to be specific for PrP$^{TSE}$ by immunoprecipitation of PrP$^{TSE}$ from infected hamster brain. As the mice had been immunized with recombinant PrP, the specificity of 15B3 for PrP$^{TSE}$ was unexpected, but it was explained in terms of a complex epitope produced when PrP$^C$ aggregates, so that contributing amino acids reside on ≥2 adjacent molecules. It has subsequently been shown that 15B3 will react with PrP$^{TSE}$ of cows, mice, deer, sheep, and humans by immunoprecipitation, can detect as little as 20 to 30 infectious units/g of infected brain tissue, reacts with both proteinase-sensitive and proteinase-resistant forms of PrP$^{TSE}$, and coprecipitates prion infectivity.[27-30] The method has been used to test plasma from small groups of symptomatic scrapie-infected sheep and BSE-infected cattle: all infected sheep and one-quarter of infected cattle tested positive, and all uninfected animals tested negative.[30]

Serbec et al[31] raised antibodies in normal BalbC mice to peptides derived from the human PrP$^C$ sequence. One resulting monoclonal antibody, designated V5B2, recognized an epitope specific to PrP$^{TSE}$. The antibody reacted with brain extracts from infected humans, cows, and sheep, but not with any form of recombinant PrP. The further properties of the antibody will be of interest.

Paramithiotis et al[32] raised a monoclonal antibody to a decapeptide of the sequence CYYRRYYRYY. The sequence was chosen because it was found that the conversion of full-length recombinant PrP to the β-sheet-rich form at low pH resulted in a great increase in the exposure of tyrosine residues, as indicated by an increase in specific fluorescence, and that the PrP sequence contains two regions in which the motif tyr-tyr-arg is repeated. Specificity was ascertained by immunoprecipitation, and, when the binding sites were cloned and expressed in a framework of dog immune globulin G (IgG), the antibody retained the same specificity in a variety of formats, including immunoprecipitation and enzyme-linked immunosorbent assay (ELISA). A blood test using this antibody has not yet been described.

Finally, Zou et al[33] described an antibody to DNA, designated OCD4, which reacted specifically with PrP^TSE that was present in CJD brain homogenates. The antibody did not precipitate denatured PrP^TSE or PrP^C in uninfected brain homogenates, and the implication is that the material in the homogenate is complexed to DNA; this is consistent with the interactions between polyionic ligands and PrP^TSE outlined in the next section. Another interesting finding was that more PrP^TSE could be captured from untreated than from PK-treated preparations, which is consistent with the existence of proteinase-sensitive forms of abnormal PrP.

In summary, a number of antibodies have been reported to react specifically with PrP^TSE in the absence of proteinase treatment. This reaction could increase the sensitivity of some assays to the point of PrP^TSE detection in blood, although currently it appears that only 15B3, described by Korth et al,[26] is being actively exploited in this way.

## PrP^TSE-Binding Ligands

The course of disease in scrapie-infected rodents is known to be prolonged by the administration of sulfated polyanionic compounds, such as pentosan sulfate or dextran sulfate, which bind to PrP^TSE in vitro. Plasminogen also binds to PrP^TSE, but not to PrP^C, which led Fischer et al[34] to suggest plasminogen binding as a means of concentrating or otherwise selectively detecting infection. However, plasminogen can bind nonspecifically to many other proteins.

Seprion (Microsens Biotechnologies, London, UK) is a ligand from the polyanionic family that, when coated onto magnetic beads, specifically captures PrP$^{TSE}$.[35] A major advantage of the method is that it does not use proteinase treatment; moreover, it is not species-specific, provided that a suitable detection antibody is available for BSE, chronic wasting disease (CWD), and other TSEs. It has been licensed for use in the United States for the diagnosis of BSE and CWD in postmortem brain specimens.

Studies of the assay for premortem use have been presented at various meetings [WHO, Geneva, 2005[30]; American Association for Clinical Chemistry, Oak Ridge, TN, 2003[35]; and IBC Second Annual Transmissible Spongiform Encephalopathies Conference, Reston, VA, 16-17 November, 2005 (unpublished data)] and are described on the Microsens Web site.[36] Tests using a crude non-red-cell fraction of blood are reported to have successfully distinguished scrapie-infected from uninfected sheep and to have yielded a proportion of positives in asymptomatic sheep in a scrapie-infected flock (it is not yet known how many of these exposed sheep will go on to develop scrapie). In humans, splenic leukocytes from a case of vCJD and a case of Gerstmann-Sträussler-Scheinker disease (GSS) were also positive, as compared with negative results in a small group of controls, and buffy coat obtained from blood was positive in one case of iatrogenic CJD and negative in a small group of controls.

A different ligand strategy has been developed by bioMérieux, Inc. (Durham, NC), in which plasma samples are subjected to proteinase digestion and precipitation or denaturation buffers, after which PrP oligomers, if present, are "reticulated" by exposure to streptomycin and then chemically captured onto plates coated with a calyx-(6)-arene (Fig 5-3); detection of the retained macromolecular aggregates is achieved by using a labeled monoclonal antibody.[30] The method has been used to detect PrP$^{TSE}$ in BSE and CJD brain

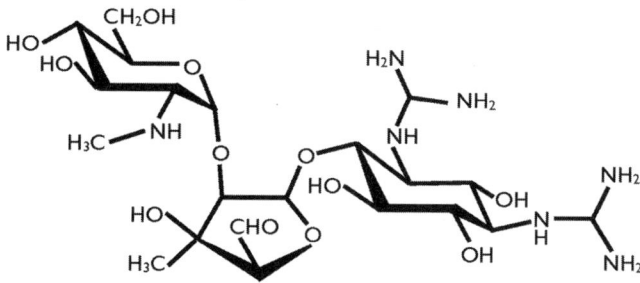

**Streptomycin**

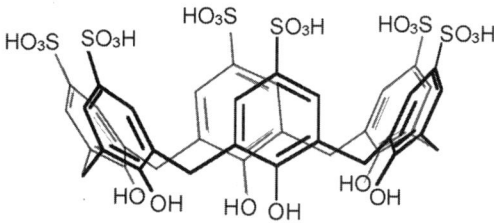

**Calyx- (6) -arene**

Figure 5-3. After a streptomycin-promoted PrP[TSE] precipitation and floccula-tion step, a calyx-(6)-arene "basket" ligand chemically bonds to the macro-molecular aggregates that are detected photometrically after incubation with a labeled PrP antibody.[29]

homogenates and in small numbers of plasma samples from scrapie-infected sheep, BSE-infected cattle, and CJD-infected humans, including those infected with the sporadic, iatro-genic, and variant forms of CJD. Two hundred normal human plasma samples tested negative.

A third ligand-based approach uses a peptide based on a re-gion of the PrP protein that is believed to be involved in the conformational transition from PrP[C] to PrP[TSE].[37] The fluores-cence-labeled polypeptide sequence from the conformationally reactive region of the PrP molecule[38] is coupled to its mirror image as a palindromic polypeptide and labeled at each end with a pyrene fluorophor. When mixed with a test specimen containing PrP$^{TSE}$, the ligand folds into a hairpin with a β-sheet conformation so that the fluorophors stack and change their fluorescence wavelength (Fig 5-4). The folded ligand induces more ligand molecules to adopt the same conformation (ie, it acts as its own amplifier).[39] The conformationally altered peptide is detected by a change in the light emission spectra of the fluorophore. Developed by Adlyfe, Inc., Rockville, MD,[40] the assay does not require either a proteinase digestion step or an antibody, and thus it has optimal detection sensitivity and broad reactivity across different species.

Data presented at recent meetings [WHO, Geneva, 2005[30]; IBC, Reston, VA, 2005 (unpublished data); and Keystone Symposium, Breckenridge, CO, 2003[40]] describe results in plasma samples from a variety of TSE infections in different animal species and humans. Successful discrimination of TSE-infected from -uninfected animals has been achieved for natural scrapie in sheep, experimental scrapie in hamsters, natural BSE in cattle, experimental GSS in mice, and experimental CJD in monkeys; the test has also discriminated a small number of patients with sCJD from uninfected control subjects. In correlative studies of test positivity and infectivity in a dilution series of GSS-infected mouse plasma, the threshold sensitivity approached 1 infectious unit.

## Amplification Methods

The accepted model of the formation of PrP$^{TSE}$ predicts that, under the correct conditions, PrP$^{TSE}$ could form in vitro from PrP$^C$ in a process seeded by preexisting PrP$^{TSE}$, and that has been shown to be possible.[41] If PrP$^{TSE}$ formed in vitro could be fragmented, it could seed a new round of PrP$^C$ conversion so that small amounts of PrP$^{TSE}$ could be amplified to detectable

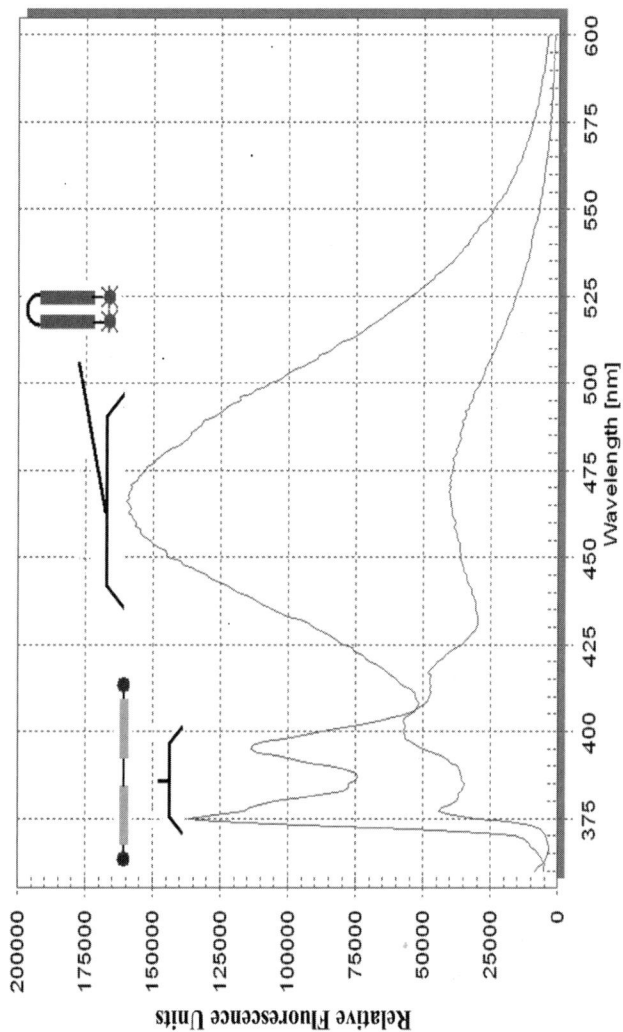

Figure 5-4. A palindromic polypeptide ligand labeled at each end with a pyrene fluorophor folds upon contact with PrP[TSE]. The folding "stacks" the fluorophors, which causes a substantial lengthening of the spectral wavelength emission that is detected by spectrophotometry.[39]

levels by repeated cycles of conversion and fragmentation. This process forms the basis of protein misfolding cyclic amplification (PMCA). As originally described,[42] brain homogenate from scrapie-infected hamsters could be amplified about 60-fold by dilution into normal hamster brain followed by five cycles of sonication and incubation. Amplification depends on the details of the incubation and sonication process and on the species from which the TSE was obtained; it has been reproduced in a number of laboratories.

If PrP$^{TSE}$ is the infectious agent, PMCA provides a means of increasing the amount of infectivity in vitro. Aliquots of amplified samples were used to seed 20 successive series of amplifications. The final material was shown to be infectious,[43] and, in view of the degree of dilution of the initial brain sample, it was concluded that the PrP$^{TSE}$ produced in vitro was indeed infectious. There would be safety implications if a method of this type were developed for routine use.

PMCA was shown to detect PrP$^{TSE}$ in the brains of presymptomatic rodents and cattle earlier than did immunoblot, and thus, by inference, it was more sensitive.[44] A modified and automated process shown to achieve amplification by more than a million-fold (Fig 5-5) was applied to blood from scrapie-infected hamsters.[45] Buffy coat from 18 clinically affected hamsters was subjected to amplification, and then an aliquot was used to seed a further round of amplification with the addition of fresh normal brain homogenate. After a single round, one of the preparations was positive; after the second round, 9 were positive, and, after six rounds, 16 were positive. There were no positives in 12 uninfected controls. Ongoing sequential sampling studies of blood after intracerebral inoculation have detected a proportion of positives beginning approximately one-third of the way through the incubation period (C Soto, communication). The method in its current form takes several days to complete, and thus it is not yet a practical screening method but clearly is very promising. As in all amplification-based methods, contamination may be an issue in the future.

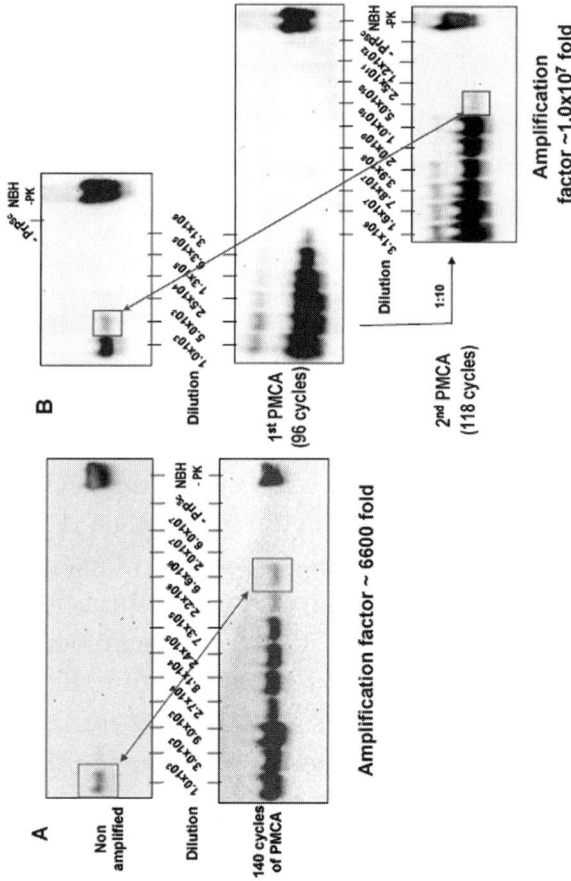

Figure 5-5. Amplification of scrapie-infected hamster brain PrP[TSE] measured by immunoblotting. (A) The two left panels show that 140 sonication cycles produced an increase in signal intensity approximately 6600-fold that of parallel dilutions of the unsonicated control specimen. (B) The upper and middle right panels compare an unsonicated control with the same sample subjected to 96 sonication cycles, at which point the limiting dilution was incubated with fresh normal brain and subjected to another 118 sonication cycles, as shown in the lower right panel. The overall amplification was approximately $10^7$-fold that of the unsonicated control.[45] NBH-PK = Normal brain homogenate, proteinase K treated; PMCA = protein misfolding cyclic amplification.

# Other Methods

Screening for intensely fluorescent targets (SIFT) is based on the discrimination of aggregates from single molecules by using confocal laser excitation of doubly labeled PrP antibody.[46] PrP$^{TSE}$ aggregates bind more antibody molecules and therefore fluoresce more strongly than does monomeric PrP$^C$. The assay is about 20 times as sensitive as immunoblot in detecting the hamster-adapted 263K scrapie agent in the form of prion rods diluted in cerebrospinal fluid (CSF). No data have been reported about the use of SIFT as a blood-screening test.

A technically simpler method that is also based on monomer-multimer forms of PrP involves the use of a single antibody or antibodies with an overlapping epitope (3F4 or 308, raised against hamster-adapted scrapie PrP). PrP is captured on an antibody-coated plate, and the same antibody (or antibody with an overlapping epitope), labeled with biotin, is used to detect the protein. With an appropriate concentration of antibody, it appears that all available epitopes of PrP$^C$ are used in the capture step, which leaves none for the detection step. However, the larger number of epitopes on the PrP$^{TSE}$ aggregate is not exhausted by the capture step, and thus the labeled antibody is bound and detected. As yet unpublished data from a study in which pooled, normal hamster blood was tested in parallel with pooled blood from symptomatic scrapie-infected hamsters showed a clean discrimination; further studies are in progress, including tests on incubation period blood from hamsters and blood from symptomatic humans with CJD (SS An, communication).

ImmunoPCR (IPCR) is a very sensitive method for detecting immune reactions, in which the antibody is conjugated to a nucleotide sequence detected by polymerase chain reaction (PCR). Extremely low levels of antigen can be detected, but concurrent amplification of background noise can be a very difficult problem to overcome. The method has been tested on scrapie-infected brain homogenates and on recombinant hamster PrP, and its threshold of sensitivity was in the femtogram range.[47]

Preliminary data based on three other approaches have also been published or presented at scientific meetings. Trieschmann et al[48] seeded plasma samples with labeled synthetic prion protein aggregates; by using flow cytometry, they detected an accelerated formation of the aggregates in plasma from BSE-infected cattle than in those from controls. A research group at Chiron, Inc,[30] captured $PrP^{TSE}$ on magnetic beads coated with a synthetic PrP polypeptide and then used a monoclonal antibody to detect $PrP^{TSE}$ in a sandwich ELISA format: human vCJD brain and sheep scrapie brain homogenates gave positive signals at a level of about 10 to 20 infectious units, and a proportion of plasma samples from scrapie-infected sheep also gave positive results. Magnetic beads coated with a streptavidin/biotin/antibody complex for capture and a second labeled antibody for detection have concentrated and quantified $PrP^{C}$ in plasma [IBC, Reston, VA, 2005 (unpublished data)]. In conjunction with proteinase digestion, $PrP^{C}$ has been distinguished from $PrP^{TSE}$ in scrapie-infected hamster brain tissue and in both buffer and plasma spiked with $PrP^{TSE}$. Other test methods are undoubtedly under development but are not sufficiently advanced to have entered the public domain.

## Cell-Based Bioassays

A reliable and rapid cell-based infectivity assay would be useful as a confirmatory test. Chronically infected murine cell lines from scrapie-infected animals have been described,[49-51] and several methods exist in which cells can be infected with exogenously supplied mouse-adapted scrapie or sheep scrapie, as shown by the persistent conversion of cell PrP to $PrP^{TSE}$ during cell passage. Some systems have been shown to be associated with an increase in infectivity, but no such system has yet been described for vCJD.

The most thoroughly studied cell line is the mouse neuro-blastoma designated N2a. Nishida et al[52] transfected the line with the wild type mouse PrP gene and obtained a number of clones producing up to six times as much PrP as did the parental line. The clones readily became persistently infected when exposed to any of several different strains of mouse-adapted scrapie.

Klohn et al[53] developed an extremely sensitive infectivity assay for the RML strain of scrapie in highly infectable sublines of N2a neuroblastoma cells. The assay has two formats. In the first, infected foci are detected by blotting, treatment with protease, and scoring by staining with antibody. In the second format, the cells are infected and passed as in the first, and then they are seeded and scored on enzyme-linked immunospot (ELISPOT) plates (Cellular Technology Ltd., Cleveland, OH). In the focus assay using a carefully titrated preparation of RML, one colony corresponded to about 10 median lethal doses ($LD_{50}$). In the ELISPOT endpoint assay, the sensitivity was the same as that of the infectivity assay in mice. In preclinical animals, the in-vitro and in-vivo assays detected infectivity at the same time. The assay takes approximately 2 weeks.

Birkett et al[54] studied the cell line SMB, which was originally derived from a mouse infected with the Chandler strain of scrapie. The SMB line is positive for PrP[TSE] and is able to infect and cause disease in animals. It was cured of infection in vitro by incubation with pentosan sulfate and then infected with a different strain of scrapie. Mice inoculated with infected cell clones had incubation periods and histologic signs consistent with those for the strains of agent with which they were infected, whereas the cured cell line did not transmit disease. The infected cells accumulated both PrP[TSE] and infectivity.

Vilette et al[55] prepared a line (Rov9) from the established rabbit line RK13, which expressed the ovine prion gene under the control of a tetracycline-inducible promoter. It could be infected with natural scrapie from the appropriate genotype of sheep and from scrapie passaged in ovinized transgenic mice.

The cells were infectious, but the removal of tetracycline to stop expression of $PrP^C$ reduced the infectivity by about $10^4$-fold. It is of particular interest that the cell is a commonly used laboratory line and not of neuronal origin.

Falanga et al[56] very recently prepared clones of this scrapie-permissive cell line with a production of $PrP^{TSE}$ approximately 10-fold that of the parental line, or 20 µg/$10^7$ cells. Infectivity bioassays of cell extracts from $10^8$ cells produced somewhat shorter incubation periods in ovinized transgenic mice than did the brain homogenate used to infect the cells, which suggests that parallel dilution series of $PrP^{TSE}$ and infectivity could yield a threshold of $PrP^{TSE}$ detection near that of bioassay detection.

Vorberg et al[57] studied acute (transient) and chronic (persistent) conversion of $PrP^C$ to $PrP^{TSE}$ in cell culture. A mouse neuroblastoma cell and a mouse fibroblast cell line were transfected with the mouse PrP gene modified to carry the epitope for the antibody 3F4, which is not found on the native murine protein. Thus, any newly formed $PrP^{TSE}$ could be detected by its resistance to proteinase and distinguished from input mouse scrapie by its reaction to 3F4. The cells were infected with a variety of mouse scrapie strains. Endogenous $PrP^C$ of both neuronal and fibroblast cell types was converted to $PrP^{TSE}$ immediately after infection, but only the fibroblast line infected with the 22L strain was capable of sustaining transmissibility of the infection to mice. Again, it is of interest that this cell line was not neuronal in origin.

Finally, Archer et al[58] established an immortalized Schwann cell culture from an ovinized transgenic mouse that is susceptible to infection with at least two strains of sheep scrapie that achieve levels of infectivity nearly equal to those of infected sheep brain homogenates. Immunoblots of serially diluted cell lysates from passaged infected cells have shown a threshold of $PrP^{TSE}$ detection in the range of 5 to 10 $LD_{50}$,[31] and, if transgenic mouse lines with similar susceptibilities to infection with bovine and human TSE strains can be established, the method could find use as a validation bioassay for blood PrP$^{TSE}$-screening tests.

## Evaluation of Approaches

The presence of infectivity in blood has been convincingly shown in mice, hamsters, and sheep with any of several kinds of TSE, and, although the level of infectivity (at least in rodents) rises at the approach of the symptomatic phase of disease, not all samples are infectious, even during the terminal illness. For example, transmission rates in the transfusion experiments involving sheep infected with scrapie or BSE are about 40% to 50%. The two instances of suspected blood-related infection in humans involved donors studied 3 years and 18 months, respectively, before they developed symptoms of disease. Donors developing disease within 12 months of disease onset have not yet been shown to transmit infection, although their blood may be thought likely to be more infectious.

To detect a single infectious dose in a unit of blood, it would be necessary to pass the entire unit through a filter with a 100% efficiency in infectivity removal and then to perform a bioassay on the extract. Such a filter does not exist, and, in any case, the performance of a bioassay is impractical by virtue of technical issues, expense, and time; thus, the need for a surrogate marker of infectivity—PrP$^{TSE}$—and, consequently, of tests for its detection. Eventually, any such surrogate will have to pass muster as an accurate index of infectivity, which will require correlative studies using animal or cell culture bioassays, but, in the interim, a number of features lend weight to the presumption of accuracy.

One means of evaluating the methods for sensitivity, specificity, and comparability to other assays would be to provide blinded panels of infected materials such as dilutions of brain or spleen. These would serve to compare the sensitivities of different methods and to evaluate the ability of the assays to score the same materials "positive" or "negative" in replicate assays of blinded samples. Although the form of PrP$^{TSE}$ in blood may be different from that in brain or spleen—which contain easily detectable levels of both PrP$^{TSE}$ and infectivity[25]—an assay able to detect PrP$^{TSE}$ in these tissues may be thought more likely also to detect it in blood. Assays could be evaluated with identical blinded samples of blood from infected or uninfected animals or persons. It would be best if the infectivity of the blood had been shown previously, but, even if it had not, the evaluation would show whether a particular assay gave consistent results. If methods based on different approaches gave the same answer with the same samples, that would support claims for the significance of surrogate detection.

A collection of materials, consisting of identical ampoules of homogenates from brain of cases of CJD including vCJD, spleen from cases of vCJD, and dilution series of infected and uninfected brain and spleen in plasma for assessment of sensitivities, has been made at the National Institute for Biological Standards and Control (NIBSC) for the purpose of assay evaluation.[59] Similar aliquots of brain, spleen, blood, and blood fractions from scrapie-infected sheep and controls have also been prepared. It is intended that these materials, which are freely available, will be used in collaborative studies of candidate methods. After this evaluation, the assays may be tested with samples of blood from vCJD cases and with samples obtained from persons potentially exposed to infection, for example, through blood transfusion from donors who later developed vCJD. Relevant human samples are extremely rare and are available in small amounts. The examination of human samples, particularly those samples from exposed but asymptomatic individuals, who may or may not be infected, also raises major ethical questions. Such samples will be crucial to the development of diagnostics for CJD. This process will provide indications of the suitability of tests but will not validate them for use in terms of specificity, sensitivity, or practicality. The European Union's approval of tests for BSE may provide a precedent for the validation process, provided common technical specifications can be agreed upon.

Should a test be found satisfactory, its implementation will be problematic. No test is completely specific or sensitive, and the action to be taken should a person be found positive in a test is not obvious. The result might be a false positive, which will require confirmation by one or more different tests for PrP$^{TSE}$ and, ultimately, an infectivity bioassay; moreover, it does not necessarily follow that a truly positive person will go on to develop disease.

## Summary and Conclusions

An increasing number of tests for the detection of PrP$^{TSE}$ in blood are reaching a serious stage of development in both academic and commercial laboratories, which raises the real possibility of a practical blood-based test for preclinical cases of vCJD and other TSEs. We have limited this review to methods on which information has been published or presented at scientific meetings. We did not pretend to be comprehensive but did provide an idea of the kinds of strategies under study and the progress being made. A valid reliable test would be invaluable in ensuring the safety of the blood supply, evaluating the epidemiology of vCJD, and developing treatments. It is essential that assays be assessed rigorously, because the consequences of introducing an unsuitable, inaccurate, or unreliable test would be far-reaching.

## References

1. Peden AH, Head MW, Ritchie DE, et al. Preclinical vCJD after blood transfusion in a PRNP codon 129 heterozygous patient. Lancet 2004; 364:527-9.
2. Hilton DA, Ghani AC, Conyers L, et al. Prevalence of lymphoreticular prion protein accumulation in UK tissue samples. J Pathol 2004; 203:733-9.
3. Cervenakova L, Yakovleva O, McKenzie C, et al. Similar levels of infectivity in the blood of mice infected with human-derived vCJD

and GSS strains of transmissible spongiform encephalopathy. Transfusion 2003;43:1687-94.

4. Bons N, Lehmann S, Mestre-Francès N, et al. Brain and buffy coat transmission of bovine spongiform encephalopathy to the primate *Microcebus murinus*. Transfusion 2002;42:513-6.

5. Hunter N, Foster J, Chong A, et al. Transmission of prion diseases by blood transfusion. J Gen Virol 2002;83:2897-905.

6. Houston F, Foster JD, Chong A, et al. Transmission of BSE by blood transfusion in sheep. Lancet 2000;356:999-1000.

7. Hadlow WJ, Kennedy RC, Race RE. Natural infection of Suffolk sheep with scrapie virus. J Infect Dis 1982;146:657-64.

8. Llewelyn CA, Hewitt PE, Knight RS, et al. Possible transmission of variant Creutzfeldt-Jakob disease by blood transfusion. Lancet 2004; 363:417-21.

9. Shaked GM, Shaked Y, Kariv-Inbal Z, et al. A protease resistant prion protein isoform is present in urine of animals and humans affected with prion disease. J Biol Chem 2001;276:31479-82.

10. Head MW, Kouverianou E, Taylor L, et al. Evaluation of urinary PrPsc as diagnostic test for sporadic variant and familial CJD. Neurology 2005;64:1794-6.

11. Seeger H, Heikenwalker M, Zeller N, et al. Coincident scrapie infection and nephritis lead to urinary prion excretion. Science 2005; 310:324-6.

12. Miele G, Manson J, Clinton M. A novel erythroid specific marker of transmissible spongiform encephalopathies. Nat Med 2001;7:641-2.

13. Schütz E, Urnovitz HB, Iakoubov L, et al. Bov-tA short interspersed nucleotide element sequences in circulating nucleic acids from sera of cattle with bovine spongiform encephalopathy (BSE) and sera of cattle exposed to BSE. Clin Diagn Lab Immunol 2005;12:814-20.

14. Safar JG, Geschwind MD, Deering C, et al. Diagnosis of human prion disease. Proc Natl Acad Sci U S A 2005;102:3501-6.

15. Silveira JR, Raymond GJ, Hughson AG, et al. The most infectious prion protein particles. Nature 2005;437:257-61.

16. Minor P, Newham J, Jones N, et al. Standards for the assay of Creutzfeldt-Jakob disease specimens. J Gen Virol 2004;85(Pt 6):1777-84.

17. Wadsworth JD, Joiner S, Hill AF, et al. Tissue distribution of protease resistant prion protein in variant Creutzfeldt-Jakob disease using a highly sensitive immunoblotting assay. Lancet 2001;358:171-80.

18. Schmerr MJ, Jenny AL, Bulgin MS, et al. Use of capillary electrophoresis and fluorescent labeled peptides to detect the abnormal prion protein in the blood of animals that are infected with a transmissible spongiform encephalopathy. J Chromatog A 1999;853:207-14.

19. Yang WC, Yeung ES, Schmerr MJ. Detection of prion protein using a capillary electrophoresis-based competitive immunoassay with laser-induced fluorescence detection and cyclodextrin-aided separation. Electrophoresis 2005;26:1751-9.

20. Cervenakova L, Brown P, Soukhartev S, et al. Failure of immuno-competitive capillary electrophoresis assay to detect disease specific prion protein in buffy coat from humans and chimpanzees with Creutzfeldt-Jakob disease. Electrophoresis 2003;24:853-9.

21. Peretz D, Williamson RA, Matsunaga Y, et al. A conformational transition at the N terminus of the prion protein features in formation of the scrapie isoform. J Mol Biol 1997;273:614-22.

22. Safar J, Wille H, Itri U, et al. Eight prion strains have PrP$^{sc}$ molecules with different conformations. Nat Med 1998;4:1157-65.

23. Safar JG, Scott M, Monaghan J, et al. Measuring prions causing bovine spongiform encephalopathy or chronic wasting disease by immuno-assays and transgenic mice. Nat Biotechnol 2002;20:1147-50.

24. Bellon A, Seyfert-Brandt W, Lang H, et al. Improved conformation de-pendent immunoassay: Suitability for human prion detection with en-hanced sensitivity. J Gen Virol 2003;84:1921-5.

25. Bruce ME, McConnell I, Will RG, Ironside JW. Detection of variant Creutzfeldt-Jakob disease infectivity in extraneural tissues. Lancet 2001;358:208-9.

26. Korth K, Stierli P, Moser M, et al. Prion (PrP$^{sc}$)-specific epitope defined by a monoclonal antibody. Nature 1997;390:74-7.

27. Kuhn F, Purro M, Zwald J, et al. Towards a live test for prion diseases. Abstract A264. Presented at the International Prion Conference, Mu-nich, Germany, October 8-10, 2003.

28. Zwald D, Kuhn D, Purro M, et al. A novel blood based TSE diagnostic test. Presented at NeuroPrion, the First International Conference of the European Network of Excellence, Paris, France, May 24-28, 2004.

29. Nazor KE, Kuhn F, Seward T, et al. Immunodetection of disease-asso-ciated mutant PrP, which accelerates disease in GSS transgenic mice. EMBO J 2005;24:2472-80.

30. World Health Organization guidelines on transmissible spongiform encephalopathies in relation to biological and pharmaceutical prod-ucts. Report of a WHO Consultation, Geneva, Switzerland, September 14-16, 2005 (in press).

31. Serbec VC, Bresjanac M, Popovic M, et al. Monoclonal antibody against a peptide of human prion protein discriminates between Creutzfeldt-Jakob disease-affected and normal brain tissue. J Biol Chem 2004;279:3694-8.

32. Paramithiotis E, Pinard M, Lawton T, et al. A prion protein epitope se-lective for the pathologically misfolded conformation. Nat Med 2003; 9:893-9.

33. Zou W-Q, Zheng J, Gray DM, et al. Antibody to DNA detects scrapie but not normal prion protein. Proc Natl Acad Sci U S A 2004;101:1380-5.

34. Fischer MB, Roeckl C, Parizek P, et al. Binding of disease-associated prion protein to plasminogen. Nature 2000;408:479-88.

35. Lane A, Stanley CJ, Dealer S, Wilson SM. Polymeric ligands with speci-ficity for aggregated prion protein (abstract). Clin Chem 2003;49: 1774-5.

36. Microsens diagnostic research focuses on the Seprion technology. London: Microsens Biotechnologies. [Available at http://www. microsens.co.uk/technology.html (accessed February 24, 2006).]

37. Hornemann S, Glockshuber R. Autonomous and reversible folding of a soluble amino terminally truncated segment of the mouse prion protein. J Mol Biol 1996;262:614-19.

38. Tcherkasskaya O, Sanders W, Chynwat V, et al. The role of hydrophobic interactions in amyloidogenesis: Example of prion-related protein polypeptides. J Biomolec Struct 2003;21:353-65.

39. Grosset A, Moskowitz K, Nelsen C, et al. Rapid presymptomatic detection of PrP$^{sc}$ via conformationally responsive palindromic PrP peptides. Peptides 2005;26:2193-200.

40. Pan T, Moskowitz K, Tcherkasskaya O, et al. Detection of PrPsc in blood using a palindromic peptide as a conformationally sensitive ligand. Presented at the Keystone Symposium on TSE Diseases, Breckenridge, CO, April 2-6, 2003.

41. Kocisko DA, Come JH, Priola SA, et al. Cell-free formation of protease resistant prion protein. Nature 1994;370:471-4.

42. Saborio GP, Permanne B, Soto C. Sensitive detection of pathological prion protein by cyclic amplification of protein misfolding. Nature 2001;411:810-13.

43. Castilla J, Saa P, Hetz C, Soto C. In vitro generation of infectious scrapie prions. Cell 2005;121:195-206.

44. Soto C, Anderes L, Suardi S, et al. Pre-symptomatic detection of prions by cyclic amplification of protein misfolding. FEBS Lett 2005;579:638-42.

45. Castilla J, Saa P, Soto C. Detection of prions in blood. Nat Med 2005;11: 982-5.

46. Bieschke J, Giese A, Schulz-Schaeffer W, et al. Ultrasensitive detection of pathological prion protein aggregates by dual color scanning for intensely fluorescent targets. Proc Natl Acad Sci U S A 2000;97:5468-73.

47. Barletta JM, Edelman DC, Highsmith WE, Constantine NT. Detection of ultra-low levels of pathological prion protein in scrapie infected hamster brain homogenates using real-time immuno-PCR. J Virol Methods 2005;127:154-64.

48. Trieschmann L, Santos AN, Kaschig K, et al. Ultra-sensitive detection of prion protein fibrils by flow cytometry in blood from cattle affected with bovine spongiform encephalopathy. BMC Biotech 2005;5:26 (Internet publication). [Available at http://www.biomedcentral. com/ 1472-6750/5/26 (accessed February 23, 2006).]

49. Race RE, Fadness LH, Chesebro B. Characterisation of scrapie infection in mouse neuroblastoma cells. J Gen Virol 1987;68:1391-9.

50. Race RE, Caughey B, Graham K, et al. Analysis of frequency of infection, specific infectivity, and prion protein biosynthesis in scrapie-infected neuroblastoma cell clones. J Virol 1988;62:2845-9.

51. Rubenstein R, Deng H, Race R, et al. Scrapie strain infection in vitro induces changes in neuronal cells. Mol Neurobiol 1994;8:129-38.

52. Nishida N, Harris DA, Vilette D, et al. Successful transmission of three mouse adapted scrapie strains to murine neuroblastoma cell lines over expressing wild-type mouse prion protein. J Virol 2000;74:320-5.

53. Klohn P-C, Stole E, Flechsig E, et al. A quantitative highly sensitive cell-based infectivity assay for mouse scrapie prions. Proc Natl Acad. Sci U S A 2003;100:11666-71.

54. Birkett CR, Henson RM, Bembridges DA, et al. Scrapie strains maintain biological phenotypes on propagation in a cell line in culture. EMBO J 2001;20:3351-8.

55. Vilette D, Andreoletti O, Archer F, et al. Ex vivo propagation of infectious sheep scrapie agent in heterologous epithelial cells expressing ovine prion protein. Proc Natl Acad Sci U S A 2001;98:4055-9.

56. Falanga PB, Blom-Potar M-C, Bittoun P, et al. Selection of ovine PrP high-producer subclones from a transfected epithelial cell line. Biophys Biochem Rec Commun 2005;340:309-17.

57. Vorberg I, Raines A, Priola SA. Acute formation of protease resistant prion protein does not always lead to persistent scrapie infection in vitro. J Biol Chem 2004;279:29218-25.

58. Archer F, Bachelin C, Andreoletti O, et al. Cultured peripheral neuroglial cells are highly permissive to sheep prion infection. J Virol 2004; 78:482-90.

59. CJD Resource Centre. Virtual Resource Centre. South Mimms, Hertfordshire, UK: National Institute for Biological Standards and Control, 2006. [Available at http://www.nibsc.ac.uk/cjd/Virtual.html (accessed May 16, 2006).]

In: Turner ML, ed.
*Creutzfeldt-Jakob Disease: Managing the Risk of
Transmission by Blood, Plasma, and Tissues*
Bethesda, MD: AABB Press, 2006

# 6

# Component Procurement and Processing Strategies to Reduce vCJD Transmission Risk

REBECCA CARDIGAN, BSc, PHD, AND LORNA M.
WILLIAMSON, BSc, MD, FRCP, FRCPATH

BLOOD DONATION CONSISTS OF the collection of 450 to 500 mL of blood into citrate anticoagulant. It is now generally accepted that there are very few clinical indications for transfusion of whole blood as it comes from the donor. Therefore, the vast majority of donations are processed into Red Blood Cell (RBC) concentrates and plasma; a high proportion of donations also provide therapeutic platelets.

*Rebecca Cardigan, BSc, PhD, Head of Component Development, National Blood Service, England and North Wales, Brentwood, Essex, United Kingdom; and Lorna M. Williamson, BSc, MD, FRCP, FRCPath, Reader in Transfusion Medicine/Clinical Director (Products), University of Cambridge/National Blood Service, Cambridge, United Kingdom*

The permitted storage temperature of whole blood between collection and manufacture depends upon the components that are to be produced from it. Because platelet function rapidly deteriorates at 4 C, whole blood intended for platelet production must be separated on the day of collection, although overnight storage at a controlled 22 C is also permitted in some countries. However, for the production of RBCs, whole blood can be stored at 4 C for up to 48 hours before separation. The plasma from whole-blood donations is either pooled and subjected to bulk fractionation into plasma products (see Chapter 7) or transfused as single-unit Fresh Frozen Plasma (FFP) or Cryoprecipitated AHF to patients with deficits of multiple coagulation factors. Generally, FFP is separated from whole blood on the day of collection or from blood stored at 22 C for up to 24 hours, because both of these methods have been shown to preserve plasma quality.

The method used to process donations intended for platelet production differs in the United States (US) and Europe. In Europe, such donations are hard-spun, and the red cells and plasma are expressed from the bottom and top of the primary pack [bottom-and-top (BAT) processing]. In the US, the platelet-rich plasma (PRP) method is used, so that whole-blood donations are first subjected to a soft spin and the PRP is removed for further processing (see the section on platelets, below).

Apheresis, a process that separates blood into its components while the donation is ongoing, is also used to collect platelets, plasma, red cells, and granulocytes. The main emphasis in the past has been the collection of platelets and plasma components, and red cells were returned to the donor. The size and complexity of the equipment, as well as the welfare of the donor, have necessitated that this activity take place in nonmobile locations. However, smaller portable machines are now available that can be used on mobile sessions to collect red cells and plasma, and similar machines for platelets are anticipated.

# Risk Assessments of Distribution of Prion Infectivity in Blood Components

One model of risk and distribution of prion infectivity that has been used to inform policy was constructed by Det Norske Veritas (DNV) Consulting (London) for the UK Department of Health.[1] It was based on literature published up to 2002 and on experimental data from mice, hamsters, and sheep. This model uses data from various animal systems to generate assumptions regarding levels of prion infectivity and its distribution in human blood. Therefore, it has to be emphasized that the mean values quoted are often conservative and associated with wide confidence intervals. In addition, the data are generated in animal systems with uncertain applicability to human transmission. Therefore, their use in policy-making should always be in the context of a sensitivity analysis, which asks whether the benefits of a proposed risk reduction step would still be robust if the true figure were, say, 10 or 100 times higher or lower than proposed in the model (see Chapter 9).

In considering how changes to blood component procurement may reduce variant Creutzfeldt-Jakob disease (vCJD) risk, four of the assumptions made in the DNV model are relevant:

1.  That blood from people incubating vCJD is infective and that infectivity is present from at least the midpoint of the incubation period.

    These observations were based on bioassays of blood from different animal and human transmissible spongiform encephalopathies (TSEs), including Gerstmann-Sträussler-Scheinker agent in mice,[2] a scrapie strain (263K) in hamsters,[3] BSE in sheep,[4] and natural scrapie in sheep.[5] There have also been two possible human-to-human transmissions of vCJD via nonleukocyte-reduced RBCs[6,7] from two donors who developed the first symptoms of vCJD 3 years, 4 months, and 18 months, respectively, after the implicated donation. A third possible transmission was reported in early 2006.[8]

2.    That overall levels of infectivity are on the order of 10 intracerebral median infective doses ($ID_{50}$/mL) and that transmission by the intravenous route is one-fifth as efficient as that by the intracerebral route.

The implications of this assumption are that human blood from an infected person would contain 2 intravenous $ID_{50}$/mL and that transmission would certainly occur if the blood component contained >2 $ID_{50}$ in total. More recent studies using hamster scrapie, however, suggest infectivity levels two to three times as high.[9,10]

3.    That infectivity is distributed between different blood components in these proportions: 24% red cells, 22% buffy coat, and 54% plasma.

This assumption was based on rodent studies in which different blood components prepared from endogenously infected mice were injected into recipients.[11] These injections were not pure preparations, and, thus, they probably contained cross-contamination from other blood elements, as is seen in normal blood component preparation. However, an alternative model is proposed in which no infectivity is carried on "pure" platelets or red cells, and all infectivity is associated with either plasma or buffy coat.[9,12]

4.    That leukocyte reduction (LR) would reduce infectivity from red cells and platelets by 2 log but that there would be no reduction in FFP.

It was recognized in the DNV risk assessment that current LR technologies had the potential to reduce leukocyte numbers by 3 log, but a conservative benefit of 2 log was proposed. On the basis of specific experiments using plasma, no benefit of LR was assumed for FFP.[13] Recently, a study of hamster scrapie suggested that the reduction in infectivity achieved by LR was approximately 40%.[10] This possibility suggests that, although LR alone will not render blood components noninfectious in current models, it could still be an essential "debulking" step before specific prion removal steps.

## Strategies Adopted to Reduce vCJD Risk Through Component Procurement and Processing

On the basis of the above assumptions, four overall strategies emerged:

1.  To reduce exposure to donor leukocytes, because they offer no benefit to the recipient.
2.  To reduce exposure to donor plasma, unless there is demonstrable or likely benefit to the recipient.
3.  To minimize the number of donors contributing to a therapeutic dose of product.
4.  To promote an evidence-based approach to prescribing donor-derived blood components and to encourage the use of alternatives.

Within these broad categories, specific approaches that have been considered or adopted in the United Kingdom (UK) are shown in Table 6-1. Some of these approaches have been adopted in other European countries, as discussed in each respective section below.

## Universal LR of Blood Components

Before 1998, leukocyte-reduced components were issued only for selective patient groups in the UK. In that year, the UK Department of Health commissioned the DNV vCJD risk assessment of transfusion and asked the UK Blood Services to assess the costs and feasibility of universal LR. A decision was taken to proceed in July 1998, and a program was rolled out over the next year to achieve LR of 100% of RBC, platelet, and FFP units. Although the risk assessment had not shown any specific benefit of LR for FFP, whole-blood filtration allowed LR FFP to be produced as a by-product. Universal LR is now undertaken in many European countries, and the appearance of vCJD was a factor in this decision. In the US, some suppliers introduced the practice, but there has been controversy regarding the cost-benefit ratio.

**Table 6-1. Strategies Adopted in the United Kingdom to Minimize the Risk of Transmission of Variant Creutzfeldt-Jakob Disease Through Blood Components**

| Strategy | How to Achieve It | Status |
|---|---|---|
| Reduce exposure to donor leukocytes | Universal leukocyte reduction of RBCs, platelets, and FFP | Implemented 1999 |
| Reduce exposure to donor plasma | | |
| From FFP | Import FFP from the United States for selected groups | |
| | MBFFP for children born on or after January 1, 1996 | Implemented summer 2004 |
| | MBFFP for all children up to age 16 years | Implemented summer 2005 |
| | Cryoprecipitate production from imported MBFFP | To be implemented 2006 |
| | SDFFP for plasma exchange for TTP | Implemented 2006 |

| | | |
|---|---|---|
| From RBCs | Process RBCs to minimize plasma contamination | Ongoing quality-improvement program 100% BAT production being considered |
| | Permit use of red cells in additive solution for large-volume transfusions in neonates | Under discussion with clinicians; BCSH guideline modified 2006 |
| | Wash all RBC units | Not considered practical at this time |
| From platelets | Manufacture pooled platelets from "drier" buffy coats | Implemented 2002 |
| | When possible, meet requests for children up to age 16 years with apheresis platelets | Apheresis "splits" used for infants since mid-1990s; for older children, implemented summer 2005 |
| | Suspend platelets in 30:70 plasma:additive solution mixture | Evaluations ongoing |
| Remove infectious prions from blood components | Pall filter for red cells CE-marked May 2005; PRDT/MacoPharma red cell filter under development | Both filters undergoing assessment by the blood services of the United Kingdom and Ireland |
| Reduce donor exposure | Increase proportion of single-donor:pooled platelets entering supply from baseline of 40% | Expected/projected to reach 50% by 2006; option appraisal ongoing of how to increase further |
| | Provide apheresis donations for children | Implemented 2005 |

(continued)

**Table 6-1. Strategies Adopted in the United Kingdom to Minimize the Risk of Transmission of Variant Creutzfeldt-Jakob Disease Through Blood Components (continued)**

| Strategy | How to Achieve It | Status |
|---|---|---|
| | Provide double-dose RBCs from apheresis collections for thalassemia patients | Pilot study completed and continued at major center; roll-out planned |
| | Provide 4 to 8 splits of RBCs for neonates, allocated to a single infant | Standard practice since late 1990s |
| Reduce donor exposure through "Better Use of Blood" program | Better management of preoperative anemia/anticoagulation; accepting lower hemoglobin trigger; intra- and postoperative cell recovery | 8% reduction in red cell use seen in 2004; further 5% reduction in 2005 |

RBCs = Red Blood Cells; FFP = Fresh Frozen Plasma; MBFFP = methylene blue-treated FFP; SDFFP = solvent/detergent-treated FFP; TTP = thrombotic thrombocytopenic purpura; CE = Council of Europe; BAT = bottom and top; BCSH = British Committee for Standards in Haematology.

## Specifications for Leukocyte-Reduced Components

Guidelines from different jurisdictions have slightly different specifications for leukocyte-reduced components. Because they are to an extent based on what can be achieved, they are not fundamentally different in practice (Table 6-2).

The UK also requires that LR should be completed within 48 hours of donation, before component storage. For whole-blood donations, this is achieved by filtration, whereas an LR step by centrifugation/elutriation is integral to some apheresis technologies. Most whole-blood LR filters remove >2 log of platelets[14] in addition to >4 log leukocytes. Therefore, to produce platelet concentrates, RBCs, plasma, and pooled buffy coat platelets must be filtered after whole blood has been processed. However, a second generation of whole-blood LR filters that permit platelets to pass through the filter is becoming available, although these filters are not yet in widespread use. LR results in a 10% to 15% loss of volume of a whole-blood or processed component, but it has minimal adverse effects on the quality of blood components.[15]

To ensure that leukocyte-reduced components meet specifications for residual leukocyte content, two complementary approaches are taken: one, prepurchase assessment of the capability and consistency of performance, and, two, regular testing of a proportion of components with statistical process monitoring to ensure ongoing compliance. The number of residual leukocytes in leukocyte-reduced components are too few to be counted by standard hematology analyzers. Manual microscopy (Nageotte) is unsuitable for large-scale use, so flow cytometry methods are employed, based on the binding of fluorescent dyes to nucleic acids in conjunction with calibrant beads. The limit of sensitivity of most methods is approximately 1 cell/$\mu$L (equivalent to $0.3 \times 10^6$/RBC unit).

Because it is logistically not feasible to sample and test 100% of leukocyte-reduced components, a proportion (typically 1% to 5%) of components is tested according to international guidelines,[16] and the LR performance is plotted on a statistical

**Table 6-2. Specifications for Leukocyte-Reduced Blood Components**

| | UK | Council of Europe/European Union Directive | AABB |
|---|---|---|---|
| Level of residual leukocytes | $<5 \times 10^6$/U | $<1 \times 10^6$/U | $<5 \times 10^6$/U for red cells and apheresis platelets; $<8.3 \times 10^5$/U for PRP platelets |
| Percentage of components in which this reduction must be attained | 99 | 90 | 95 |
| Statistical confidence that this reduction is attained | 95% | Not stated | Not stated |

UK = United Kingdom.

process monitoring chart.[17] In this way, poor performance can be identified before a large number of units that will fail to meet specification are produced. Systems with poor LR capability will result in the testing of a large proportion of components. Examples of routine quality-monitoring data collated nationally are given in Table 6-3.

Because LR was instituted as a safety step, it is important to assess the risk that a given LR system will result in the issuing of blood components that fail to meet the required specification for residual leukocytes. The chance of this happening is dependent upon a number of factors—the capability of the LR system, the frequency of potential manufacturing defects in the LR filter or pack system, the proportion of components that are tested for residual leukocytes, and donor-related causes. Although most donor-related causes of filter failure are poorly understood, it is known that the blood of donors with sickle cell trait is more likely either to block LR filters or to fail to be leukocyte reduced.[17] Thus, in the UK, 100% of hemoglobin AS donations are assessed for residual leukocytes. An estimation has been made of the likelihood that components that exceed certain levels of residual leukocyte content will be issued, as shown in Table 6-4.

These figures are taken from UK quality-monitoring data for an 18-month period. Residual risk can be calculated by using this formula: residual risk = number of units issued/(number of units not tested/number of units tested) × number of units that have residual leukocytes above a defined level.

## Leukocyte Subsets and Microparticles

At the time of implementation of universal LR, evidence from a murine genetic knock-out model suggested that circulating B lymphocytes might be a reservoir of infectious prion.[18] Although these observations turned out to have another explanation,[19] studies were performed to examine the removal of different leukocyte subsets during LR processes. Initial studies used flow cytometry and immunophenotyping of residual

**Table 6-3. National Leukocyte-Reduction Quality-Monitoring Data from England***

| Component | Number Tested | Residual Leukocytes (mean ± SD) | Percentage of Components >1 × 10⁶/U | Percentage of Components >5 × 10⁶/U |
|---|---|---|---|---|
| Red cells in additive solution, whole-blood-derived | 14,456 | 0.35 ± 0.29 | 2.21 | 0.04 |
| Red cells in additive solution, apheresis | 399 | 0.26 ± 0.02 | 0 | 0 |
| Red cells | 1,909 | 0.35 ± 0.22 | 1.26 | 0.05 |
| Platelets, whole-blood-derived | 3,570 | 0.32 ± 0.08 | 0.11 | 0 |
| Platelets, apheresis | 10,859 | 0.29 ± 2.68 | 1.36 | 0.11 |
| Fresh Frozen Plasma | 3,492 | 0.28 ± 0.02 | 0 | 0 |

*Data are from a 3-month period in 2005, taken from national quality-monitoring information from the National Blood Service.

## Table 6-4. Estimation of the Residual Risk of Issue of a Leukocyte-Reduced Component Containing Residual Leukocytes Above Defined Levels

| | >1 × 10⁶/U | >5 × 10⁶/U | >100 × 10⁶/U |
|---|---|---|---|
| Apheresis platelets | 1:175 | 1:1,352 | 1:6,381 |
| Pooled platelets | 1:202 | 1:2,028 | <1:22,304 |
| Red cells in additive solution | 1:160 | 1:1,522 | 1:7,250 |
| Fresh Frozen Plasma | 1:1,072 | 1:18,251 | <1:14,783 |

leukocytes to show that, after LR of whole blood or RBCs, most of the residual leukocytes were neutrophils, whereas, in leukocyte-reduced platelets, lymphocytes tended to predominate.[20,21] A later study used real-time reverse transcriptase polymerase chain reaction (RT-PCR) to quantitate mRNA encoding proteins specific to leukocyte subsets. This showed at least $3.5_{10}$ log reduction of all subtypes by red cell filtration and at least $2_{10}$ log reduction from platelet LR, whether in pools or apheresis platelets.[22] However, because the leukocyte load in pooled platelets is already reduced during processing, all processes have similar residual leukocyte levels.

One concern about LR processes was that the number of cellular microparticles in blood components may be increased if leukocytes (or platelets) were fragmented by the filter fibers. If such particles carried infectious prions, the benefits of universal LR may be entirely eliminated. Therefore, a comprehensive study was performed to measure microparticles derived from red cells, platelets, and leukocytes in blood components manufactured by all LR processes in use by UK Blood Services. Fortunately, this study showed no overall generation of cellular microparticles by LR processes and did not show any individual filters or processes that were extreme outliers.[23]

# Minimizing Plasma Exposure Through Red Cell Transfusion

## Modifying Red Cell Processing

For the vast majority of RBC units processed, an additive solution containing adenine is added after separation to achieve a hematocrit of 50% to 70% and to maintain red cell quality during the storage period, which is 35 days in the UK and 42 days in other European countries and the US. RBCs produced from donations from which the buffy coat has been removed to make platelets have a slightly lower volume and hemoglobin content because of the loss of red cells into the buffy coat.

The amount of residual plasma in an RBC unit in additive solution is dependent on the hematocrit of the donor and how hard the red cells were centrifuged. During consideration of strategies to reduce exposure of patients to donor plasma, it was noted that RBC units processed by top-and-top methods contained significantly more plasma than those processed by BAT methods (Table 6-5). Attempts have been made to reduce the volume of plasma in top-and-top RBC units by modification of the centrifuge conditions.

### Review of the Need for Nonadditive Red Cells for Large-Volume Transfusions in Neonates

Red cell components used for intrauterine and exchange transfusions in neonates are normally manufactured in 100% plasma because of theoretical concerns about the potential toxic effects of adenine and mannitol.[24] A recent UK guideline for transfusion of neonates and older children reflected this and also recommended that infants less than 6 months old who undergo cardiac bypass surgery should not receive red cells collected into optimal additive solutions [ie, saline-adenine-glucose-mannitol (SAG-M)].[25] The same recommendation was made for extracorporeal membrane oxygenation, and, in this case, the point was made that the fresh semi-packed red cells recommended will include a significant amount of relatively fresh plasma containing useful levels of all clotting factors other than Factors VIII and V. However, such practices expose children to large volumes of plasma.

There has been recent evidence of the possible safety of mannitol and adenine in neonatal cardiac surgery. A prospective randomized trial compared whole blood with reconstituted blood in 200 infants undergoing cardiac surgery.[26] The reconstituted blood was made up of red cells in Adsol or Optisol combined with FFP, and, therefore, it contained adenine and mannitol. The group that received reconstituted blood had a better outcome than the group that received fresh whole blood, with a shorter stay in intensive care and a lower

## Table 6-5. Specifications from Different Sources, and Typical Values for Volume and Hemoglobin Content for Leukocyte-Reduced Red Cell Components

| | Specification | | | | | | Typical Values[†] | | |
| | Volume (mL) | | | Hemoglobin Content (g/unit) | | | | | |
| | UK | EU | AABB | UK | EU | AABB | Volume (mL) | Hemo-globin (g/unit) | Plasma Volume (mL) |
|---|---|---|---|---|---|---|---|---|---|
| Red cells in additive solution, leukocyte reduced, all methods | >75%* 220–340 | NS | NS | >75%* >40 | >40 | NS | 282 ± 32 | 55 ± 8 | 17 |
| Red cells in additive solution, leukocyte reduced, apheresis | >75%* 220–340 | NS | >95%* >128 mL red cells | >75%* >40 | >40 | >95% >42.5 | 261 ± 15 | 54 ± 5 | 22 |
| Red cells in plasma, leukocyte reduced, for exchange | NS | | | >75%* >40 | NS | | 324 ± 27 | 62 ± 5 | 116 |

| | | | | |
|---|---|---|---|---|
| Red cells in additive solution, leukocyte reduced, buffy coat removed | As above | 250 ± 19 | 49 ± 6 | 6 |
| Red cells in additive solution, leukocyte reduced | As above | 304 ± 17 | 58 ± 5 | 28 |

*Percentage of units tested that must be of the value shown.
†Taken from national quality-monitoring data from the English National Blood Service; they are likely to vary between countries.
NS = not specified; UK = United Kingdom; EU = European Union.

perioperative fluid overload. Moreover, there was no significant difference in the numbers of infants requiring renal replacement therapy. Neonates (<28 days old) constituted 39%
of the study group, and a post hoc subgroup analysis by patient age, comparing those ≤28 days old with those >28 days
old, also found no difference in outcome by the type of blood
received. This study therefore provides evidence of the apparent safety of mannitol and adenine for neonatal cardiac surgery, and the authors suggest that it is possible that mannitol's
antioxidant properties may have a protective effect. An infor-
mal survey of cardiac surgery units revealed mixed practice,
with some centers using SAG-M blood as the standard without apparent detriment. Discussions are ongoing with some
cardiac units in the UK regarding a switch to SAG-M red cells,
and an addendum to the UK guidelines that takes the above
study into account has been released stating "In this context,
the British Committee for Standards in Haematology (BCSH)
Transfusion Task Force recommends that pediatric cardiac
centers already using SAG-M blood should continue to do so,
and that those using citrate-phosphate-dextrose (CPD) should
consider switching to SAG-M blood."[27]

## Red Cell Washing

Red cell washing with removal of >90% plasma and saline
resuspension is used in three settings: for patients with immunoglobulin A (IgA) deficiency with IgA antibodies; for patients with severe anaphylactic reactions to red cells; and for
reconstitution of cryopreserved red cells provided to patients
with rare phenotypes. Such red cells are now provided by a
new generation of cell-washing equipment that offers a closed
system and thus allows the extension of shelf life beyond 24
hours. However, the product has been validated only for a
7-day shelf life. Therefore, although this might appear to be an
attractive option for vCJD risk reduction, the short shelf life

precludes the use of large-scale washing of the entire red cell supply at present.

## Prion Reduction Technology

Two companies (Pall Corp., East Hills, NY; MacoPharma, Tourcoing, France) approached the UK and Irish blood services in 2004 to report that they were developing prion-removal filtration-type technology. The companies have taken different approaches to the development of such technology, but, at this writing, the only blood component for which a prion-reduction filter is available is LR RBCs.

### Pall

The Pall Leukotrap Affinity Prion Reduction Filter (LAPRF) contains polyester fibers that are surface modified with proprietary chemistry to allow the removal of abnormal prion in plasma by mechanisms that include cation/anion exchange, nonspecific ionic interaction, and hydrogen bonding. Although the filter is designed to remove abnormal prion from RBC units that have already been leukocyte reduced, the nonwoven fibers are constructed to remove any remaining leukocytes along with any associated abnormal prion. They also have a sieving action to remove prion aggregates and other prion-containing heterotypic aggregates. The filter can be used on any day 1 red cells and has been validated for red cells stored in CPD/SAG-M, CPD, and citrate-phosphate-dextrose-adenine-1 (CPDA-1).

Two main methods have been used to validate the prion reduction capability of the LAPRF: exogenous study, which involves human blood spiked with scrapie-infected, homogenized brain tissue, and endogenous study, which involves peripheral blood from scrapie-infected hamsters. There is more than 90% homology between human and hamster protein, and, in addition, prion proteins (PrP) from different species share similar physicochemical properties, antigenicity, and degrees of resistance to proteinase K digestion.[28-30] Therefore, the properties of hamster scrapie isoform PrP (PrP$^{Sc}$) make it a suitable model for investigating filter performance. In the exogenous PrP$^{Sc}$ removal study, scrapie-infected hamster brain homogenate (SIHBH) was added to RBC units (CPD, CPDA-1, and CPD/SAG-M). The red cells were then filtered at 4 C or 22 C ± 2 C at 15" to 40" filtration head height. The concentration of PrP$^{Sc}$ in the red cells before and after filtration was measured by using either a Western blot assay (with 3F4 as the primary monoclonal antibody and goat anti-mouse immunoglobulin G conjugated to horseradish peroxidase with a chemiluminescent substrate) or a bioassay. Results of the Western blot assay show that the LAPRF removed 2.9 ± 0.7 log abnormal prion. In the bioassay, prefiltration and postfiltration red cell samples were 10-fold diluted with phosphate-buffered saline (PBS). Hamsters were injected intracerebrally with either pre- or postfiltration samples. The animals are being monitored, and the titration will be ascertained when the animals show clinical signs of scrapie disease (eg, head bobbing, wobbling gait, and weight loss). The concentration of infectious prions in the sample will be calculated from the score at the highest dilution by using the Reed-Muench method.[31] The results will be calculated and expressed as a log reduction. Published spike plus bioassay data from studies using a prototype prion-reduction filter showed 3.7 log reduction in infectivity.[32]

For the endogenous study, blood was collected into CPD or CPDA-1 from scrapie-infected Syrian hamsters at the onset of clinical symptoms. This was then pooled and processed into human-sized RBC units by using standard blood-processing conditions. RBC units were filtered by using the LAPRF at 30" filtration head height. Forty-µL aliquots of either pre- or postfiltration samples were injected intracranially into both sides of the brain of normal Syrian hamsters for each treatment condition. The animals are being maintained and will be monitored for 400 days; those that develop clinical symptoms of scrapie will be sacrificed, and the brains of all animals (including survivors) will be tested for the presence of PrP$^{Sc}$ by using Western blot. Endogenous infectivity studies using a prototype prion-reduction filter showed that 6 of 43 animals receiving nonfiltered blood had symptoms of scrapie and/or PrP$^{sc}$ in their brains, in contrast to 0 of 35 ($P = 0.03$) that had received prion-filtered blood.[32]

Prion-reduction filtration is a new technology, and there are no specific guidelines (other than those for non-prion-treated red cells) to define the quality of the resultant blood components either immediately after filtration or during component storage. RBC units produced with the LAPRF have been evaluated by using standard in-vitro markers of red cell quality (ie, percentage of hemolysis, ATP, K+, and pH). Saunders et al[33] reported that filtered units showed no differences from control units, and they met European Union requirements for hemoglobin content of LR RBCs (75% had >40 g/unit). Filtered units were found, however, to have significantly higher percentages of hemolysis than do controls, but all were well within the permitted 0.8% level at the end of storage. The LAPRF has also been shown to have no effects on microvesicle formation, band 3 protein, CD47, or red cell antigen expression (manufacturer's data). Finally, satisfactory 24-hour in-vivo red cell recovery data have been shown for CP2D/AS3 red cells[34] and in-vivo red cell recovery and survival data for CPD red cells (manufacturer's data).

It is obviously not possible to perform routine quality control to assess the level of prion removal in filtered RBC units. Therefore, a surrogate marker that is readily detectable by using easily implemented techniques is needed. The manufacturer found that the LAPRF removes Factor IX from RBC units. The removal of Factor IX can be correlated with the number of LAPRF media layers and also with abnormal prion removal (K Wilkins, personal communication). LAPRF therefore has the potential to be used in blood centers as a surrogate marker for quality-monitoring purposes. The Pall Leukotrap Affinity Prion Reduction Filter was Council of Europe (CE) marked for claims relating to the spiking experiments in May 2005.

## PRDT/MacoPharma

The MacoPharma P-Capt Filter is a prion-specific filter that consists of established, biocompatible filter media incorporating patented PRDT (Pathogen Removal and Diagnostic Technology, Falls Church, VA) ligand technology. The ligand is integrated into a filter housing (MacoPharma) for use as a sterile, single-use, prion-reduction filter for LR RBCs. Affinity interactions selectively adsorb and concentrate targeted proteins and pathogens on immobilized supports. In an evaluation of millions of different chemical structures, PRDT identified multiple strong binders of prion proteins. From these, a ligand was selected that binds human, hamster, and mouse prions in both their normal and protease-resistant forms and in the presence of human plasma, red cells, and whole blood. The ligand adsorbs the abnormal forms of the prion protein from both sporadic and vCJD-infected human brain, familial CJD-infected mouse brain, and scrapie-infected hamster brain with high affinity ($Kd = 10^{-9} M$). Reactivity with the rodent prion proteins and infectivity was used as a tool to develop and validate the filter.

Two bioassays have been performed to assess the ability of the immobilized ligand to remove TSE infectivity from blood. The first study used a highly infectious preparation derived from TSE-infected hamster (263K) brain spiked into a human RBC unit. The infected unit was passed over the immobilized ligand and the PrP-depleted red cell preparation was subsequently inoculated into noninfected animals to measure the level of removal of infectivity. Removal of the infection-specific form of the PrP from spiked RBCs was shown to the limit of detection of the Western blot and a 4 $\log_{10}$ ID$_{50}$/mL reduction in infectivity in the in-vivo bioassay. Because the concentration of TSE infectivity in whole blood is only approximately 10 ID/mL, even during symptomatic disease, this level of reduction would provide a large margin of safety, presuming that the infectivity endogenously present in blood behaves similarly to that spiked into blood from brain preparation. The second study used the sensitive and precise "limiting-dilution titration" method developed in the Rohwer Laboratory (Veterans Affairs Medical Center, Baltimore, MD) to measure, to the extent possible, the reduction of the low levels of infectivity present in endogenously infected blood. A large cohort of hamsters infected with 263K scrapie was phlebotomized into CP2D over approximately 2 hours to generate a 500-mL pool of infected blood. The whole blood was leukocyte reduced and then passed over the immobilized ligand. Five-milliliter samples of LR and prion-filtered whole blood were inoculated at a rate of 50 $\mu$L per animal into large cohorts ($n = 100$) of hamsters via the intracranial route, and the animals were observed for 18 months for the presence of disease. The study showed that a titer of approximately 2.8 ID/mL was reduced below the limit of detection of the bioassay (<0.2 ID/mL), which represents >1.1 $\log_{10}$ reduction in infectivity. Thus, the ligand also removes the form of the infectivity that is present in blood.

The filter material and ligand technology have no impact on selected plasma protein activation, platelet activation, or complement activation. In addition, RBCs treated with the ligand technology showed acceptable red cell stability over a 42-day storage period.

## Approval Mechanisms for Prion Reduction Filters

Such filters will be licensed in Europe as medical devices through the CE marking process, which does not require clinical trials as part of the approval process. Because this is a new technology of unknown safety and uncertain efficacy, the UK Blood Services have agreed on a process for the independent assessment of this technology. This process has five parts.

1.  Requirement for manufacturers to show 3 log prion removal. Current assumptions regarding levels of in-

fectivity suggest that, to have a good chance of preventing transmission, removal of $\geq 3$ log infectious prion must be shown. This requires studies in which human blood components are spiked with animal brain homogenate of a high titer (commonly 263K scrapie in hamsters), with removal shown both by sensitive Western blot and by bioassay that uses a limiting-dilution approach. Removal of endogenous infectivity, in which blood from infected rodents is pooled and passed through the prion-reduction device, also should be shown. However, the low levels of infectivity in animal blood limit the sensitivity of this method to about 1 log reduction.

2.    Independent evaluation of prion removal. An evaluation will be performed in an independent laboratory, consisting of spiking studies using both 263K scrapie brain homogenate (in crude, microsomal, and sonicated forms) and, if the titer permits, 301V BSE spleen. Removal of both types of spike will be evaluated by both Western blot and bioassay. An endogenous infectivity study may also be performed. It should be noted that the Food and Drug Administration (FDA) recently also concluded that data on prion reduction should be obtained from two independent laboratories.

3.    Assessment of red cell quality. Storage to 42 days is assessed in vitro by using standard assays to measure hemolysis—ie, adenosine triphosphate (ATP) and 2,3-diphosphoglycerate.[35] These assays are applied to red cells stored in CPD/SAG-M additive solution, CPD/plasma, and ACD to cover red cells collected by apheresis. It also should be shown that prion reduction can be safely combined with gamma irradiation and red cell washing.

Because of the presence of normal $PrP^c$ in the red cell membrane, there is a potential for subtle interactions between the cells and the filter that might either generate neoantigens or shorten in-vivo efficacy. Therefore, manufacturers are required to show normal red cell recovery (and, ideally, survival) by radiolabeling studies in volunteers and to assess red cell surface changes by assays of normal red cell antigens, band 3, and CD47. Compatibility testing with large panels of normal sera or plasma samples is also required to ensure that prion-treated red cells can be crossmatched by the standard gel-card methods now in use in hospitals. For hospitals that have replaced physical crossmatching with an antibody screen, consideration will have to be given to performing the screen with prion-reduced red cells, at least until more is known about the possible existence of naturally occurring antibodies to prion-treated cells.

4.   Operational assessments and surrogate markers for process monitoring. As with any new filter, small- and large-scale operational assessments are needed to ensure usability, ergonomic safety, and consistency of performance. The challenge here is to identify for each type of filter a surrogate marker that can be measured in processing laboratories to ensure that the process can be shown to be in control. This will require the presence in normal plasma of a marker in a high concentration, which is removed by the filter by approximately 3 log and which can be assayed by a general transfusion laboratory.

5.   Clinical safety studies. As with any new technology, it is necessary to show that there are no new risks associated with the product. LR filters have proved remarkably safe, but there were early reports of "red eye syndrome" with one filter type and of bradykinin-induced hypotension in patients on angiotensin-converting-enzyme-inhibitor treatment who received bedside-filtered RBCs. It is not predictable whether prion reduction might cause an increase in the incidence of the normal type of transfusion reactions or whether new types of side effects may be seen. In addition, there is concern that red cells exposed to prion-reduction filters may be capable of triggering unusual alloantibody responses, either to standard red cells or to neoantigens.

Therefore, clinical studies are planned in three phases, for which the endpoints are transfusion reactions and red cell alloantibodies: 1) dose-escalation studies in which small numbers of patients receive 1, 2, or 3 units of prion-treated red cells; 2) a nonrandomized study of single transfusion episodes in surgical patients; and 3) a randomized study of six transfusions in transfusion-dependent patients. Because of the serious implications of red cell alloantibodies, patients with hemoglobinopathies will not be included in these early studies.

## Reducing Exposure to Multiple Donors and to Donor Plasma in the Preparation of Platelets

Platelets may be procured either from whole-blood donations or from apheresis collections. There are two basic methods for producing platelets from whole blood donations—the "buffy coat" method favored in Europe and the PRP method favored in North America. Specifications for platelet components are given in Table 6-6. In the buffy coat method, whole blood is subjected to a hard spin and separated into plasma, red cells, and a buffy coat that contains most of the platelets, but also some leukocytes and red cells. Buffy coats from four to six donations are then pooled with approximately 300 mL plasma (or a platelet additive solution:plasma mixture) and subjected to a soft spin; the platelets are then removed and passed through a LR filter.

For a therapeutic dose, six to eight packs of PRP platelets are required. Until recently, these could not be pooled before storage, so they had to be either pooled in the blood bank just before being issued to the patient or administered singly at the bedside. However, the FDA has now approved prestorage pooling of PRP platelets.

Apheresis and buffy coat platelets are considered therapeutically equivalent, and the most obvious difference between them is the number of donor exposures each type of product involves. Therefore, optimal strategies for platelet procure-

## Table 6-6. Specifications and Typical Values for Volume and Platelet Content for Leukocyte-Reduced Platelet Components

| Platelet Processing Method | Number of Donors per ATD | Specifications Volume (mL)* UK | Specifications Volume (mL)* EU | Specifications Volume (mL)* AABB | Platelet Content ($\times 10^9$/U) UK | Platelet Content ($\times 10^9$/U) EU | Platelet Content ($\times 10^9$/U) AABB | Typical Values[†] Volume (mL) | Typical Values[†] Platelet Content ($10^9$/U) |
|---|---|---|---|---|---|---|---|---|---|
| Platelet-rich plasma-derived, pooled | 5 to 10 | — | >40 mL per $60 \times 10^9$ platelets | Not speci-fied | — | >60 | >55[‡] | | |
| Apheresis | 1 to 2 | Locally defined | >40 mL per $60 \times 10^9$ platelets | Not speci-fied | >240[‡] | >200 | >300[§] | $191 \pm 50$ | $290 \pm 40$ |

(continued)

## Table 6-6. Specifications and Typical Values for Volume and Platelet Content for Leukocyte-Reduced Platelet Components (continued)

| Platelet Processing Method | Number of Donors per ATD | Specifications | | | | | | | Typical Values[†] | |
| | | Volume (mL)* | | | Platelet Content (× 10⁹/U) | | | Volume (mL) | Platelet Content (10⁹/U) |
| | | UK | EU | AABB | UK | EU | AABB | | |
| Buffy-coat-derived, pooled | 4 to 8 | Locally defined | >40 mL per 60 × 10⁹ platelets | Not speci-fied | >240‡ | >60 per single unit equiva-lent | — | 310 ± 33 | 311 ± 50 |

*The volume is partly dictated by a requirement to keep the pH of platelet components within specified limits during storage.
†Typical values are taken from national quality-monitoring data from the English National Blood Service and are likely to vary between other countries.
‡>75% of components must meet this criterion.
§>90% of components must meet this criterion.
ATD = adult therapeutic dose; UK = United Kingdom; EU = European Union.

ment have been considered, both to reduce donor exposure overall and to minimize exposure to plasma. These strategies consist of:

• Preparing small platelet units for infants by splitting apheresis packs.

• Using apheresis packs for older children who need an adult dose.

• Shifting the ratio of whole blood to apheresis platelets from 40:60 to 50:50 in the first instance and developing options for further increases. It could be asked whether such a strategy may increase the risk by potential infection of many recipients from a single apheresis donor who is providing platelets every 3 to 4 weeks. However, at an assumed prevalence of asymptomatic carriage of 1 in 10,000, it has been calculated that the overall benefit of a potential fourfold reduction in donor exposure will outweigh this slight risk.

• Changing the processing of buffy coats from a method in which all four donors each contribute an equal volume of suspending plasma to one in which >90% of the plasma comes from one of the four buffy coat donors. The opportunity has been taken to use "male plasma" when possible for platelet suspension to minimize the risk of transfusion-related acute lung injury (TRALI). Currently, this is achieved approximately 80% of the time.

• Consideration of the use of platelet additive solutions. For either buffy-coat-derived or apheresis platelets, 65% to 70% of the plasma in the platelet concentrate can be replaced with a platelet additive solution, which is designed to maintain platelet function during storage. Although platelet additive solutions differ in their composition, key elements are acetate or glucose as a substrate for platelet metabolism, phosphate to buffer lactate production, citrate to prevent coagulation and lactate production, and potassium and magnesium to improve platelet function during storage.[36] Three such solutions are CE-marked in Europe, and some European blood centers routinely produce and store platelets in them. In some countries, this practice has accompanied the extension of shelf life to 7 days, provided the platelets are screened for bacterial contamination.

The effect on vCJD risk of removing 65% to 70% of the plasma is uncertain. Because the level of infectivity in plasma is assumed to be high, and because platelets themselves may carry infectious prions, this step alone may be insufficient to have a predictable effect on preventing transmission from platelets. However, it may still be a worthwhile initiative, because it is relatively low in cost and has the possibility that the reduction in prion load achieved may prolong the incubation period beyond the survival period of most platelet recipients.

Platelets in 100% platelet additive solution are provided for patients with severe anaphylactic reactions to platelets caused by contaminating plasma proteins. However, these "washed" platelets have a shelf life of only 24 hours because of the rapid deterioration of platelet quality in the complete absence of plasma, so this is not an option for routine platelet provision.

## Strategies for Frozen Plasma Components

In most countries, plasma from whole-blood donations or apheresis is used to prepare plasma components for direct clinical transfusion (ie, FFP, cryoprecipitate, and cryosupernatant) or fractionated to produce pure plasma proteins. However, because of vCJD, plasma has not been fractionated in the UK since 1999 (see Chapter 7). The freezing of plasma for FFP production is usually performed within 8 hours of donation in order to preserve the activity of coagulation Factors V and VIII, which are relatively labile. However, FFP can be produced from whole blood that has been stored at 4 C or 22 C for 24 hours. To minimize the risk of virus transmission, FFP is not manufactured from the blood of first-time donors or of those who have lapsed for more than 24 months. Although the number of leukocytes in FFP is usually $<10^6$/unit, a decision was made that all FFP should undergo a specific LR step. In practice, most FFP can be manufactured via whole-blood filtration with supplementation by LR of plasma units if required to maintain the supply.

### Use of Imported, Pathogen-Inactivated FFP for Children

More than 300,000 units of FFP are produced in the UK annually, requiring an estimated 100 tonnes of plasma. Consideration has been given to obtaining all of this plasma from countries with no BSE or vCJD. At the time of writing, imported FFP obtained from volunteer donors in the US has been made available to selected UK patients in three stages: from 1999, to replace congenital single coagulation factor deficiencies only when purified factor concentrates are not available (Factors V and XI; UK Haemophilia Directors Organisation recommendation); from 2004, for children born on or after January 1, 1996, a date after which the UK food supply has been deemed safe from BSE by the Department of the Environment, Food and Rural Affairs; and from 2005, for all children up to age 16 years. As with platelet suspension, the opportunity was taken to request male donor plasma only to reduce the risk of TRALI.

The relative residual viral risks for UK and US plasma also had to be considered. Partly because of the UK policy of using only repeat donors for FFP production, the residual risk per unit of human immunodeficiency virus (HIV), hepatitis C virus (HCV), and hepatitis B virus (HBV) has been calculated to be 1 in 5, 35, and 0.5 million, respectively.[37] Because of the higher background viral risk and the inclusion of first-time donors, the residual risks of these three viruses was calculated as 4 to 9 times as high in the imported plasma. Therefore, a decision was made to treat individual plasma units on arrival in the UK with the methylene blue (MB)/light photodynamic method of virus inactivation. This method, which works by generating short-lived but highly reactive oxygen species, would not be predicted to have any direct effect on infectious prions, but it is highly effective against HIV, HBV, and HCV. Efficacy of the MB system against West Nile virus has also been shown.[38] The disadvantage is that there is approximately 20% loss of Factor VIII and fibrinogen[39] (Table 6-7).

## Cryoprecipitated AHF

Cryoprecipitate is produced by slowly thawing FFP at 4 C. This causes precipitation of the so-called cryoproteins (Factor VIII, fibrinogen, von Willebrand factor (vWF), fibronectin, and Factor XIII). By centrifuging and removing the supernatant plasma, the cryoprecipitate left is a rich source of these cryoproteins in a small volume of plasma. Because of the widespread availability of purified or recombinant concentrates of Factor VIII and vWF, cryoprecipitate is rarely used to replace these factors and is mainly used in the treatment of hypo- or dysfibrinogenemia. For an adult, a total dose of 10 bags (1 to 2 g) is indicated. This means exposure to plasma from a considerable number of UK donors; therefore, it has been investigated whether cryoprecipitate could be manufactured from non-UK MB-treated plasma. Although recoverable fibrinogen was reduced by 40% in cryoprecipitate prepared from MB-treated FFP, absolute recovery doubled from 24% to 42% when the units underwent an extra freeze-thaw cycle.[40] This product is now in routine use in some parts of the UK.

## Plasma Exchange for TTP

Plasma exchange for thrombotic thrombocytopenic purpura (TTP) can be performed with either whole FFP or the supernatant plasma removed from cryoprecipitate (cryoprecipitate-depleted plasma). There are theoretical advantages of using cryoprecipitate-depleted plasma, because it contains lower levels of high-molecular-weight multimers of vWF, but this benefit has not been proven clinically.[41] A plasma exchange schedule of 3 L/day for 14 days exposes a TTP patient to >100 donors. Consideration is being given, therefore, to the use of imported FFP for this patient group also. However, there is very little experience with the use of MB-treated FFP for TTP. The levels of the vWF-cleaving protease are normal, as are

**Table 6-7. Specifications and Typical Values for Residual Cellular and Coagulation Factor Content of Frozen Plasma Components**

| Specification | Residual Cellular Content ($\times 10^9$/L)* | | | Coagulation Factor Content | | |
| | UK† | EU | AABB | UK† | EU | AABB |
|---|---|---|---|---|---|---|
| FFP | Platelets <30 | Platelets <50<br>Red cells <6 | None | Factor VIII<br>>0.70 IU/mL | Factor VIII<br>>0.70 IU/mL | None |
| Methylene blue-treated and removed FFP | Platelets <30 | Component not defined | | Factor VIII<br>>0.50 IU/mL | Component not defined | |
| Solvent/detergent-treated FFP | Negligible as removed by SD process | | | Defined by manufacturer as 0.5 IU/mL for all factors | | |
| Cryoprecipitate | None | Platelets <50<br>Red cells <6 | None | Fibrinogen<br>>140 mg/<br>unit<br>Factor VIII<br>>70 IU/unit | Fibrinogen<br>>140 mg/<br>unit<br>Factor VIII<br>>70 IU/unit | Fibrinogen<br>>150 mg/<br>unit<br>Factor VIII<br>>80 IU/unit |

(continued)

## Table 6-7. Specifications and Typical Values for Residual Cellular and Coagulation Factor Content of Frozen Plasma Components (continued)

| Residual Cellular Content | Typical Values[‡] | |
| | Coagulation Factor Content | Total Volume (mL) |
| --- | --- | --- |
| Platelets <3 × 10⁹/L<br>Red cells 0.63 ± 0.50 × 10⁹/L | Factor VIII 1.16 ± 0.35 IU/mL | 273 ± 17 |
| Platelets <3 × 10⁹/L<br>Red cells <0.05 × 10⁹/L | Factor VIII 0.96 ± 0.30 IU/mL | 232 ± 18 |
| | Factor VIII 168 ± 82 IU/unit | 34 ± 4 |
| | Fibrinogen 440 ± 181 mg/unit | |

*Specifications for residual white cells are as per Table 6-2.
[†]>75% of components must meet these criteria.
[‡]Typical values are taken from national quality-monitoring data from the English National Blood Service and are likely to vary between countries.
UK = United Kingdom; EU = European Union.

those of the vWF multimers,[42] but clinical data are limited.[43,44] Therefore, it has been recommended that TTP patients in the UK be treated with US plasma that has been virus inactivated by the pooled solvent/detergent (SD)-treated method. Although the method involves pooling and therefore the amplification of the risk of an SD-resistant infectious agent, it has been calculated that, with the current pool size of 500 to 1000 units and the absence of vCJD in the US, the overall benefit:risk ratio of this approach is high. SDFFP has a long track record of safety, and there have been no convincing cases of TRALI with this product.

### Appropriate Prescription of FFP

Most FFP is used to treat acquired multiple coagulation factor deficiencies, usually in a clinical setting of massive transfusion, liver disease, or disseminated intravascular coagulation (BCSH guidelines). However, the level of evidence for many statements in the guidelines is low, and a recent systematic review failed to find a single controlled trial in any clinical setting in which FFP was proven to show benefit.[45]

## Acknowledgments

The authors are grateful to Neil Beckman for quality-monitoring data and to Karen Wilkins from Pall and Peter Edwardson from PRDT for data on those companies' filters.

## References

1. DNV Consulting 2003. Risk assessment of exposure to vCJD infectivity in blood and blood products. [Available at http://www.dnv.com/binaries/vCJD_Update_Report_tcm4-74414.pdf (accessed March 23, 2006).]
2. Brown P, Cervenakova L, McShane LM, et al. Further studies of blood infectivity in an experimental model of transmissible spongiform encephalopathy, with an explanation of why blood components do not transmit Creutzfeldt-Jakob disease in humans. Transfusion 1999; 39:1169-78.

3. Rohwer R. New data on blood-borne TSE infectivity. Presented at Cambridge Healthtech Institute Meeting on Transmissible Spongiform Encephalopathies, February 4-7, 2002, Washington, DC.

4. Houston F, Foster JD, Chong A, et al. Transmission of BSE by blood transfusion in sheep. Lancet 2000;356:999-1000.

5. Hunter N, Foster J, Chong A, et al. Transmission of prion diseases by blood transfusion. J Gen Virol 2002;83:2897-905.

6. Llewelyn CA, Hewitt PE, Knight RS, et al. Possible transmission of variant Creutzfeldt-Jakob disease by blood transfusion. Lancet 2004; 363:417-21.

7. Peden AH, Head MW, Ritchie DL, et al. Preclinical vCJD after blood transfusion in a PRNP codon 129 heterozygous patient. Lancet 2004; 364:527-9.

8. UK Blood Services and the National CJD Surveillance Unit. Transfusion medicine epidemiology review. Edinburgh, UK: National Creutzfeldt-Jakob Surveillance Unit, 2006. [Available at http:// www.cjd.ed. ac.uk/TMER/results.htm (accessed May 17, 2006).]

9. Holada K, Vostal JG, Theisen PW, et al. Scrapie infectivity in hamster blood is not associated with platelets. J Virol 2002;76:4649-50.

10. Gregori L, McCombie N, Palmer D, et al. Effectiveness of leucoreduction for removal of infectivity of transmissible spongiform encephalopathies from blood. Lancet 2004;364:529-31.

11. Brown P, Rohwer RG, Dunstan BC, et al. The distribution of infectivity in blood components and plasma derivatives in experimental models of transmissible spongiform encephalopathy. Transfusion 1998;38: 810-16.

12. Cervenakova L, Yakovleva O, McKenzie C, et al. Similar levels of infectivity in the blood of mice infected with human-derived vCJD and GSS strains of transmissible spongiform encephalopathy. Transfusion 2003;43:1687-94.

13. Prowse CV, Hornsey VS, Drummond O, et al. Preliminary assessment of whole-blood, red-cell and platelet-leucodepleting filters for possible induction of prion release by leucocyte fragmentation during room temperature processing. Br J Haematol 1999;106:240-7.

14. Williamson LM, Rider JR, Swann ID, et al. Evaluation of plasma and red cells obtained after leucocyte depletion of whole blood. Transfus Med 1999;9:51-61.

15. Dumont L, Dzik WH, Rebulla P, et al. Practical guidelines for process control and validation of leukoreduced components: Report of BEST working party of ISBT. Transfusion 1996;36:11-20.

16. Beckman N, Cardigan R, Wallington T, Williamson LM. Value of central analysis of leucocyte depletion quality control data within the National Blood Service, England. Vox Sang 2002;83:110-18.

17. Beard MJ, Cardigan R, Seghatchian J, et al. Variables determining blockage of leukocyte depleting filters by hemoglobin sickle cell donations. Transfusion 2004;44:422-30.

18. Klein MA, Frigg R, Flechsig E, et al. A crucial role for B cells in neuroinvasive scrapie. Nature 1997;390:687-90.
19. Klein MA, Frigg R, Raeber AJ, et al. PrP expression in B lymphocytes is not required for prion neuroinvasion. Nat Med 1998;4:1429-33.
20. Rider JR, Want EJ, Winter MA, et al. Differential leucocyte subpopulation analysis of leucodepleted red cell products. Transfus Med 2000;10:49-58.
21. Sowemimo-Coker SO, Kim A, Tribble E, et al. White cell subsets in apheresis and filtered platelet concentrates. Transfusion 1998;38: 650-7.
22. Pennington J, Garner SF, Sutherland J, Williamson LM. Residual subset population analysis in WBC-reduced blood components using real-time PCR quantitation of specific mRNA. Transfusion 2001;41: 1591-600.
23. Krailadsiri P, Seghatchian J, MacGregor I, et al. The effects of leucodepletion on the generation and removal of microvesicles and prion-protein in blood components. Transfusion 2006;46:407-17.
24. Luban NLC, Strauss RG, Hume HA. Commentary on the safety of red cells preserved in extended-storage media for neonatal transfusions. Transfusion 1991;31:229-35.
25. British Committee for Standards in Haematology. Transfusion guidelines for neonates and older children. Br J Haematol 2004;124:433-53.
26. Mou SS, Giroir BP, Molitor-Kirsch EA, et al. Fresh whole blood versus reconstituted blood for pump priming in heart surgery in infants. N Engl J Med 2004;351:1635-44.
27. British Committee for Standards in Haematology guidelines. Oxford, UK: Blackwell Publishing, 2006. [Available at www.bcshguidelines. com (accessed February 24, 2006).]
28. Lee DC, Stenland CJ, Miller JLC, et al. A direct relationship between the portioning of the pathogenic prion protein and transmissible spongiform encephalopathy infectivity during the purification of plasma proteins. Transfusion 2001;41:449-55.
29. Liao YC, Lebo RV, Clawson GA, Smuckler EA. Human prion protein cDNA: Molecular cloning, chromosomal mapping, and biological implications. Science 1986;233:364-7.
30. Bendheim PE, Bockman JM, McKinley MP, et al. Scrapie and Creutzfeldt-Jakob disease prion proteins share physical properties and antigenic determinants. Proc Natl Acad Sci U S A 1985;82:997-1001.
31. Reed LJ, Muench H. A simple method for estimating fifty percent endpoint. Am J Hyg 1938;27:493-7.
32. Sowemimo-Coker S, Kascsak R, Kim A, et al. Removal of exogenous (spiked) and endogenous prion infectivity from red cells with a new prototype of leukoreduction filter. Transfusion 2005;45:1839-44.
33. Saunders C, Herbert P, Rowe G, et al. In-vitro evaluation of PALL Leukotrap Affinity Prion Reduction Filter as a secondary device following primary leucoreduction. Vox Sang 2005;89:220-8.

34. Nelson E, Taylor H, Whitley P, Lieu T. Evaluation of in vivo red blood cell recovery after processing with a new filter designed to remove prions. Vox Sang 2005;89(Suppl 2):220.

35. Guidelines for UK Transfusion Services. 6th ed. London, UK: The Stationery Office, 2002.

36. Gulliksson H, AuBuchon JP, Cardigan R, et al. Storage of platelets in additive solutions: A multicentre study of the in vitro effects of potassium and magnesium. Vox Sang 2003;85:199-205.

37. Soldan K, Davison K, Dow B. Estimates of the frequency of HBV, HCV, and HIV infectious donations entering the blood supply in the United Kingdom, 1996 to 2003. Euro Surveill 2005;10:17-19.

38. Mohr H, Knuver-Hopf J, Gravemann U, et al. West Nile virus in plasma is highly sensitive to methylene blue-light treatment. Transfusion 2004;44:886-90.

39. Garwood M, Cardigan R, Drummond O, et al. The effect of methylene blue photoinactivation and methylene blue removal on the quality of fresh frozen plasma. Transfusion 2003;43:1238-47.

40. Hornsey VS, Young DA, Docherty A, et al. Cryoprecipitate prepared from plasma treated with methylene blue plus light: Increasing the fibrinogen concentration. Transfus Med 2004;14:369-74.

41. Rock G, Anderson D, Clark W, et al. Does cryosupernatant plasma improve outcome in thrombotic thrombocytopenic purpura? No answer yet. Br J Haematol 2005;129:79-86.

42. Cardigan R, Allford S, Williamson LM. Levels of von Willebrand factor-cleaving protease are normal in methylene-blue treated fresh-frozen plasma. Br J Haematol 2002;117:253-4.

43. de la Rubia J, Arriaga F, Linares D, et al. Role of methylene blue-treated or fresh-frozen plasma in the response to plasma exchange in patients with thrombotic thrombocytopenic purpura. Br J Haematol 2001;114:721-3.

44. Alvarez-Larran A, Del Rio J, Ramirez C, et al. Methylene blue-photo-inactivated plasma vs. fresh-frozen plasma as replacement fluid for plasma exchange in thrombotic thrombocytopenic purpura. Vox Sang 2004;86:246-51.

45. Stanworth SJ, Brunskill SJ, Hyde CJ, et al. Is fresh frozen plasma clinically effective? A systematic review of randomized controlled trials. Br J Haematol 2004;126:139-52.

In: Turner ML, ed.
*Creutzfeldt-Jakob Disease: Managing the Risk of
Transmission by Blood, Plasma, and Tissues*
Bethesda, MD: AABB Press, 2006

# 7

# Plasma Products

PETER R. FOSTER, BSc, MSc, PhD,
CS, CSci, CEng, FIChemE

MORE THAN 500 metric tons of protein are administered annually to patients worldwide in the form of biopharmaceutical products derived from human plasma. These products include immunoglobulins for the treatment of immune disorders, albumin for volume and protein replacement, coagulation factor concentrates for the treatment of disorders of hemostasis, and other specific proteins, such as alpha-1-antitrypsin, for the treatment of inherited or acquired deficiencies. The possible transmission of human blood-borne pathogens is a risk that is intrinsic to treatment with any product derived from human blood. The possibility that human prion diseases might be transmissible by blood was first suggested by Preece,[1] after the transmission of sporadic Creutzfeldt-Jakob disease (sCJD) to patients treated with growth hormone derived from human pituitaries. The subsequent emergence of variant CJD (vCJD) and its association with the epidemic of bovine spongiform enceph-

*Peter R. Foster, BSc, MSc, PhD, CS, CSci, CEng, FIChemE, Development Manager, SNBTS Protein Fractionation Centre, Edinburgh, United Kingdom*

alopathy (BSE) in the United Kingdom (UK)[2] has led to concern that blood components[3] and plasma products[4] could provide routes for continued secondary transmission of this disease in the human population.

There are two major concerns with plasma products. The first is the large volumes of pooled plasma from which products are manufactured, which raise the potential for one infected donation to contaminate all products derived from a pool and infect large numbers of patients. The second is the chronic treatment of patients with hemophilia or immunologic disorders, which raises the possibility that infection may result in recipients after repeated exposure to subinfectious doses of a prion agent.[5]

Precautionary measures that have been introduced to address the risk of vCJD transmission by plasma products include a decision that plasma collected in the UK should not be used to manufacture fractionated plasma products[6] and, in many countries, the deferral from donation of individuals who were resident in the UK in the period from 1980 to 1996.[7] Although vCJD has not been diagnosed in recipients of plasma products, infection has been diagnosed in two individuals who had received nonleukocyte-reduced red cells from donors who had developed clinical vCJD themselves some years after donating.[8,9] Although other routes of infection cannot be excluded, these cases are consistent with transfusion studies in sheep,[10] and they provide compelling evidence that vCJD is transmissible to humans via blood transfusion.

By November 2005, a total of 188,027 cases of BSE had been diagnosed in 26 countries, with the vast majority (97%) from the UK. Definite or probable vCJD has been diagnosed in a total of 185 persons to date, of whom 158 are from the UK and 15 from France. However, the full extent and distribution of prion diseases in animals that enter the human food chain are not known, nor is the prevalence of vCJD in blood donor populations known, either in the UK or elsewhere.

The safety of plasma products is dependent on the exclusion of human pathogens from the plasma pool or their elimination during manufacture.[11] Generally, prion agents have been found to have a low aqueous solubility, to form aggregates readily, and to adhere strongly to surfaces, properties that may be exploited to remove prion infectivity during the manufacture of plasma products.[12] In the absence of suitable procedures for screening blood donors and given the high resistance of prion agents to inactivation, attention has been focused on ascertaining the extent to which established separation technologies used in plasma fractionation may be able to eliminate prion infectivity.

## Experimental Systems

A number of experimental studies have been undertaken to ascertain the extent to which prion agents may be removed by processes used in the preparation of plasma products. Most investigations have been carried out by adding an aliquot of high-titer prion infectivity to a small volume of feedstock and then processing this mixture by using procedures that have been downscaled to simulate full-scale manufacturing. The subsequent partitioning or distribution of the prion agent has been established in vitro immunochemically by Western blotting[13,14] or by conformation-dependent immunoassay (CDI)[15] or in vivo by using rodent bioassays designed to measure infectious dose-50 ($ID_{50}$).[16,17]

The high-titer materials used to "spike" starting solutions have been derived from infected brain in the form of either a brain homogenate (BH),[13] a microsomal fraction (MF)[18] derived from BH, caveola-like domains (CLD),[19] or semipurified fibrils of abnormal prion protein ($PrP^{Sc}$).[19] These exogenous preparations have been obtained from a number of different strains of prion agent, including hamster-passaged scrapie (strains 263K and Sc237), murine-passaged scrapie (strain ME7), and murine-passaged BSE (strain 301V).

Plasma fractionation studies have also been performed with endogenous infectivity by using blood from infected rodents as starting material.[16,17] The low level of infectivity available required distribution of the prion agent to be determined by bioassay using the method of limiting-dilution titration.[17] Prion agents used in such studies have included murine-passaged Gerstmann-Sträussler-Scheinker (GSS) syndrome (Fukuoka-1 strain), hamster-passaged scrapie (strain 263K), and murine-passaged BSE (strain 301V) (Rohwer RG, unpublished observations; Reichl HE, unpublished observations).

The limited availability of suitable prion agents and the biohazards that face those working with infected materials mean that investigational studies are undertaken in containment laboratories at a scale many orders of magnitude smaller than full-scale industrial manufacture. For experimental results to be meaningful, it is therefore necessary to ensure that procedures are correctly scaled down to simulate the performance of full-scale manufacturing processes as accurately as possible. The extent to which small-scale experiments have been able to represent routine industrial processing accurately is a critical consideration in assessing the relevance of the results obtained.

Most prion removal studies have examined the partitioning behavior of the prion agent over individual process operations studied in isolation. Fractionation procedures investigated in this manner include protein precipitation operations, depth filtration processes, adsorption chromatography with different matrices, and nanofiltration using different types and grades of membrane filter. Some investigators have studied successive process operations being run in combination; these include multiple precipitation steps,[16,17,20] protein precipitation followed by either one or two depth filtration processes,[21] two depth filtration processes in sequence,[21] protein precipitation plus added filter aid with phase separation by centrifugation,[22,23] and two combined procedures involving the addition of filter aid with phase separation by centrifugation.[22,23]

The extent to which a prion agent is removed by a separation process is usually described by the degree of removal expressed as a reduction factor (RF). RF values are derived for each resultant fraction by subtracting the total quantity ($\log_{10}$ transformed) of prion agent measured in each fraction from the total quantity of prion agent measured in the starting material. When no prion agent is detected in a fraction after processing, a "≥" sign precedes the $\log_{10}$ RF value. RF values of <1 $\log_{10}$ are viewed as not significant because of the degree of error associated with assays used for the measurement of prion agents.[24]

# Plasma Fractionation

The manufacture of plasma products involves the extraction of a number of proteins from human plasma and then their purification and preparation into suitable pharmaceutical dose forms. A range of bioseparation processes is used for this purpose. A typical overall fractionation scheme by which these separation processes are arranged is shown in Fig 7-1; it includes a number of process operations that have been shown to have a potential for prion removal.

## Protein Precipitation

The solubility of a protein is related to its physicochemical characteristics, and differences in solubility behavior can be used to separate proteins from one another by selective precipitation and then phase separation.[25] Most plasma fractionators prepare human albumin and human immunoglubulin by cold-ethanol (Cohn) fractionation,[26] a sequence of precipitation processes in which changes in pH, ethanol concentration, ionic strength, and temperature are exploited to selectively partition specific proteins into different precipitate fractions, which are then separated from proteins in solution by centrifugation or by filtration.[26-28]

Significant RF values have been reported for a number of cold-ethanol precipitation steps studied individually in spiking experiments (Table 7-1). Precipitation of prion agents into Fraction (I)+II+III and Fraction IV in the preparation of human albumin and into Fraction (I)+III in the preparation of human

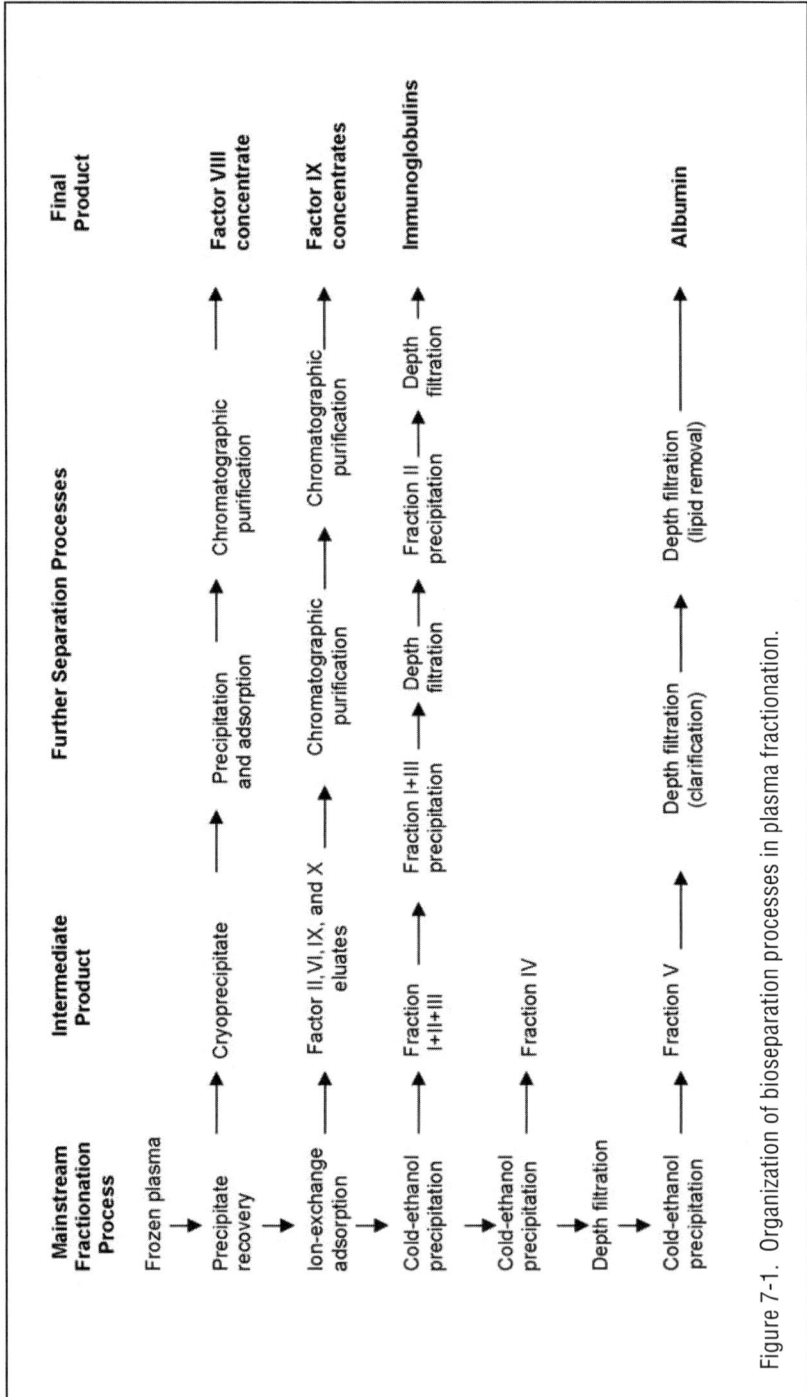

Figure 7-1.  Organization of bioseparation processes in plasma fractionation.

## Table 7-1. Removal of Prion Agents by Cold-Ethanol (Cohn) Precipitation

| Precipitation Step | Resultant Product | Prion Agent | Prion Spike | Prion Assay | Prion Reduction Factor (Log$_{10}$) | Reference |
|---|---|---|---|---|---|---|
| Fraction (I) + II + III | Albumin | 263K | MF | Western blot | 1.3 | Foster et al[18] |
| | Albumin | 263K | BH | Western blot | ≥4.7 | Lee et al[13] |
| | Albumin | 263K | BH | Bioassay | 6.0 | Lee et al[29] |
| | Albumin | Sc237 | BH/MF/CLD/PrP$^{Sc}$ | CDI | 3.6/3.1/3.1/4.0 | Vey et al[19] |
| | Albumin | 263K | BH | Bioassay | 2.2* | Gregori et al[23] |
| | Albumin | 263K | MF | Western blot | ≥2.8* | Flan et al[30] |
| Fraction (I)+III | IgG | 263K | MF | Western blot | ≥3.7 | Foster et al[18] |
| | IgG | 263K | BH | Western blot | ≥4.3 | Lee et al[13] |
| | IgG | 263K | BH | Bioassay | 5.3 | Lee et al[29] |
| | IgG | 301V | MF | Bioassay | 2.1 | Reichl et al[21] |

(continued)

## Table 7-1. Removal of Prion Agents by Cold-Ethanol (Cohn) Precipitation (continued)

| Precipitation Step | Resultant Product | Prion Agent | Prion Spike | Prion Assay | Prion Reduction Factor ($Log_{10}$) | Reference |
|---|---|---|---|---|---|---|
| | IgG | 263K | BH | Bioassay | 3.5* | Gregori et al[23] |
| | IgG | 263K | MF | Western blot | ≥3.5* | Flan et al[30] |
| Fraction IV | Albumin | 263K | BH | Western blot | ≥3.0 | Foster et al[18] |
| (IV$_1$/IV$_4$) | Albumin | 263K | BH | Western blot | ≥4.2/≥4.1 | Lee et al[13] |
| | Albumin | 263K | BH | Bioassay | 3.7/4.6 | Lee et al[29] |
| | Albumin | Sc237 | BH/MF/CLD/PrP$^{Sc}$ | CDI | 3.2/3.4/3.2/2.2 | Vey et al[19] |
| | Albumin | 263K | BH | Bioassay | 3.0* | Gregori et al[23] |
| | Albumin | 263K | MF | Western blot | ≥4.3* | Flan et al[30] |

*Includes the addition of filter-aid to precipitate suspension.
MF = microsomal fraction; BH = brain homogenate; CLD = caveola-like domains; PrP$^{Sc}$ = purified abnormal prion protein; CDI = conformation-dependent immunoassay; IgG = immunoglobulin G.

immunoglobulin is of particular interest, because these fractions are removed from the particular product stream. Although high RF values usually were obtained for these steps (Table 7-1), it should be noted that, when a more sensitive assay was used, such as a bioassay or the CDI, the prion agent was detectable in the product supernatant, which indicated that separation was incomplete. Whether this was due to the fact that a fraction of the prion agent remained soluble under the precipitation conditions employed or to the fact that the particulate residues remained in the supernatant because of limitations of phase separation remains to be ascertained.

A wide range of other agents and techniques is available for protein precipitation.[25] Some of them that have been shown to be capable of significant precipitation of prion agents include polyethylene glycol (PEG) precipitation in the preparation of Factor VIII concentrate and alpha-1-antitrypsin[13,29,31] and caprylic acid precipitation in the preparation of intravenous immunoglobulin.[32] Although cryoprecipitation is used in the manufacture of Factor VIII concentrate, most investigators have found the RF for prion removal at this stage to be on the order of $1 \log_{10}$ or less and therefore of marginal significance.[33]

When cold-ethanol precipitation steps have been studied in combination, a progressive reduction of prion agent by precipitation into successive precipitate fractions has been generally observed, both in exogenous experiments using brain-derived material for spiking and in endogenous experiments in which infected rodent plasma was processed (Table 7-2). However, substantial differences in the starting titers of prion agent and differences in the way results have been expressed make precise comparisons between these endogenous and exogenous experiments difficult.

Further points to note are that the downscaling of precipitation[25] and of centrifugation[34] is not straightforward and that individual industrial-scale protein precipitation operations are not highly selective procedures for purifying proteins. Particles of protein precipitate are composed of loose amorphous flocs in which supernatant is retained, with the result that

**Table 7-2. Partitioning of Prion Agents from Plasma into Successive Precipitate Fractions**

| | Brown et al[16,17] | Rohwer* | Reichl† | Brown et al[16] | Cai et al[20] | Cai et al[20] |
|---|---|---|---|---|---|---|
| Type of study | Endogenous | Endogenous | Endogenous | Exogenous | Exogenous | Exogenous |
| Prion agent | Fukuoka-1 | 263K | 301V | 263K | 263K | 263K |
| Prion spike | None | None | None | BH | BH | BH |
| Prion assay | Bioassay | Bioassay | Bioassay | Bioassay | Bioassay | Western blot |
| Prion determined in fraction (units) | (IU/mL plasma) | (IU/mL plasma) | (IU/mL plasma) | ($\log_{10}$ reduction)‡ | ($\log_{10}$ reduction)‡ | ($\log_{10}$ PrP$^{Sc}$)§ |
| Plasma | 10.3-34.4 | 3.9 | 5 | — | — | 4.4 |
| Cryoprecipitate | 1.2-2.6 | 0.6 | 2.5 | 2.1 | — | — |
| Fraction I | — | — | — | — | 0.8 | 4.5 |

| | | | | | | |
|---|---|---|---|---|---|---|
| Fraction (I)+ II+III | 0.8 | 0.3 | 2.5 | 2.1 | 5.0 | 4.1 |
| Fraction (I)+III | 6.2 | — | — | — | 5.3 | 4.2 |
| Fraction IV | <0.11-0.5 | ND | ND | 4.2 | — | ND |
| Fraction II | 0.3 | ND | — | — | — | — |
| Fraction V | <0.15-0.3 | ND | ND | 5.4 | — | — |

*Rohwer RG, unpublished observations.
†Reichl HE, unpublished observations.
‡All values expressed as $\log_{10}$ reduction from plasma.
§Arbitrary units.
BH = brain homogenate; PrP$^{Sc}$ = purified abnormal prion protein; ND = not detected; IU = international unit.

about half of a precipitate mass can be made up of supernatant that is carried over with the recovered paste. Industrial phase-separation technology may not be capable of removing fine precipitate particles, and they may be retained in the supernatant phase. The solids-holding capacity of most industrial centrifuges is relatively small, which often necessitates the use of multiple centrifuges per product batch, and incomplete removal of solids can occur when a centrifuge approaches the limit of its capacity. It is for these reasons that critical supernatants are normally clarified by depth filtration after centrifugation to ensure that any residues of precipitate are removed from the product stream.[12,18]

## Depth Filtration

Depth filtration processes are most commonly used to clarify solutions of human immunogloblin and human albumin after the precipitation of Fraction III and Fraction IV, respectively, and after resuspension of the intermediate-product precipitates Fraction II (immunoglobulin G, or IgG) and Fraction V (albumin). One advantage of depth filtration is that depth filter media are inexpensive and are discarded after each use, which avoids the possibility that adsorbed prion infectivity will contaminate future product batches. Many types and grades of depth filter are available, and a number of them have been shown to exhibit significant prion removal (Table 7-3). In some studies, prion infectivity was not detected in the filtrate, even when the most sensitive methods of detection were used, which suggests that depth-filtration technology may remove prion agents more effectively than other bioseparation technologies. In contrast, Vey et al[19] found no significant removal of prions from Supernatant I by depth filtration, even though the particular depth filter employed was effective in removing prions from solutions of albumin and immunoglobulin (Table 7-3). Supernatant I contains a broad mixture of plasma proteins; it is probable, therefore, that a class of protein was present that adsorbed preferentially to the filter matrix and

## Table 7-3. Removal of Prion Agents by Depth Filtration

| Solution Filtered | Resultant Product | Prion Agent | Prion Spike | Prion Assay | Depth Filter Type | Prion Reduction Factor ($Log_{10}$) | Reference |
|---|---|---|---|---|---|---|---|
| Supernatant I | IgG, albumin | Sc237 | BH/MF/CLD/ PrP$^{Sc}$ | CDI | Seitz Supra P80 | 0.1/–0.1/0/0* | Vey et al[19] |
| Supernatant III | IgG | 301V | MF | Bioassay | Seitz KS80P | ≥3.1 | Reichl et al[21] |
| | IgG | 301V | MF | Bioassay | Millipore AP20 | 2.4 | Reichl et al[21] |
| | IgG† | 263K | BH | Western blot | Cuno Zetaplus | ≥3.3 | Van Holten et al[35] |
| Fraction II solution | IgG | 263K | MF | Western blot | Seitz K200 | ≥2.8 | Foster et al[18] |

(continued)

**Table 7-3. Removal of Prion Agents by Depth Filtration (continued)**

| Solution Filtered | Resultant Product | Prion Agent | Prion Spike | Prion Assay | Depth Filter Type | Prion Reduction Factor ($Log_{10}$) | Reference |
|---|---|---|---|---|---|---|---|
|  | IgG[‡] | 263K | BH | Bioassay | Cuno | ≥6.9 | Trejo et al[32] |
|  | IgG | 263K | MF | Bioassay | Cuno | 2.5 | Flan et al[30] |
| Supernatant IV | Albumin | Sc237 | BH/MF/CLD/PrP$^{Sc}$ | CDI | Seitz Supra P80 | ≥0.9/≥1.1/ ≥0.9/≥2.4* | Vey et al[19] |
| Fraction V solution | Albumin | 263K | MF | Western blot | Seitz KS80P | ≥4.9 | Foster et al[18] |
|  | Albumin | 263K | MF | Western blot | Cuno delipid-1 | 2.3 | Foster et al[18] |
|  | Albumin | 263K | MF | Western blot | Seitz AKS5 | ≥2.9 | Flan et al[30] |

*Prion spike added prior to cold-ethanol precipitation step, with resultant supernatant clarified by depth filtration.
[†]Fractionation by precipitation with methanol.
[‡]Derived via caprylate precipitation of Cohn Fraction II+III.
IgG = immunoglobulin G; BH = brain homogenate; MF = microsomal fraction; CLD = caveola-like domains; PrP$^{Sc}$ = purified abnormal prion protein; CDI = conformation-dependent immunoassay.

prevented adsorption of the prion agent. If this is the case, prion removal capability will have to be determined experimentally for both the application and the type of filter used; it is also possible that depth filtration may be most effective for prion removal when applied to purified or semipurified proteins.

## Adsorption Chromatography

The removal of prion infectivity during chromatographic purification has been examined in a number of bioprocess applications, with reported RF values ranging from 2 to 5 $\log_{10}$.[12] In a range of studies of plasma products, RF values were found to be approximately 3 $\log_{10}$ with the use of either anion exchange or cation exchange (Table 7-4).[18,36] Despite these relatively high RF values, it is important to note that, in most of these studies, some prion agent was detected in product eluates. Whether this was because the chromatography bed had been overloaded by the use of a high-titer prion spike or because a subfraction of prion material copurified with the plasma product in question is not known.

Significant removal of prion infectivity has also been reported for the preparation of Factor VIII concentrate by immunoaffinity chromatography,[37] with the total removal of prion infectivity ($ID_{50}$) being 4.6 $\log_{10}$ $ID_{50}$ by immunoaffinity chromatography and 3.5 $\log_{10}$ by quaternary-aminoethyl-ion exchange chromatography. A lower degree of prion removal was observed when a heparin-affinity matrix was used in the purification of Factor IX concentrate,[18] when elution of Factor IX from the affinity matrix was at relatively high ionic strength and pH (Table 7-4).

In all of these studies, it has not been possible to account for more than a very small proportion of the prion agent that was added to the starting material; this suggests that most infectivity remained bound to the chromatography matrix after product elution. The high cost of chromatographic matrices means that they are reused many times, sometimes for many

## Table 7-4. Removal of Prion Agents by Adsorption Chromatography

| Prion agent | | | Prion Reduction Factor (Log$_{10}$) | | | | | |
|---|---|---|---|---|---|---|---|---|
| Prion assay | | | Factor VIII | | Fibrinogen | | Factor IX | Thrombin |
| | | | 263K | 301V | 263K | 301V | 263K | 263K |
| | | | Western blot | Bioassay | Western blot | Bioassay | Western blot | Western blot |
| Prion spike | NaCl (mM) | pH | MF | MF | MF | MF | MF | MF |
| Anion exchange matrix | | | | | | | | |
| Toyopearl DEAE-650M* | 110 | 7.0 | 3.1 | | | | | |
| Toyopearl DEAE-650M | 250 | 7.0 | | 2.7 | ≥3.5 | ≥2.9 | | |
| DEAE-Cellulose | 200 | 6.9 | | | | | 3.0 | 3.0 |
| DEAE-Sepharose | 360 | 7.8 | | | | | 3.0 | 3.0 |
| Cation exchange matrix | | | | | | | | |
| S-Sepharose* | 500 | 6.5 | | | | | | 2.9 |
| Affinity matrix | | | | | | | | |
| Heparin-Sepharose* | 500 | 7.5 | | | | | 1.4 | |

*Inclusive of solvent/detergent treatment before chromatography.
MF = microsomal fraction.

years. Therefore, suitable sanitization of chromatographic materials after each use is a critical issue if the subsequent contamination of product batches by one infected pool is to be prevented. In a study of a regimen used to clean an anion exchange matrix used in the preparation of Factor VIII concentrate, it was found that a significant quantity of prion infectivity was desorbed by using a 2$M$ NaCl wash and that no infectivity was detected after treatment with 0.1$M$ NaOH or after a further wash with 2$M$ NaCl.[36]

## Nanofiltration

Filtration that uses membranes with a mean pore diameter of 35 nm or less has been shown to remove transmissible spongiform encephalopathy (TSE) agents to a significant degree (Table 7-5) in experiments using solutions spiked with BH. Whether prion infectivity that is naturally present in blood would behave in the same way as that derived from BH is not known. In some studies, the BH extract was treated by sonication and 0.1-μm membrane filtration,[38] by the addition of 0.5% sarkosyl detergent,[41] or by detergent treatment plus ultrasonication (Sato T and Rohwer RG, unpublished observations) in attempts to both disaggregate and to solubilize infectivity associated with brain tissue so that the spike might better represent the state of endogenous infectivity in blood. Should any vCJD infectivity be present at this stage in fractionation processes, it would be expected to be soluble and well dispersed, so BH treated in this manner may provide an appropriate challenge for studies of nanofiltration, even if this treatment is not performed in routine manufacturing. When the BH spike was solubilized and a bioassay was used for prion determination, removal of prion infectivity was incomplete; infectivity was detected after filtration even at 15 nm (Table 7-5). The pore size by which nanofilters are specified is a mean diameter, not the widest diameter; thus, these results may not be inconsistent with a finding that solubilized BH

## Table 7-5. Removal of Prion Agents by Nanofiltration

| Solution Filtered | Prion Agent | Prion Spike | Prion Assay | Nanofilter Type | Prion Reduction Factor ($Log_{10}$) | Prion in Filtrate | Reference |
|---|---|---|---|---|---|---|---|
| IgG | 263K | BH* | Western blot | Millipore, Viresolve 180 | ≥3.0 | No | Van Holten et al[38] |
| Albumin | 263K | BH | Western blot | Millipore, Viresolve 180 | ≥5.0 | No | Gilligan et al[39] |
| Albumin | 263K | BH | Bioassay | Millipore, Viresolve 180 | 5.0 | Yes | Gilligan et al[39] |
| Albumin | CJD | BH | Bioassay | Asahi, Planova 35N | ≥5.9 | No | Tateishi et al[40] |
| Albumin | ME7 | BH | Bioassay | Asahi, Planova 35N | 4.9 | Yes | Tateishi et al[41] |
| Albumin | ME7 | BH† | Bioassay | Asahi, Planova 35N | 1.6 | Yes | Tateishi et al[41] |
| Albumin | ME7 | BH | Bioassay | Asahi, Planova 15N | ≥5.9 | No | Tateishi et al[41] |
| Albumin | ME7 | BH† | Bioassay | Asahi, Planova 15N | ≥4.2 | No | Tateishi et al[41] |
| Protein | 263K | BH‡ | Bioassay | Asahi, Planova 15N | | Yes | Sato and Rohwer§ |

*BH disaggregated by sonication and clarified by membrane filtration to 0.1 µM before being spiked into immunoglobulin G solution.
†Anionic detergent (0.5% Sarkosyl) added to BH to disaggregate prion protein before being spiked into albumin solution.
‡BH treated with detergent (Sarkosyl) and by ultrasonication before being spiked into protein solution.
§Sato T and Rohwer RG, unpublished observations.
BH = brain homogenate; CJD = Creutzfeldt-Jakob disease; IgG = immunoglobulin G.

prion particles with the highest specific infectivity were 17 to 27 nm in diameter.[42]

## Cleaning of Equipment

The complete separation of product batches from one another is necessary to avoid the potential for cross-contamination by blood-borne pathogens. Effective cleaning of equipment and reusable materials between batches is critical to achieving this separation. Items to be cleaned in this manner include chromatographic matrices, ultrafiltration membranes, miscellaneous equipment such as pumps and valves, and fractionation vessels.

Prion agents are regarded as highly resistant to physical and chemical methods of inactivation, and procedures recommended for cleaning equipment include autoclaving at 134 to 138 C for 18 minutes in a porous-load autoclave, treatment with 1$M$ sodium hydroxide at 20 C for 1 hour, and treatment with 2% sodium hypochlorite at 20 C for 1 hour,[43] conditions that may be too severe for some materials or items of equipment to withstand. It is important to appreciate that these recommendations were based on studies involving the inactivation of large quantities of infected brain tissue.[43] The challenge facing the fractionation industry is the possible contamination of equipment with much lower concentrations of prion protein. In studies more representative of those in plasma fractionation, treatment with 0.1$M$ sodium hydroxide was effective in abolishing abnormal prion protein in a 0.125% solution.[44] Similarly, removal of prion infectivity from an ion exchange matrix was obtained by treatment with 2$M$ sodium chloride and then with 0.1$M$ sodium hydroxide.[36] These results suggest that, in most cases, established cleaning procedures in plasma fractionation may already be satisfactory; however, further studies are required to confirm these findings.

# Plasma Products

Each plasma product is prepared by using one or more process operations for which significant prion RFs (ie, >1 $\log_{10}$) have been reported. Whether prion infectivity can be removed completely by any of these steps, performed either individually or in combination, is not known. The process operations that are expected to contribute the most to prion removal are identified below for the major plasma products.

## Human Factor VIII Concentrate

Process operations used in the preparation of Factor VIII concentrates for which significant RF values have been obtained include the fractionation of cryoprecipitate extract by aluminium hydroxide adsorption and/or precipitation[18,29,31] and further purification by immunoaffinity chromatography[37] and/or ion exchange chromatography.[18,37]

## Human Factor IX Concentrate

Process operations used in the preparation of Factor IX concentrates for which significant RF values have been obtained include primary ion exchange purification, secondary ion exchange purification, and affinity chromatography.[18]

## Human Immunoglobulin

Process operations used in the preparation of immunoglobulins for which significant RF values have been obtained include precipitation of Fraction I+III/Fraction III,[13,18,21,29] depth filtration of Supernatant III,[21,35] depth filtration of resuspended Fraction II,[18,32] and nanofiltration of immunoglubulin solution.[38]

## Human Albumin

Process operations used in the preparation of albumin for which significant RF values have been obtained include precipitation of Fraction I+II+III/Fraction I+III,[13,18,19,29] precipitation of Fraction IV,[13,18,19,29] depth filtration of Supernatant IV,[19] depth filtration (clarification) of resuspended Fraction V,[18] and depth filtration (lipid removal) of albumin solution.[18]

# Remaining Issues

Although there are no known cases of vCJD transmission by plasma products, the risk of transmission cannot be discounted. To estimate this risk, it is necessary to know the quantity of infectivity in the plasma pool, the degree of clearance achieved by the manufacturing process, the dose required for infection, and the quantity of infective material administered to the patient. The prevalence of subclinical infection in blood donor populations and the vCJD dose required to cause infection in clinically relevant circumstances are not known. Clearance of prions by manufacturing processes has been measured experimentally by a number of investigators, but the value of these data remains uncertain because of experimental limitations. These limitations are discussed below.

### Physicochemical Form of the Prion Agent

To determine the capability of a manufacturing process to clear a pathogen present in the starting material, it is preferable to measure clearance by both the whole process and by relevant steps operated individually and in combination.[45] The test material should possess a sufficient titer of infectivity for this purpose, and infectivity should be present in the physicochemical state in which it would exist naturally at the relevant stage of the manufacturing process.

Most prion studies to date have employed infectivity obtained either from rodent blood (endogenous) or from rodent brain tissue (exogenous). Experiments with endogenous material are limited by the very low titer of infectivity present, which means that few process steps can be studied and that it is difficult to show significant prion removal. A high titer can be obtained by using exogenous infectivity, but the relevance of the results obtained with this type of material is uncertain, because it is not known how accurately exogenous infectivity can represent the vCJD agent in human plasma.

Endogenous infectivity present in rodent plasma could not be removed by high-speed centrifugation (30 minutes at $17,000 \times g$)[17] or by leukocyte filtration of either plasma[17] or whole blood,[46] which led Brown et al[17] to conclude that plasma infectivity "must be partly in the form of very small, unsedimentable particles, molecular aggregates, or individual molecules." Brain-derived infectivity appears to partition in a manner similar to that of endogenous infectivity in cold-ethanol fractionation (Table 7-2) and in leukocyte filtration.[47] However, equivalent comparisons have not been performed for chromatographic adsorption, depth filtration, or nanofiltration, which leaves continued uncertainty over the relevance of RF values obtained for these technologies by using exogenous material for spiking.

To address this concern, BH has been treated to disaggregate and to solubilize prion infectivity by using various combinations of sonication, ultrasonication, detergent treatment, and membrane filtration (Table 7-5); the use of enzyme degradation has also been proposed.[48] High-titer infectivity prepared from brain tissue in this manner could provide an ideal spike for process validation studies; however, to ensure its suitability, the behavior of such a material would have to be compared first with that of endogenous infectivity for each of the process technologies of interest.

## Design of Investigational Studies

Pocchiari[45] has advised that two types of experiment should be performed: one type to show the absence of residual infectivity over the complete process and another type to ascertain clearance factors for individual steps. Most studies of plasma products have measured RF values only in individual steps, and very few whole-process studies have been performed. Because the technologies being examined involve separation processes, as opposed to methods of inactivation, the outcomes are determined by relationships of state—that is, by solubility relationships for precipitation processes, by adsorption isotherms for chromatographic separations/adsorptive filtration, and by sieving coefficients for nanofiltration. It is these relationships that will establish whether prion infectivity will be present or absent in the final product. RFs provide little or no information concerning such relationships (eg, a partitioning coefficient) and could be misleading when a high RF value is merely a reflection of the high titer of prion agent used for spiking. Therefore, although significant RFs are necessary, they may not be sufficient to show absence of infectivity.

## Application of Reduction Factors to Multiple Process Steps

All plasma products are prepared by using multiple bioseparations and bioprocess operations. However, because of technical limitations, most prion removal studies have dealt only with clearance in the course of individual steps. The extent to which these data can be extrapolated to multiple steps operated in sequence is uncertain. A progressive reduction in the concentration of prion agent has been observed through successive precipitation steps (Table 7-2), but when depth filtration was combined with precipitation[21] or when two different filtration procedures were combined,[21,32] the degree of prion removal through the combined steps was greater than that through the first step but less than the RF values for the individual steps added together. These observations suggest that multiple steps may be complementary but that RF values cannot be assumed to be additive without experimental confirmation.

## Detection of Prions

Knowledge of the partitioning behavior of prion agents in the manufacture of plasma products is restricted by limitations in the methods of prion determination—in particular, the inadequate sensitivity of both in-vitro and in-vivo assays and by specialist bioassays that are expensive, lengthy, and constrained by ethical considerations. The sensitivity of bioassays is limited by the need to dilute samples to ensure tolerability and by the small volumes that can be injected. The development of in-vitro infectivity assays using cell culture[49] together with improvements in sensitivity of detection[50] may provide a less costly and quicker alternative to bioassays and would have fewer restrictions on sample size and concentration.

## Conclusion

A large body of experimental data is available showing that conventional bioseparation processes used in plasma product manufacture are capable of removing prion agents to a significant extent. Results obtained by different investigators have been similar, despite the use of slightly different manufacturing methods and different experimental models, which indicates that many of the findings are robust and may be applied generically. Consequently, the risk of transmission of vCJD by plasma products is considered to be low. Nevertheless, uncertainties remain because of limitations in the experimental systems employed and insufficient sensitivity of prion assays. Therefore, the possibility that vCJD might be transmitted by plasma products cannot be discounted, and further research is required to better define the safety of plasma products in this regard.

## References

1. Preece MA. Creutzfeldt-Jakob disease: Implications for growth hormone-deficient children. Neuropathol Appl Neurobiol 1986;12:509-15.
2. Will RG, Ironside JW, Zeilder M, et al. A new variant of Creutzfeldt-Jakob disease in the UK. Lancet 1996;347:921-5.
3. Dealler S. A matter for debate: The risk of bovine spongiform encephalopathy to humans posed by blood transfusion in the UK. Transfus Med 1996;6:217-22.
4. Ludlam CA. New-variant Creutzfeldt-Jakob disease and treatment of haemophilia (letter). Executive Committee of the UKHCDO. United

Kingdom Haemophilia Centre Directors' Organisation. Lancet 1997; 350:1704.

5.  Jacquemot C, Cuche C, Dormont D, Lazarini F. High incidence of scrapie induced by repeated injection of subinfectious prion doses. J Virol 2005;79:8904-8.

6.  Foster PR. Prions and blood products. Ann Med 2000;32:501-13.

7.  Farrugia A. Risk of variant Creutzfeldt-Jakob disease from factor concentrates: Current perspectives. Haemophilia 2002;8:230-5.

8.  Llewelyn CA, Hewitt PE, Knight RSG, et al. Possible transmission of variant Creutzfeldt-Jakob disease by blood transfusion. Lancet 2004; 363:417-21.

9.  Peden AH, Head MW, Ritchie DL, et al. Preclinical vCJD after blood transfusion in a PRNP codon 129 heterozygous patient. Lancet 2004; 364:529-31.

10.  Hunter N, Foster J, Chong A, et al. Transmission of prion diseases by blood transfusion. J Gen Virol 2002;83:2897-905.

11.  Foster PR, Cuthbertson B, McIntosh RV, MacLeod AJ. Safer clotting factor concentrates. In: Forbes CD, Aledort L, Madhok R, eds. Hemophilia. London, UK: Chapman and Hall Medical, 1997:307-32.

12.  Foster PR. Assessment of the potential of plasma fractionation processes to remove causative agents of transmissible spongiform encephalopathy. Transfus Med 1999;9:3-14.

13.  Lee DC, Stenland CJ, Hartwell RC, et al. Monitoring plasma processing steps with a sensitive Western blot assay for the detection of the prion protein. J Virol Methods 2000;84:77-89.

14.  Hartwell RC, Nelson MS, Kislan MM, et al. An improved Western blot assay to assess the clearance of prion protein from plasma-derived therapeutic proteins. J Virol Methods 2005;125:187-93.

15.  Bellon A, Seyfert-Brandt W, Lang W, et al. Improved conformational-dependent immunoassay: Suitability for prion detection with enhanced sensitivity. J Gen Virol 2003;84:1921-5.

16.  Brown P, Rohwer RG, Dunstan BC, et al. The distribution of infectivity in blood components and plasma derivatives in experimental models of transmissible spongiform encephalopathy. Transfusion 1998;38:810-6.

17.  Brown P, Cervenakova L, McShane LM, et al. Further studies of blood infectivity in an experimental model of transmissible spongiform encephalopathy, with an explanation of why blood components do not transmit Creutzfeldt-Jakob disease in humans. Transfusion 1999; 39:1169-78.

18.  Foster PR, Welch AG, McLean C, et al. Studies on the removal of abnormal prion protein by processes used in the manufacture of human plasma products. Vox Sang 2000;78:86-95.

19.  Vey M, Baron H, Weimer T, Gröner A. Purity of spiking agents affects partitioning of prions in plasma protein purification. Biologicals 2002; 30:187-96.

20.  Cai K, Miller JLC, Stenland CJ, et al. Solvent-dependent precipitation of prion protein. Biochim Biophys Acta 2002;1597:28-35.

21. Reichl HE, Foster PR, Welch AG, et al. Studies on removal of a bovine spongiform encephalopathy-derived agent by processes used in the manufacture of human immunoglobulin. Vox Sang 2002;83:137-45.

22. Morgenthaler J-J, Maring J-A, Rentsch M, inventors; ZLB Bioplasma AG (Bern, Switzerland), assignee. Method for the removal of causative agent(s) of transmissible spongiform encephalopathies from protein solutions. US Patent 6,407,212. June 18, 2002.

23. Gregori L, Maring J-A, MacAuley C, et al. Partitioning of TSE infectivity during ethanol fractionation of human plasma. Biologicals 2004;32:1-10.

24. Committee for Medicinal Products for Human Use, for the European Medicines Agency. Guideline on the investigation of manufacturing processes for plasma-derived medicinal products with regard to vCJD risk. CPMP/BWP/5136/03 (October 21, 2004). London, UK: EMEA, 2004.

25. Foster PR. Protein precipitation. In: Weatherley LR, ed. Engineering processes for bio-separations. Oxford, UK: Butterworth-Heinemann, 1994:73-109.

26. Cohn EJ, Strong LE, Hughes WL, et al. Preparation and properties of serum and plasma proteins IV: A system for the separation into fractions of the protein and lipoprotein components of biological tissues and fluids. J Am Chem Soc 1946;68:459-75.

27. Oncley JL, Melin M, Richert DA, et al. The separation of the antibodies, isoagglutinins, prothrombin, plasminogen, and $\beta_1$-lipoprotein into subfractions of human plasma. J Am Chem Soc 1949;71:541-50.

28. Kistler P, Nitschmann H. Large-scale production of human plasma fractions. Eight years' experience with the alcohol fractionation procedure of Nitschmann, Kistler and Lergier. Vox Sang 1962;7:414-24.

29. Lee DC, Stenland CJ, Miller JLC, et al. A direct relationship between partitioning of the pathogenic prion protein and transmissible spongiform encephalopathy infectivity during the purification of plasma proteins. Transfusion 2001;41:49-55.

30. Flan B, Aubin J-T. Evaluation de l'efficacité des procédés de purification des protéines plasmatiques à éliminer les agents transmissibles nonconventionnels. Virologie 2005;9:S45-56.

31. Stenland CJ, Lee DC, Brown P, et al. Partitioning of human and sheep forms of the pathogenic prion protein during the purification of therapeutic proteins from human plasma. Transfusion 2002;42:1497-500.

32. Trejo SR, Hotta JA, Lebing W, et al. Evaluation of virus and prion reduction in a new intravenous immunoglobulin manufacturing process. Vox Sang 2003;84:176-87.

33. Foster PR. Removal of TSE agents from blood products. Vox Sang 2004;87(Suppl 2):7-10.

34. Boychyn M, Yim SS, Bulmer M, et al. Performance prediction of industrial centrifuges using scale-down models. Bioprocess Biosyst Eng 2004;26:385-91.

35. Van Holten RW, Autenrieth SM. Evaluation of depth filtration to remove prion challenge from an immune globulin preparation. Vox Sang 2003;85:20-4.

36.  Foster PR, Griffin BD, Bienek C, et al. Distribution of a bovine-spongiform encephalopathy-derived agent over ion exchange chromatography used in the preparation of concentrates of fibrinogen and factor VIII. Vox Sang 2004;86:92-9.
37.  Cervenakova L, Brown P, Hammond DJ, et al. Factor VIII and transmissible spongiform encephalopathy: The case for safety. Haemophilia 2002;8:63-75.
38.  Van Holten RW, Autenrieth S, Boose JA, et al. Removal of prion challenge from an immune globulin preparation by use of a size-exclusion filter. Transfusion 2002;42:999-1004.
39.  Gilligan KJ, Pizzi VF, Stenland C, et al. The use of size exclusion composite membrane remove TSE infectious particles from a model protein solution filtration. Poster PS1020EN00. Bedford, MA: Millipore Publications, 2002 . [Available at http://www.millipore.com/publications.nsf/docs/ps1020en00 (accessed February 13, 2006).]
40.  Tateishi J, Kitamoto T, Ishikawa G, Manable S. Removal of causative agent of  Creutzfeldt-Jakob disease (CJD) through membrane filtration method. Membrane 1993;18:357-62.
41.  Tateishi J, Kitamoto T, Mohri S, et al. Scapie removal using Planova virus removal filters. Biologicals 2001;29:17-25.
42.  Silveira JR, Raymond GJ, Hughson AG, et al. The most infectious prion protein particles. Nature 2005;437:257-61.
43.  Taylor DM. Inactivation of TSE agents: Safety of blood and blood-derived products. Transfus Clin Biol 2003;10:23-5.
44.  Käsermann F, Kempf C. Sodium hydroxide renders the prion protein $PrP^{Sc}$ sensitive to proteinase K. J Gen Virol 2003;84:3173-6.
45.  Pocchiari M. Methodological aspects of the validation of purification procedures of human/animal-derived products to remove unconventional slow viruses. In: Horaud F, Brown F, eds. Virological aspects of the safety of biological products. Developments in biological standardization, vol 75. Basel, Switzerland: S Karger AG, 1991:87-95.
46.  Gregori L, McCombie N, Palmer D, et al. Effectiveness of leucoreduction for removal of infectivity of transmissible spongiform encephalopathies from blood. Lancet 2004;364:529-31.
47.  Prowse CV, Bailey A. Validation of prion removal by leucocyte-depleting filters: A cautionary tale (letter). Vox Sang 2000;79:248.
48.  Brown P. Blood infectivity, processing and screening tests in transmissible spongiform encephalopathy. Vox Sang 2005;89:63-70.
49.  Klohn PC, Stoltze L, Flechsig E, et al. A quantitative, highly sensitive cell-based assay for mouse scrapie prions. Proc Natl Acad Sci U S A 2003;100:11666-71.
50.  Barletta JM, Edelman DC, Highsmith WE, Constantine NT. Detection of ultra-low levels of pathogenic prion protein in scrapie infected hamster brain homogenates using real-time immuno-PCR. J Virol Methods 2005;127:154-64.

In: Turner ML, ed.
*Creutzfeldt-Jakob Disease: Managing the Risk of
Transmission by Blood, Plasma, and Tissues*
Bethesda, MD: AABB Press, 2006

# 8

# Cell, Tissue, and Organ Transplantation

GEORGE GALEA, MD(ABER), FRCP(ED), FRCPATH, AND
MARC L. TURNER, MB, CHB, PHD, FRCP, FRCPATH

AS LIFE EXPECTANCY continues to increase in most developed societies and as the incidence of death from infectious disease and privation decreases, neoplastic and degenerative diseases have become the preeminent causes of morbidity and mortality. Although modern pharmaceuticals make a significant contribution to the prevention and amelioration of degenerative conditions, little exists that will facilitate tissue and organ regeneration. Xenotransplantation may play a future role, but, at this time, compatibility and ethical concerns still significantly constrict its widespread use.

The transplantation of human cells, tissues, and organs, both as therapeutic products in their own right and as part of

*George Galea, MD(Aber), FRCP(Ed), FRCPath, Medical Director, Scottish Na-
tional Blood Transfusion Service, Tissue Services; and Marc L. Turner, MB, ChB,
PhD, FRCP, FRCPath, Senior Lecturer in Immunohematology and Transfusion
Medicine, University of Edinburgh, and Clinical Director, Edinburgh Blood Transfusion Centre; Edinburgh, United Kingdom*

medical devices and engineered products, therefore is steadily increasing. Estimates of the use of various tissues in the United States (US) and elsewhere are provided in Table 8-1.

There are numerous ways of defining cells, organs, and tissues, but perhaps it is simplest to use the definitions from the European Union Tissues and Cells Directive (2004/23/EC).[3] These definitions and the range of such products are summarized in Table 8-2. Some, such as cell products used for hematopoietic stem cell (HSC) transplantation, are derived only from live donors. Some, such as cornea, are derived only from cadaveric donors. Whereas most organs are derived from live donors or those declared dead by brain-stem testing, tissues may be derived from living, brain-stem-dead or non-heart-beating donors. Shortages exist for many if not most cells, tissues, and organs; for cells and organs, these shortages are compounded by the requirement of a degree of blood group and HLA matching. Moreover, although most cell and tissue products can be stored, cornea, pancreatic islet cells, and organs have limited ex-vivo viability. Tissues and organs derived from a single donor can often be transplanted to multiple recipients, which will compound the effect of disease transmission if that donor is infected.[1] Finally, the range of clinical indications varies from the acutely life-threatening to the life-enhancing. There is, therefore, a great deal of variability in the availability, nature, and volume of the products transplanted, the window of opportunity (eg, for testing), the robustness of the response to manipulation, the severity and urgency of clinical indication, and the age or health status of the recipient. This variability obviates a simple extrapolation of risk management strategies from the fields of blood components and plasma products.

## Distribution of Infectivity in Cells, Tissues, and Organs

The World Health Organization has recently reviewed the evidence on the distribution of infectivity and abnormal prion

**Table 8-1. Estimated Number or Volume of Allografts Transplanted Annually in the United States (USA), the United Kingdom (UK), and Other European Countries**

| Tissue | USA* | UK[†] | Netherlands | France | Italy |
|---|---|---|---|---|---|
| **Cadaveric Tissue** | | | | | |
| Bone[‡] (n) | 675,000 | 6000 | 6000 | 14,000 | 3000 |
| Corneas (n) | 50,000 | 3500 | 1450 | 4400 | 5500 |
| Skin | 1020 $m^2$ | 28 $m^2$ | 20 $m^2$ | NA | 24 $m^2$ |
| Heart valves (n) | 5500 | 350 | 480 | 280 | 140 |
| Vessels (n) | 400 | NA | — | — | — |
| Pericardium (n) | 5300 | NA | — | — | — |
| **Living Donor Tissues** | | | | | |
| Unrelated-donor marrow stem cells (n) | 1100 | — | — | — | — |
| Peripheral blood stem cells (n) | 500 | 772[§] | 300 | 275 | 300 |
| Cord blood stem cells (n) | 60 | NA | 10 | — | 12 |

* Data for the USA from 2001-2002 (modified from Eastlund and Strong[1]).
[†] Data for the UK from the World Health Organization.[2]
[‡] Not all bone in all countries is derived from cadaveric donors.
[§] All hematopoietic stem cell transplants, ie, marrow and peripheral blood.
NA = data not available.

## Table 8-2. Cells, Tissues, and Organs in Therapeutic Use*

**Cells†**
Marrow (autologous and allogeneic)
Peripheral blood stem cells (obtained by leukapheresis)
Donor leukocyte infusions (also obtained by leukapheresis)
Umbilical cord blood
Occasional research preparations such as dendritic cells, T-cell
    infusions, and adult stem cells for tissue repair
Pancreatic islet cells

**Tissues‡**
Musculoskeletal tissues
    Bones
    Tendons
    Ligaments
Cardiovascular tissues
    Heart valves
Ocular tissues
    Cornea
    Cornea epithelial stem cells
    Sclera
Epidermal tissues
    Amniotic membrane
    Skin

**Organs§**
Kidneys                    Pancreatata
Liver                      Small intestine
Heart

---

*Definitions of cells, tissues, and organs are taken from Directive 2004/23/EC of the European Parliament and Council.[3]
†Individual human cells or a collection of human cells when not bound by any form of connective tissue. Red cell, platelet, and granulocyte concentrates would (correctly) be classified as "human cell therapies" under the terms of this definition, but they are deliberately excluded and remain classified as "blood components."
‡All constituent parts of the human body formed by cells. Some are used therapeutically in an acellular form.
§An organ is a differentiated and vital part of the human body, formed by different tissues, that maintains its structure, vascularization, and capacity to develop physiologic functions with an important level of autonomy.

protein (PrP$^{TSE}$) transmissible spongiform encephalopathies (TSE) in animals (naturally occurring disease or primary experimental infection) and man[4] and has grouped these into tissues with higher infectivity, tissues with lower infectivity, and tissues with no detectable infectivity (Tables 8-3, 8-4, and 8-5, respectively). Two observations should be made. The first is that the sensitivity of detection of infectivity and PrP$^{TSE}$ will depend on the precise assay method; therefore, a negative result cannot necessarily be equated with a complete absence of infection. The second, a related point, is that categories of infection are not the same as categories of risk of transmission, which may depend on other factors, including the volume of material transplanted.

Most human TSEs show evidence of infectivity and PrP$^{TSE}$ in neural tissue and limited evidence of lymphoid and muscular tissue involvement (Tables 8-3 and 8-4). In variant Creutzfeldt-Jakob disease (vCJD), infectivity and PrP$^{TSE}$ have been found in neural tissue and lymphoid tissues of the tonsil, appendix, lymph nodes, and spleen as early as 2 years before the development of clinical neurologic disease (Tables 8-3 and 8-4).[5,6] Similarly, in the second case of probable transmission of vCJD prions by blood transfusion, the patient died of unrelated causes, but abnormal PrP accumulation was shown in the spleen and one cervical lymph node, but not the central nervous system (CNS).[7]

These findings are consistent with the evidence from peripheral transmission of TSEs in animal models, which suggests that infectivity is present in the lymphoid tissue early in the course of infection, well before it becomes detectable in the CNS and before clinical disease develops (Fig 8-1) (see Chapter 2).

In an effort to extend these observations, immunohistochemical analysis was undertaken in a large anonymized UK survey in the United Kingdom (UK) of 16,700 surgically removed tonsillectomy and appendectomy specimens, most of which were from patients 10 to 30 years old at the time of operation. Three appendectomy samples showed lymphoreticular

**Table 8-3. High-Infectivity Tissues\*†**

| Tissues | Human TSEs | | | | Cattle | | Sheep and Goats | |
|---|---|---|---|---|---|---|---|---|
| | vCJD | | Other TSEs | | BSE | | Scrapie | |
| | Infectivity | PrP^TSE | Infectivity | PrP^TSE | Infectivity | PrP^TSE | Infectivity | PrP^TSE |
| Brain | + | + | + | + | + | + | + | + |
| Spinal cord | + | + | + | + | + | + | + | + |
| Retina | NT | + | + | + | + | NT | NT | + |
| Optic nerve | NT | + | NT | + | + | NT | NT | + |
| Spinal ganglia | + | + | NT | + | + | NT | NT | + |
| Trigeminal ganglia | + | + | NT | + | + | NT | NT | + |
| Pituitary gland | NT | + | + | + | – | NT | + | NT |
| Dura mater | NT | – | + | – | NT | NT | NT | NT |

\*Central nervous system (CNS) tissues that attain a high titer of infectivity in the later stages of TSE and certain tissues anatomically associated with the CNS.

†Used with permission from WHO Guidelines on Tissue Infectivity Distribution in Transmissible Spongiform Encephalopathies, September 2005. [Available at http://www.who.int/bloodproducts/tse/WHO%20TSE%20Guidelines%20FINAL-22%20JuneupdatedNL.pdf.]

TSEs = transmissible spongiform encephalopathies; vCJD = variant Creutzfeldt-Jakob disease; BSE = bovine spongiform encephalopathy; PrP = prion protein; + = presence of infectivity or PrP^TSE; – = absence of detectable infectivity or PrP^TSE; NT = not tested.

**Table 8-4. Lower-Infectivity Tissues*†**

| Tissues | Human TSEs | | | | Cattle | | Sheep and Goats | |
| | vCJD | | Other TSEs | | BSE | | Scrapie | |
| | Infectivity | PrP$^{TSE}$ | Infectivity | PrP$^{TSE}$ | Infectivity | PrP$^{TSE}$ | Infectivity | PrP$^{TSE}$ |
|---|---|---|---|---|---|---|---|---|
| **Peripheral Nervous System** | | | | | | | | |
| Peripheral nerves | + | + | (−) | + | + | + | + | + |
| Enteric plexuses | NT | + | NT | (−) | NT | + | NT | + |
| **Lymphoreticular Tissues** | | | | | | | | |
| Spleen | + | + | + | + | − | − | + | + |
| Lymph nodes | + | + | + | − | − | − | + | + |
| Tonsil | + | + | NT | − | + | − | + | + |
| Nictitating membrane | NA | NA | NA | NA | + | − | NT | + |
| Thymus | NT | + | NT | − | − | NT | + | NT |

(continued)

**Table 8-4. Lower-Infectivity Tissues*† (continued)**

| | Human TSEs | | | | Cattle | | Sheep and Goats | |
| | vCJD | | Other TSEs | | BSE | | Scrapie | |
| Tissues | Infectivity | PrP$^{TSE}$ | Infectivity | PrP$^{TSE}$ | Infectivity | PrP$^{TSE}$ | Infectivity | PrP$^{TSE}$ |
|---|---|---|---|---|---|---|---|---|
| **Alimentary Tract** | | | | | | | | |
| Esophagus | NT | – | NT | – | – | NT | NT | + |
| Fore-stomach (ruminants only) | NA | NA | NA | NA | – | NT | NT | + |
| Stomach/abomasum | NT | – | NT | NT | – | NT | NT | + |
| Duodenum | NT | – | NT | NT | – | NT | NT | + |
| Jejunum | NT | + | NT | – | – | NT | NT | + |
| Ileum | NT | + | NT | – | + | + | + | + |
| Appendix | – | + | NT | – | NA | NA | NA | NA |
| Large intestine | + | + | NT | – | – | NT | + | + |
| **Reproductive Tissues** | | | | | | | | |
| Placenta | NT | – | (+) | – | – | NT | + | + |

**Other Tissues**

| Tissue | | | | | | | |
|---|---|---|---|---|---|---|---|
| Lung | NT | – | – | – | NT | – | – |
| Liver | NT | – | – | – | NT | + | NT |
| Kidney | NT | – | – | – | – | – | – |
| Adrenal | NT | + | – | NT | NT | + | NT |
| Pancreas | NT | – | – | – | NT | + | NT |
| Bone marrow | – | (–) | – | (+) | NT | + | NT |
| Skeletal muscle | NT | (–) | + | (+) | NT | – | + |
| Tongue | NT | + | – | – | NT | NT | + |
| Blood vessels | NT | + | + | – | NT | + | + |
| Nasal mucosa | NT | NT | + | – | NT | + | + |
| Salivary gland | NT | – | NT | – | NT | + | NT |
| Cornea | NT | – | – | NT | NT | + | NT |

**Body Fluids**

| Fluid | | | | | | | |
|---|---|---|---|---|---|---|---|
| Cerebro-spinal fluid | – | + | NT | – | – | + | NT |
| Blood | + | – | ? | – | ? | + | ? |

*Peripheral tissues that have tested positive for infectivity and/or $PrP^{TSE}$ in at least one form of TSE.

†Used with permission from WHO Guidelines on Tissue Infectivity Distribution in Transmissible Spongiform Encephalopathies, September 2005. [Available at http://www.who.int/bloodproducts/tse/WHO%20TSE%20Guidelines%20FINAL-22%20JuneupdatedNL.pdf.]

TSEs = transmissible spongiform encephalopathies; vCJD = variant Creutzfeldt-Jakob disease; BSE = bovine spongiform encephalopathy; PrP = prion protein; + = presence of infectivity or $PrP^{TSE}$; – = absence of detectable infectivity or $PrP^{TSE}$; NT = not tested; NA = not available; ( ) = limited or preliminary data; ? = controversial results.

**Table 8-5. Tissues with No Detected Infectivity or PrP$^{TSE}$ ***

| Tissues | Human TSEs | | | | Cattle | | Sheep and Goats | |
| | vCJD | | Other TSEs | | BSE | | Scrapie | |
| | Infectivity | PrP$^{TSE}$ | Infectivity | PrP$^{TSE}$ | Infectivity | PrP$^{TSE}$ | Infectivity | PrP$^{TSE}$ |
|---|---|---|---|---|---|---|---|---|
| **Reproductive Tissues** | | | | | | | | |
| Testis | NT | – | (–) | – | – | NT | – | NT |
| Prostate, epididymis, or seminal vesicle | NT | – | (–) | – | – | NT | – | NT |
| Semen | NT | – | (–) | – | – | NT | NT | NT |
| Ovary | NT | – | NT | – | – | NT | – | NT |
| Uterus (nongravid) | NT | – | NT | – | – | NT | – | NT |
| Placental fluids | NT | NT | (–) | NT | – | NT | NT | NT |
| Fetus | NT | NT | NT | NT | – | NT | – | – |
| Embryos | NT | NT | NT | NT | – | NT | ? | NT |

| | | | | | | | | | |
|---|---|---|---|---|---|---|---|---|---|
| **Musculoskeletal Tissues** | | | | | | | | | |
| Bone | NT | NT | NT | NT | – | NT | NT | NT | |
| Heart or pericardium | NT | – | – | – | – | NT | – | NT | |
| Tendon | NT | NT | NT | NT | – | NT | NT | NT | |
| **Other Tissues** | | | | | | | | | |
| Gingival tissue | NT | – | – | NT | – | NT | NT | NT | |
| Dental pulp | NT | – | NT | NT | – | NT | NT | NT | |
| Trachea | NT | – | NT | – | – | NT | NT | NT | |
| Skin | NT | – | NT | – | – | NT | – | NT | |
| Adipose tissue | NT | – | (–) | – | – | NT | NT | NT | |
| Thyroid gland | NT | – | (–) | – | NT | NT | – | NT | |
| Mammary gland or udder | NT | NT | NT | NT | – | NT | – | NT | |
| **Body Fluids, Secretions, and Excretions** | | | | | | | | | |
| Milk | NT | NT | (–) | NT | – | – | – | NT | |
| Colostrum | NT | NT | (–) | NT | (–) | – | – | NT | |

(continued)

**Table 8-5. Tissues with No Detected Infectivity or PrP$^{TSE}$ (continued)**

| Tissues | Human TSEs | | | | Cattle | | Sheep and Goats | |
| | vCJD | | Other TSEs | | BSE | | Scrapie | |
| | Infectivity | PrP$^{TSE}$ | Infectivity | PrP$^{TSE}$ | Infectivity | PrP$^{TSE}$ | Infectivity | PrP$^{TSE}$ |
|---|---|---|---|---|---|---|---|---|
| Cord blood | NT | NT | (−) | NT | − | NT | NT | NT |
| Saliva | NT | − | − | NT | NT | NT | − | NT |
| Sweat | NT | NT | − | NT | NT | NT | NT | NT |
| Tears | NT | NT | − | NT | NT | NT | NT | NT |
| Nasal mucus | NT | − | − | NT | NT | NT | NT | NT |
| Bile | NT | NT | NT | NT | NT | NT | NT | NT |
| Urine | NT | NT | − | − | − | NT | NT | NT |
| Feces | NT | NT | − | NT | − | NT | − | NT |

*Used with permission from WHO Guidelines on Tissue Infectivity Distribution in Transmissible Spongiform Encephalopathies, September 2005. [Available at http://www.who.int/bloodproducts/tse/WHO%20TSE/WHO%20Guidelines%20TSE%20FINAL-22%20JuneupdatedNL.pdf.]
TSEs = transmissible spongiform encephalopathies; vCJD = variant Creutzfeldt-Jakob disease; BSE = bovine spongiform encephalopathy; PrP = prion protein; + = presence of infectivity or PrP$^{TSE}$, − = absence of detectable infectivity or PrP$^{TSE}$, NT = not tested; ? = controversial results; ( ) = limited or preliminary data.

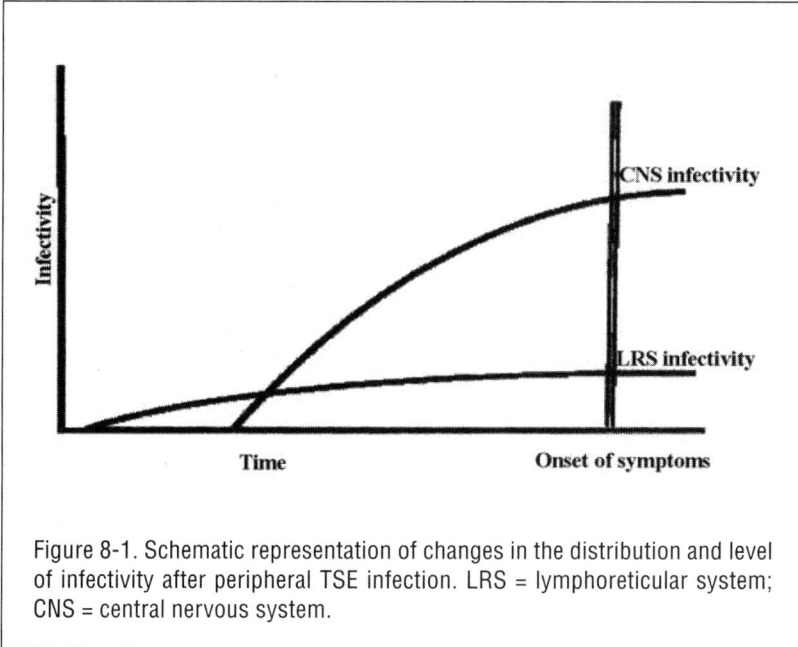

Figure 8-1. Schematic representation of changes in the distribution and level of infectivity after peripheral TSE infection. LRS = lymphoreticular system; CNS = central nervous system.

accumulation of prion protein, giving an estimated prevalence of 3 per 12,674 or 237 per million (95% CI: 49–692 per million). Although there are some uncertainties about the degrees of sensitivity and specificity of the assay in this setting, these findings suggest that the prevalence of subclinical disease may be significantly higher than the current incidence of clinical disease would suggest.

## Iatrogenic Transmission of CJD

Iatrogenic CJD is a rare disease, but it is important from the transplantation perspective. There have been approximately 406 cases of iatrogenic CJD transmission, over 197 of which involved dura mater that had been processed from human cadavers[8-15] (P Brown, personal communication). The dura mater allograft was obtained from a single manufacturer and transplanted worldwide, mainly in 1984 and 1985.[15,16] Several factors contributed to this outbreak, including the pooling of dura mater from many different cadavers during processing and the possibility that the dura mater came from persons who may have been demented.

The other major source of such iatrogenic transmissions was therapeutically used growth hormone (194 instances) and gonadotrophins (4 cases) purified from cadaveric pituitary glands[17,18] (P Brown, personal communication). The latter were in use in the late 1940s and early 1950s as potential therapies for female infertility, and pooling in those instances was also thought to contribute to the size of the outbreak. Both these sources were interrupted by the banning of dura mater use and by the use of recombinant growth hormone instead of human-derived growth hormone.

The ability of the cornea to transmit CJD has been reported.[19] In that case, a patient received a cornea from a donor; both donor and recipient died of CJD, and the diagnosis was confirmed histologically at autopsy. It is important to note that the donor had antemortem neurologic signs that currently would make him ineligible for tissue donation. However, Manuelidis et al[20] clearly showed that CJD can be transmitted experimentally via corneas in guinea pigs, thus duplicating infection with the CJD agent after corneal transplantation in humans. It is clear, therefore, that CJD can be and has been transmitted by a variety of tissues.

In addition, instruments may be contaminated with prion agents during contact with infected tissues during surgery, as evidenced by iatrogenic transmission of CJD via contaminated neurosurgical instruments and intracranial electroencephalogram electrodes. As discussed below, prions are extremely resistant to normal cleaning and decontamination processes; therefore, instruments may remain infective when they are used in other procedures. There is a concern that cross-contamination of tissues could occur during ex-vivo processing if fully disposable instruments are not used.

# Risk Assessment

The paucity of both animal and human data on the temporal and spatial distribution of TSE infectivity in tissue and organs during the subclinical phase of infection makes assessment of the risk of transmission of disease via cell, tissue, or organ transplantation highly problematic. The UK risk assessment took the approach of estimating the volume of material transplanted during these procedures and projecting the concentration of infectivity above which transmission would occur. For most cells, tissues, and organs, the mass of tissue transplanted is such that the concentration of infectivity would have to be well below the sensitivity limits of current biochemical and biologic assays to avoid transmission (Tables 8-6 and 8-7). In the absence of robust epidemiologic data, it is therefore prudent to assume that TSEs are transmissible by these products until proven otherwise.

To place the values in Table 8-6 in context, they can be compared with the postulated levels detectable by current assays—ie, 10,000 intracerebral $ID_{50}$/g. In every case, infectivity concentrations well below this limit would be sufficient to give doses >2 $ID_{50}$, which implies a very high risk of transmission should the donor be infected.

Table 8-7 shows the potential dose of infectivity administered if the donor is infected and assuming a similar concentration and distribution of infectivity to that thought to exist in peripheral blood. Again, the total amount of infectivity would be very large, well above a 2 $ID_{50}$ threshold.

# Risk-Reduction Measures

The risks of CJD transmission via tissues can be attributed to two sources—cross-contamination and endogenous infection. Cross-contamination is associated with the retrieval and processing of the tissues; endogenous infection is associated with the donor cell, tissue, or organ itself.

## Table 8-6. Threshold Dose Calculations for Tissues

| Tissue | Typical Mass | Threshold for 2 $ID_{50}$ Dose | Specific Infectivity (Intracerebral $ID_{50}$/g) Threshold for 0.02 $ID_{50}$ Dose* | Risk Assessment |
|---|---|---|---|---|
| **Ocular Tissue** | | | | |
| Cornea | 0.04 g (8-mm button) | 500 | 5 | Midrange |
| Sclera | 1.2 g (shell) | 1.7 | 0.017 | Midrange |
| Limbal stem cells | 0.04 g (maximum) | 500 | 5 | Midrange |
| **Amniotic Membrane** | | | | |
| Ophthalmic tissue | 0.02 g (for 4 cm$^2$) | 1000 | 10 | Lower range |
| Vaginoplasty | 5 g (for A5 size) | 4 | 0.04 | Lower range |
| **Skin** | 75 g (for 2500-cm$^2$ graft) | 0.25 | 0.0025 | Lower range |
| **Bone** | 180 g (approx. 20 mL marrow) | 0.11 | 0.0011 | Lower range |
| **Heart Valves** | 14.5 g | 1.4 | 0.014 | Low or zero |
| **Tendons** | 70.4 g (patellar tendon graft) | 0.28 | 0.0028 | Low or zero |

*See Chapter 9.
$ID_{50}$ = median infective dose.

### Table 8-7. Potential Infectivity Associated with Cells

| Harvest | Total Nucleated Cells Administered | Total Potential Infectivity (Intravenous $ID_{50}$) |
|---|---|---|
| Peripheral blood stem cells | $10 - 30 \times 10^9$ | $2000 - 6000$ |
| Marrow | $4 - 8 \times 10^9$ | $800 - 1600$ |
| Donor lymphocytes | $30 - 90 \times 10^9$ (per procedure)* | $6000 - 18{,}000$ |
| Cord blood | $0.17 - 1.8 \times 10^9$ | $34 - 360$ |
| CD34 | $0.14 - 0.28 \times 10^9$ | $28 - 56$ |

$ID_{50}$ = median infective dose.

## Avoidance of Cross-Contamination

Most tissue establishments have adopted measures to minimize the risk of cross-contamination. Instruments are used during various stages of tissue grafting. Depending on the source and type of tissue, control of the instruments used will be under the auspices of either clinicians or tissue establishments (see Table 8-8).

Significant progress has been made by tissue establishments in identifying suitable disposable equipment to replace (whenever possible) previously reusable instruments for both tissue retrieval and processing. The implementation of disposable equipment in tissue processing would exceed the UK Department of Health requirement that disposable equipment be introduced only for procedures that involve contact with neural and lymphatic tissues.[21] However, it is believed that the effect of this intervention on CJD transmission is low because, in all instances of implantation and in many retrievals, the surgical instruments used are nondisposable and, in the main, are nondedicated.

### Table 8-8. Instrument Use During Tissue Retrieval, Processing, and Grafting

| Donor | Retrieval | Processing | Grafting |
|---|---|---|---|
| Living (eg, bone) | C | NA | C |
| Living (explant) | C | T | C |
| MOD ( eg, tendon) | T | T | C |
| MOD (eg, heart valve) | C | T | C |
| Mortuary (eg, heart valve) | T | T | C |

C = clinician; NA = not applicable; T = tissue establishment; MOD = multiorgan donor.

Many tissue banks use decontamination procedures at a level above that recommended by the UK Department of Health,[22] which applies only to nondisposable equipment that is in direct contact with brain tissue. In UK tissue establishments, it is common practice, whenever possible, that nondisposable instruments that come into contact with any human tissue are sterilized by using hypochlorite and then wet-autoclaved above 121 C. Moreover, each instrument tray containing nondisposable instruments includes instruments that are individually labeled and dedicated to a particular tray. This practice minimizes donor exposure and makes the audit trail easier.

### Endogenous Infectivity

Several approaches have been taken to manage the risk posed by endogenous infection.

### Donor Selection

Donor selection guidelines for cells, tissues, and organs have fairly closely followed those that apply to blood donors. In most countries, the following donors would be excluded from donation:

- Donors with CJD or those who received human pituitary-derived growth hormones or underwent treatment for infertility with gonadotrophins.
- Donors exposed to other human pituitary extracts.
- Donors with a family history of CJD.
- Donors who received a corneal transplant.
- Donors who have had brain surgery or have undergone an operation for a tumor or spinal cyst. (This exclusion criterion was introduced after a review of the uses of dura mater. It became clear that dura mater was used extensively in operations ranging from pelvic floor repair to bladder surgery. Therefore, a decision was taken that, because the greatest risk of CJD transmission via dura mater was from its implantation in close proximity to the brain, the biggest impact on safety would derive from exclusion as donors patients who received dura mater during a neurosurgical operation. Moreover, it is acknowledged that most patients who have undergone such a procedure would not know whether dura mater had been used; therefore, all such patients need to be excluded. It should be noted that the banking of dura mater in the UK was stopped in 1992.)
- Donors with a history of degenerative neurologic disease of unknown etiology.

These selection criteria will not identify individuals in the preclinical or subclinical phase of variant CJD, however.

In the UK, a decision was taken to exclude living bone donors who have received blood or tissue products (HSC and organ transplant recipients would already be excluded on the grounds of their underlying condition). However, implementation of that decision has proved more problematic than at first envisaged.

Unpublished data from numerous tissue banks in the UK indicate that between 15% and 30% of live bone donors have been transfused with red cell concentrates or other blood components such as Fresh Frozen Plasma or Platelets. Excluding these donors would represent a significant loss of donations, particularly in the context of a borderline sufficiency of supply. The impact of this intervention is lessened to a certain extent if the transfusion history is limited to that after 1980, the year in which the BSE epidemic is generally considered to have begun. With that change, the impact would be a 13% to 22% loss, which is still a very significant drop in donations and much higher than the 3% to 5% figure for blood donors. Nevertheless, in view of the importance attached to limiting tertiary transmissions, this policy was implemented in the UK in 2005 for donors with a definite history of transfusion.

Bone losses would be increased even further if the exclusion criteria were widened to exclude donors who have probably (rather than definitely) received a transfusion. This exclusion was implemented for blood donors in August 2005, and it is clear that there are issues with donors' recollection of transfusion events. It may be that asking about major surgery and trauma would be more valuable in this context.

The situation with cadaveric tissue donors is even more difficult. Risk-benefit analyses and supply-and-demand concerns have necessitated a critical look at the implications of adopting such a criterion for cadaver-derived tissue donations. An important distinction between recent and historical transfusions in the context of vCJD transmission has been made by the UK Spongiform Encephalopathy Advisory Committee. Taking into account the likely changes in the level and distribution of infection after peripheral infection, it is thought that a perimortem transfusion is less likely to pose a risk of tertiary or higher order transmission than is historical transfusion with potentially established infection in the recipient/donor. The impact on cadaver tissue donations of excluding recipients of historical transfusions only is thought to be in the order of 4%, and such an exclusion is being considered for bone and other musculoskeletal tissues. This criterion, however, would have a much bigger impact on cornea donations (>11%), because the cornea-donor population is very different from the population of donors of other tissues, in terms of both age and medical selection criteria (UK Transplant, unpublished observations). Furthermore, a history of transfusion is likely to be far less accurate when provided by a relative.

Exclusion of transfused donors is unlikely to be applied to donors of HSCs or solid organs for whom the risk-benefit criteria are entirely different—in particular, the paucity of supply, the need for a degree of ABO and/or HLA matching, and the life-saving nature of the procedure. In addition, skin is a life-saving tissue that is in short supply.

A further possibility is the selection of donors on the basis of age, on the grounds that it seems likely that younger donors may have a higher prevalence of subclinical vCJD than the more elderly (see Chapter 10). Data collected in recent years indicate that 97% of living bone donors are more than 50 years old, and 80% are more than 60. Some tissues, such as heart valves or tendons, cannot be obtained from older donors because of the inferior quality of the product. Moreover, this age criterion would not apply to donors of organs or HSCs. The impact of excluding cornea donors on the basis of age would be very significant, because, currently, there are no age limits for donors of ocular tissue.

It should be appreciated that donor selection criteria are, at best, only a partially effective risk-reduction measure in terms of both sensitivity and specificity. The criteria may be differentially applied, depending on the potential risk of transmission associated with a particular tissue, the offset against other risks (such as that of failure of supply), and the potential benefit of the procedure to the patient.

*Importation of Tissues from Countries without Known vCJD or Low Dietary Exposure to BSE*

For those countries with a significant risk of vCJD transmission, importation is, in a sense, a form of donor selection and may be a very effective way to reduce the risk of transmission. The incidence of reports of vCJD from European countries is increasing; therefore, such countries may not be considered "safe" with respect to vCJD.

It should also be noted that, although Food and Drug Administration regulation of US tissue banks has been in place for some years, and although numerous requirements have been stipulated by the agency,[23-25] deaths have occurred through bacterially contaminated grafts,[26] and there have also been some good-manufacturing-practice concerns as recently as October 2005 (see www.fda.gov/cber/recalls.html). Therefore, any imported tissue may be considered safe with respect to vCJD, but that probability should be balanced by the overall quality and safety of the imported tissues.

The only tissues that may be adequately available for importation are bone and skin. Security of supply cannot be guaranteed, which raises real concerns about whether full importation would lead to the suspension of internal procurement programs. In practice, it is likely that the UK will import tissues on a limited scale for selected "most vulnerable" recipients, such as children born after 1996, who are likely to have experienced the least exposure to BSE and who have long potential life spans. In the case of other tissues, either there is no worldwide surplus, as in the case of heart valves, or significant issues arise, as in the case of corneas, for which emergency transplantation of matched corneas would not be possible.

Currently, there are no restrictions across borders for the import and export of HSCs, because their movement is most often dependent on the HLA type. Organs are very infrequently imported because of worldwide shortages.

## Applying CJD Testing to Tissue Donors

To date, test systems for $PrP^{TSE}$ detection have been available for postmortem diagnosis but not for antemortem screening.[27] Prion accumulation can be detected by immunohistochemistry or by Western blot analysis.[28] The latter can be used as a test for vCJD by obtaining a biopsy of either lymphoid or neurologic tissue.

Clearly, it would be unacceptable to take either brain or tonsil tissue from a live donor for screening. It would be feasible, in principle, to obtain a lymph node from the operative site during a hip replacement. However, lymph nodes are not thought to be the best site for prion detection, and there are ethical considerations with respect to extending surgical procedures in this way for the benefit of the recipient (not the donor). However, if a validated CJD blood test becomes available and the ethical issues are resolved, the test will also be used in donors of tissues.

Although it is technically challenging, obtaining splenic or tonsil tissue for biopsy during the retrieval of tissue from a cadaveric donor is possible. The ethical issues surrounding donor information in such cases are less severe, and serious consideration is being given to testing this specific group of tissue donors.

The situation is clearly far more complex if tissues are obtained from a multiorgan donor, because organs would be transplanted before a test result is available. The procurement of lymphoid tissue from cornea donors is also problematic. Therefore, it is not thought likely that testing will be carried out in these situations in the near future.

The potential availability of a "tested" product, albeit one with uncertain sensitivity and specificity, raises the possibility that cadaveric tissues could be regarded as safer with respect to vCJD than are those from live donors. However, other considerations include the fact that the medical history of live donors is obtained by direct questioning of the donor, rather than by questioning relatives under very stressful circumstances; therefore, it may be considered less robust. Moreover, the availability of antemortem blood samples that have been validated for mandatory microbiologic markers is an important consideration. It is well known that, unless precautions are taken during testing, false-positive and false-negative results may be obtained when using samples obtained after death.

*Pooling and Tissue Processing*

In the UK, most surgical bone is stored frozen and issued in that state. However, to recover the proportion of collected bone that may be bacterially contaminated, a final sterilization step is required. The advantages of processing include the removal of lipids and marrow (which may be toxic and delay incorporation), the eradication of bacteria, and the reduction of the infectivity of viruses.[29] For operational and cost reasons, all processing of surgical (fresh frozen) femoral heads in the UK was formerly done on a pooling basis. A 2004 UK assessment of the various risk-reduction measures that could be undertaken on bone in the context of vCJD concluded that as much of the marrow and blood as possible should be removed, without pooling (UK Department of Health, unpublished observations). Extensive validations have been carried out to achieve a product from which at least 99% of the cellular content of the bone has been removed.[30,31] It has also been shown that pulse washing of morselized bone in the operating room removes at least 50% of the bone marrow. Although it seems doubtful that the risk of transmissibility would be significantly reduced by this measure alone, any marrow removal may be considered beneficial.

Generally, other musculoskeletal tissues are considered to be avascular or to have low levels of cellularity, eg, tendons and ligaments. When bacterially contaminated, they are processed by decontamination, but neither they nor the processing method are thought to have an impact on their potential prion infectivity (Table 8-2). Similar considerations apply to cardiovascular tissues, because heart valves are generally considered to be composed of mostly fibrous tissue with a thin layer of endothelial cells.

Although it is possible, through CD34 cell selection, to reduce the volume of cells transplanted during an HSC transplantation, it is still likely that the numbers of cells transplanted would suffice to transmit infection unless levels of infectivity were very low (Table 8-7). Moreover, CD34 cell selection has other implications in terms of the graft's effects on disease, which should be given appropriate weight by the attending clinicians.

## Decontamination Regimens

Unlike other infectious agents, prions resist inactivation by agents that destroy nucleic acids. It has been shown, for example, that a radiation dose of 50 kGy reduces the PrP$^{TSE}$ levels only by 1.5 logs.[32] They are also resistant to endogenous protease, to temperatures >100 C, to formalin, to extremes of pH, and to nonpolar organic solvents.[33] Moreover, they are able to pass through 0.1-μm filters. Infectivity of prions can be destroyed only by exposure to 0.1 to 1 $M$ NaOH for 1 hour at room temperature,[34] to a 0.5% solution of sodium hypochlorite for 1 hour, or to wet autoclaving for 1 hour at 130 C. Clearly, such steps cannot be undertaken in the production processes of labile cells, tissues, or organs, because they would have significant detrimental effects on the viability of the transplanted material. However, there are also concerns that these treatments may be toxic to collagenous matrices, rendering even acellular tissues exposed to them biologically and clinically ineffective.[35]

## Increasing Clinical Awareness of Appropriate Cell and Tissue Use

Autologous bone is seen as the gold standard for bone grafting. However, increased morbidity and pain are associated with the bone removal site. Moreover, the autologous bone is often not sufficient to fill the defects. The average issue for bone impaction grafting is in revision hip surgery 2.5 femoral heads or the equivalent.

Use of bone is very much driven by clinical demand and the various techniques used by different surgeons. Crude data (UK tissue banks, unpublished observations) show that, for revision hip surgery, there is quite a wide variation, and that mean femoral head use varies between 1.53 and 2.63 per revision hip arthroplasty. Clearly, the complexity of the surgery may play a role, but clinical audit and discussion with clinicians will be important in ensuring that bone is used in an effective and most appropriate way.

There is a wide range of synthetic bone material on the market, ranging from hydroxyapatite to tissue-engineered, bone-void filler. These substances have been used for several years.[36] However, surgical consensus is that human allograft is a very close second to autografts and superior to many synthetic products. Acceptance of that view should depend on evidence-based results, which are lacking in this field and should be encouraged. It is important to note that a few meta-analyses in the field of bone grafting are being conducted.

The clinical indications for human heart valve allografts are very specific. Not only are the operations (eg, Ross procedures) selective, but also they are used in specific types of patients for particular reasons. For example, these grafts are highly resistant to infection and are therefore suitable in cases of valve replacement when bacterial endocarditis is present. Patients who receive human heart valves do not need maintenance anticoagulation, in contrast to those who receive mechanical valves. Therefore, these grafts are particularly suitable in children and in pregnant women.

Skin is used in a variety of clinical situations—some chronic, such as the treatment of diabetic foot ulcers, and some acute, such as life-saving situations after massive burns. The historical gold standard has been and continues to be the split-thickness autograft. However, the use of this graft requires a second injury, and, in some instances, as in the case of a severely burnt patient, this is impossible. There are numerous commercially available skin substitutes. It remains to be seen which (if any) will be successful in the long term. The grafting to date has fallen short of that seen with human skin. Therefore, the split-thickness skin graft will remain the tissue of choice for the foreseeable future.

# Conclusions

CJD and its variants are a relatively rare set of clinical diseases. The lack of knowledge about the level and distribution of infectivity in different tissues, the likely existence of long subclinical periods, and the absence of a screening test and/or easily applicable decontamination processes have produced a set of challenging problems with respect to the possible transmission of these diseases via cell, tissue, and organ allografting. A series of interventions, following a set of measures that were applied to blood, have been undertaken by the tissue and organ transplant community. These interventions have been further complicated by the variety of risks perceived for different tissues, their clinical benefit (life-saving versus life-enhancing), and the availability of alternative therapeutic approaches. Moreover, because, in many instances, organs and tissues are derived from the same donor, significant ethical challenges must be addressed: eg, whereas tissues can be banked, organs cannot. As further measures are contemplated, the issues become more complex and resource-intensive. There is no doubt that, once the "precautionary principle" is applied to protect public health, tensions about the best policies to be applied and the trade-off with other risks and opportunity costs become evident.

# References

1. Eastlund T, Strong DM. Infectious disease transmission through tissue transplantation. Adv Tissue Bank 2004;7:51-131.
2. First global consultation on regulatory requirements for human cells and tissues for transplantation. Ottawa, Canada, 29 November - 1 December 2004. Geneva, Switzerland: World Health Organization, 2005. [Available at https://www.who.int/transplantation/Report Ottawa CTTx.pdf (accessed April 17, 2006).]
3. Directive 2004/23/EC of the European Parliament and of the Council of 31 March 2004 on setting standards of quality and safety for the donation, procurement, testing, processing, preservation, storage and distribution of human tissues and cells. Official Journal of the European Union 2004;7:48-58.
4. World Health Organization guidelines on transmissible spongiform encephalopathies in relation to biological and pharmaceutical prod-

ucts. Report of a WHO consultation. Geneva, Switzerland, 14-16 September 2005 (in press).

5. Hilton DA, Ghani AC, Conyers L, et al. Prevalence of lymphoreticular prion protein accumulation in UK tissue samples. J Pathol 2004;203: 733-9.

6. Hilton DA, Ghani AC, Conyers L, et al. Accumulation of prion protein in tonsil and appendix: Review of tissue samples. BMJ 2002;325:633-4.

7. Peden AH, Head MW, Ritchie DL, et al. Preclinical vCJD after blood transfusion in a PRNP codon 129 heterozygous patient. Lancet 2004; 364:527-9.

8. Centers for Disease Control and Prevention. Rapidly progressive dementia in a patient who received a cadaveric dura mater graft. MMWR Morb Mortal Wkly Rep 1987;36:49-55.

9. Centers for Disease Control and Prevention. Update: CJD in a patient receiving a cadaveric dura mater graft. MMWR Morb Mortal Wkly Rep 1987;36:324-5.

10. Centers for Disease Control and Prevention. Update: CJD in a patient receiving a cadaveric dura mater graft. MMWR Morb Mortal Wkly Rep 1989;38:37-43.

11. Centers for Disease Control and Prevention. CJD in a patient receiving a cadaveric dura mater graft. MMWR Morb Mortal Wkly Rep 1993;42: 560-3.

12. Lane KL, Brown P, Howell DN, et al. Creutzfeldt-Jakob disease in a pregnant woman with an implanted dura mater graft. Neurosurgery 1994;34:737-9; discussion 739-40.

13. Masullo C, Pocchiari M, Macchi G, et al. Transmission of Creutzfeldt-Jakob disease by dural cadaveric graft. J Neurosurg 1989;71:954-5.

14. Thadani V, Penar PL, Partington J, et al. Creutzfeldt-Jakob disease probably acquired from a cadaveric dura mater graft. Case report. J Neurosurg 1988;69:766-9.

15. Yamada S, Aiba T, Endo Y, et al. Creutzfeldt-Jakob disease transmitted by a cadaveric dura mater graft. Neurosurgery 1994;34:740-3; discussion 743-4.

16. Lang CJ, Schuler P, Engelhardt A, et al. Probable Creutzfeldt-Jakob disease after a cadaveric dural graft. Eur J Epidemiol 1995;11:79-81.

17. Brown P, Preece M, Brandel JP, et al. Iatrogenic Creutzfeldt-Jakob disease at the millennium (review). Neurology 2000;55:1075-81.

18. Cochius JI, Burns RJ, Blumbergs PC, et al. Creutzfeldt-Jakob disease in a recipient of human pituitary-derived gonadotrophin. Aust N Z J Med 1990;20:592-3.

19. Duffy P, Wolf J, Collins G, et al. Possible person-to-person transmission of Creutzfeldt-Jakob disease (letter). N Engl J Med 1974;290:692-3.

20. Manuelidis EE, Angelo JN, Gorgacz EJ, et al. Experimental Creutzfeldt-Jakob disease transmitted via the eye with infected cornea. N Engl J Med 1977;296:1334-6.

21. Frosh A, Joyce R, Johnson A. Iatrogenic vCJD from surgical instruments. BMJ 2001;322:1558-9.

22. Advisory Committee on Dangerous Pathogens and the Spongiform Encephalopathy Advisory Committee (UK). Transmissible spongiform encephalopathy agents: Safe working and the prevention of infection. London: The Stationery Office, 1998.

23. Food and Drug Administration. Human tissue intended for transplantation. Title 21 CFR Part 1270. Fed Regist 1997;62:40,429-47.

24. Food and Drug Administration. Current good tissue practice for manufacturers of human cellular and tissue-based products. Title 21 CFR Part 1271. Fed Regist 2001;66:1508.

25. Food and Drug Administration. Human cells, tissues and cellular and tissue-based products: Established registration and listing. Title 21 CFR Part 1271. Fed Regist 2001;66:5447-69.

26. Food and Drug Administration. Guidance for industry. Validation of procedures for processing of human tissue intended for transplantation. Title 21 CFR Part 1270.3. Fed Regist 2002;67:677-9.

27. Aguzzi A, Heikenwalder M, Miele G. Progress and problems in the biology, diagnostics, and therapeutics of prion diseases. J Clin Invest 2004;114:153-60.

28. Armstrong RA, Cairns NJ, Ironside JW, Lantos PL. Quantification of vacuolation ("spongiform change"), surviving neurones and prion protein deposition in eleven cases of variant Creutzfeldt-Jakob disease. Neuropathol Appl Neurobiol 2002;28:129-35.

29. Galea G, Kearney JN. Clinical effectiveness of processed and unprocessed bone. Transfus Med 2005;15:165-74.

30. Lomas R, Drummond O, Kearney JN. Processing of whole femoral head allografts: A method for improving clinical efficacy and safety. Cell Tissue Bank 2000;1:193-200.

31. Yates P, Thomson J, Galea G. Processing of whole femoral head allografts: Validation methodology for the reliable removal of nucleated cells, lipid and soluble proteins using a multi-step washing procedure. Cell Tissue Bank 2005;6:277-85.

32. Miekka SI, Forng RY, Rohwer RG, et al. Inactivation of viral and prion pathogens by gamma-irradiation under conditions that maintain the integrity of human albumin. Vox Sang 2003;84:36-44.

33. Hilmy N, Lina M. Effects of ionising radiation on viruses, proteins and prions. In: Nather A, ed. Advances in tissue banking, vol. 5: The scientific basis of tissue transplantation. Singapore: World Scientific, 2001; 5:358-75.

34. Brown P, Rohwer RG, Gajdusek DC. Sodium hydroxide decontamination of Creutzfeldt-Jakob disease virus (letter). N Engl J Med 1984;310: 727.

35. Kearney JN, Johnson C. Evaluation of NaOH treatment of human dura mater implants to obviate Creutzfeldt-Jakob disease transmission. Biomaterials 1991;12:431-2.

36. Kocialkowski A, Wallace WA, Prince HG. Clinical experience with a new artificial bone graft: Preliminary results of a prospective study. Injury 1990;21:142-4.

In: Turner ML, ed.
*Creutzfeldt-Jakob Disease: Managing the Risk of
Transmission by Blood, Plasma, and Tissues*
Bethesda, MD: AABB Press, 2006

# 9

# Risk Assessments for Variant Creutzfeldt-Jakob Disease and Blood Transfusion: A Perspective from the United Kingdom

PETER BENNETT, BSC, MSC, PHD, AND
STEPHEN DOBRA, BSC, MSC, MSC, MBA

FROM THE FIRST identification of variant Creutz-feldt-Jakob disease (vCJD) as a new disease, policy within the United Kingdom (UK) has been based on the presumption that infection *might* be transmissible from person to person, and that blood transfusion might be one possible route. This has led to the implementation of a series of precautionary steps. Analysis has been used to estimate the possible risk of infection by blood transfusion, its wider implications, and the effectiveness of possible risk reduction steps. Acknowledging great uncertainty both about the preva-

*Peter Bennett, BSc, MSc, PhD, Head of Operational Research; and Stephen Dobra,
BSc, MSc, MSc, MBA, Principal Operational Research Analyst; Standards and
Quality Analytical Team, Department of Health, London, United Kingdom*

lence of vCJD in the UK population and the probability of transmission via blood has led to application of the precautionary principle. Decisions have necessarily been taken on available information, prior to hard scientific evidence on the level of risk being available. Nevertheless, such decisions need to be proportionate to the potential risk, consistent, and appropriately prioritized and targeted. These judgments may often rely on consensus expert opinion, but decisions have typically been underpinned by analysis of the potential risk reductions across a range of scenarios for both infectivity and prevalence. A good deal of this underpinning analysis has been undertaken by the Department of Health (DH), though often drawing heavily on other research and modeling.

The aim of this chapter is to outline the DH risk assessments carried out to date. Much of this work is necessarily provisional. Understanding of the nature and risk of infection has increased over time, but great uncertainty remains. Steps to reduce infection are continually reviewed in the light of new evidence. New measures become possible as technology moves forward, for example in the field of prion removal, and will need to be evaluated.

Analysis has been used to assess both general risks to public health and the consequences of specific "incidents." These typically occur when someone subsequently found to have vCJD has undergone certain forms of surgery, or has donated blood, organs, or tissues. For blood-borne transmission, analyses include both "forward" risk assessments—ie, estimating the possible consequences for recipients if a donor develops vCJD—and the "reverse" situation in which a recipient later develops vCJD while the donor (or donors) so far remain free of symptoms.

This chapter focuses on work carried out in the UK. However, vCJD transmission is to a significant extent an "international" issue, a point underlined both by the progressive—if slow—international spread of both bovine spongiform encephalopathy (BSE) and vCJD and by the various precautionary measures introduced in the United States (US), Canada, Europe, and elsewhere.

# Background

The work outlined here forms part of a larger whole. A coherent approach to minimizing the risks of vCJD requires attention to both primary and secondary transmission routes. So alongside steps to ensure that the food chain was free of BSE, consideration also quickly turned to possible secondary infection routes. A series of models have been developed to assess the risks of secondary transmission, all starting from the proposition that an unknown number of people may be carrying vCJD without showing any symptoms of the disease. Evidence from animal models suggests that transmission requires affected protein to come into direct contact with protein in another person's body, so the main potential routes were identified as being via residues on surgical instruments and via donated blood, tissues, or organs.

The relative importance of these routes, in terms of their possible impact on public health, is influenced by two basic factors. One is the frequency with which "risk events" (eg, blood donation from an infected donor or an operation on an infected patient) might be expected to occur, for any given prevalence of vCJD infection. The other is the likely consequence of such an event, in terms of the additional secondary infections that might be caused. On that basis, the two most important potential routes were identified as blood transfusion and surgery—especially operations involving the brain or back of the eye and possibly also including certain dental procedures. This chapter outlines the risk assessments carried out with respect to donated blood, those dealing with surgery and dentistry being covered elsewhere.[1-4]

Potential vCJD transmission has become a focus of concern beyond the UK, with some concerns applying whether or not a given country has any (detected) incidence of vCJD or BSE.

For example, what risks might be introduced by accepting donors who have lived in the UK, or by the historical importation of plasma products sourced from UK donors? Risk assessments have been carried out by relevant authorities in countries including the US, Canada, France, and Australia.[5-11] This chapter touches on some points of comparison.

To cope with the many uncertainties affecting the risks of vCJD transmission, DH risk assessments have used scenario-based models that consider wide ranges of assumptions. One key question is obviously the prevalence of vCJD infection within the population. DH analysis has drawn on continuing efforts by other researchers to assess the likely scale of the primary vCJD outbreak, as discussed briefly at the end of this chapter. However, it is worth stressing immediately that *secondary transmission risks are driven by the existing prevalence of infection within the population, not the predicted number of vCJD cases*. This is a key distinction. Many of those infected may die of other causes without ever developing symptoms of vCJD, but may still have acted as sources of onward infection—eg, by donating blood—during the pre- or subclinical stage of the disease. So using projected numbers of primary vCJD cases to assess the risks of secondary transmission could seriously underestimate the scale of such risks.

On the specific question of blood-borne transmission risks, the risk of blood-borne transmission will clearly depend on whether the blood of a donor incubating the disease would actually carry vCJD infection. There was initially no direct evidence on this basic point: however, there is relatively long-standing evidence for transmission of prion diseases in many animal models—although not all.[12-15] Until recently, a case could be made against vCJD being transmissible via human blood, just as sporadic CJD appears not to be. However, human-to-human transmission of vCJD unfortunately now appears to be established beyond reasonable doubt.[16,17] Nevertheless, key questions remain, including the following:

- How infective is blood within the incubation period, when does infectivity appear, and how does it grow?
- How is infectivity distributed across the major components within a donation? This is of particular importance, given that transfusions now hardly ever consist of whole blood.
- What does a therapeutic unit "as given" actually comprise? For example, a unit of Red Blood Cells (RBCs) will contain a significant proportion of plasma, but the exact amount varies according to the production process used.
- What are the effects of pooling donations? This is a key question with regard to plasma derivatives, where there might be one infective donation in a pool of many thousand. But the question is also relevant to Platelets, some units of which are made up by pooling buffy coats from four donors.
- How do manufacturing processes such as fractionation and filtration affect the residual infectivity in Plasma products?
- What is the age profile of those infected in the primary outbreak, and how does it relate to that of the blood donor base?
- What further factors affect the chance of anyone infected by a secondary route going on to become a source of further infection?

In the face of these many unknowns, it would be futile to aim for precise estimates of risk, or to expect any model to predict the future course of the outbreak. Rather, risk assessment has been scenario-based. The aim has been to arrive at conclusions that are as *robust* as possible—roughly valid across a wide range of scenarios consistent with current evidence. One can then evaluate possible risk reduction measures as realistically as possible. This requires models to be "fit for purpose" in each case—the appropriate level of complexity often depending on the options being considered. These include:

- Reducing "avoidable use"—ie, ensuring that allogeneic blood is used only when necessary.
- Imports from outside the UK—eg, of Plasma for fractionation, and some Fresh Frozen Plasma for transfusion.
- Restrictions on eligibility to donate—eg, preventing donations from those who have previously been transfused.

- Changing production processes—eg, introducing leukocyte reduction (removal of white cells from donations), reducing the plasma content of red cell and platelet packs, or sourcing of platelets from single rather than pooled donations.
- Introducing appropriate additional precautions for anyone identified as being at increased risk of carrying vCJD infection—eg, as a result of receiving blood from a donor who later developed the disease, or through reuse of surgical instruments used on such a patient.

As well as considering individual options, the authors have worked with the UK blood services—especially the National Blood Service (NBS) in England—to help develop an overall strategy addressing the risks of vCJD transmission. This involves comparing the effectiveness of different risk reduction measures and placing them in the more general context of blood safety and supply. All risk assessments have been subject to discussion by the relevant advisory committees.* This allows modeling to inform recommendations and decisions while also exposing methodology and assumptions to expert scrutiny and critique.

The next section outlines, in rough chronological order, modeling of steps to reduce the general risks of blood-borne vCJD transmission. This part of the discussion takes a population-based perspective. Next, the discussion addresses the use of modeling to inform decisions about specific incidents involving identifiable individuals. This raises additional ques-

---

*Throughout this period, advice to the Department of Health has been channeled through the committee on the Microbiological Safety of Blood and Tissues for Transfusion (MSBT), now extended to cover Microbiological Safety of Blood, Tissues and Organs (MSBTO). Discussion within the former National Blood Service (NBS), now part of The National Health Service (NHS) Blood and Transplant, has been led by the Blood and Tissue Safety Assurance Group (BTSAG). Across the UK blood services, a key body is the Standing Advisory Committee on Transfusion-Transmitted Infections (SACTTI), which has a subgroup specifically dealing with vCJD. Questions on the risk posed to specific individuals and appropriate actions on notification are dealt with by the CJD Incidents Panel, as described further below. Throughout, scientific advice regarding vCJD itself has been provided by the Spongiform Encephalopathy Advisory Committee (SEAC).*

tions about the information to be given to anyone who may be at increased risk, and how to balance the harm that such notification might cause them with the need to protect public health. Finally, the chapter outlines some current questions for analysis, including both new risk reduction measures and outstanding issues regarding vCJD itself.

## Assessing and Reducing Risks to the Population

As a general principle, the potential risks to public health for any vCJD transmission route can be analyzed by considering in turn:

- *The consequences of a single "risk event"*—eg, transfusion with blood from an infected donor, use of instruments on an infective patient—under different scenarios for infectivity.
- *The resulting rate of new infections* within the population, based on scenarios for the prevalence of vCJD infection.
- *Implications for the long-term dynamics of the disease*—for example, whether new infections would cease altogether as the primary outbreak runs its course or whether vCJD could become self-sustaining within the population.

The third stage of analysis brings in many other factors affecting the chance of someone infected by a secondary route unknowingly passing the infection on. For blood-borne transmission, key questions include the typical incubation period for this route, patients' life expectancy after transfusion, their eligibility to donate blood or tissues, and the likelihood of their doing so if eligible. It is also important to bear in mind the potential compounding effects of various transmission routes rather than merely considering each separate route in isolation. For example, someone infected via blood transfusion might have neurosurgery before developing symptoms, creating a risk of further onward infections as instruments were reused. However, these compounding effects are particularly difficult to quantify.

Initial modeling work was undertaken both within DH and by external consultants DNV Technica (now known simply as DNV). The two groups worked independently but in liaison. In general, the DNV team concentrated mainly on the first two stages outlined above, whereas the DH analysis put more emphasis on longer-term dynamics of infection. They thus provided complementary perspectives. The key output of DNV's work was a report published in 1999 and updated in 2002-2003.[18] This did not address the question of *whether* human blood is infective. Rather, it assessed likely levels and distribution *if* infectivity were present, primarily by reviewing the research literature using animal models. The report also drew together data from the UK blood services on the donation and use of blood and the manufacture and use of blood products.

These early studies emphasized the distinction between the risks arising from transfusion of blood components (and the rare use of Whole Blood) and those from use of plasma derivatives. These are subject to very different calculations.[12,19]

- For *blood components*, each unit exposes the recipient to a substantial volume of material, in most cases sourced from a single donor. A key finding of the DNV study was that if blood was infective, the dose contained in a unit of any component from an infected donor was likely to be high—more than sufficient to infect the recipient. This finding was judged to be quite robust. However, there was no explicit assessment of *when* infectivity might appear within the donor's incubation period—DNV made the simple "precautionary" assumption it would be present throughout. This is discussed further below.

- By contrast, recipients *of plasma derivatives* are exposed to thousands of donors on each occasion, with a tiny volume of material coming from each. The levels of infectivity in such products were (and are) considered much more uncertain. DNV offered various alternative bases for calculating the effects of the various manufacturing steps: in the UK, policy has been based on the most precautionary (conservative) of these. In addition, assumptions have to be made about the effect of any single infective donation being diluted within a large pool.

On the basis of these initial findings,[†] the UK took two key steps, both fully implemented in 1999. The first, heavily influenced by the DNV study, was to remove white cells from all donations—the process of leukocyte reduction. This was done on the understanding that a significant proportion of blood-borne infectivity would be associated with the leukocytes. However, it was realized that some residual infectivity might remain—eg, within the plasma element. So leukocyte reduction would be unlikely to eliminate any transmission risk and would need to be complemented by other measures.

The other major step was to import plasma used for fractionation. As already noted, considerations of potential risk here are very different. Because the pool sizes are so large, even a small prevalence of vCJD among donors would imply a significant likelihood of any given pool containing at least one infected donation. The effects of dilution, and of steps within the manufacturing process, might suggest that a unit produced from such a pool would contain only a very small infective dose. But unless there is a significant "lower threshold" dose for vCJD, below which the chance of infecting each recipient would be strictly zero (rather than just proportionately small), the impact at a population level could still be substan-

---

[†]*The main practical findings cited here are echoed by subsequent assessments carried out outside the UK (see references[5-11] already cited). Although different specific inputs on levels of infectivity are used, there seems to be consensus that a full unit of any blood component sourced from an infected but preclinical donor could contain a high infective dose, at least in the latter stages of the incubation period. By contrast, there is a much greater spread of conclusions on the risks from plasma products. This is largely because experimental investigations have had to rely on "spiking" infective material—eg, from brain—into the blood tested. The results suggest that manufacturing processes greatly reduce levels of infectivity (ie, produce high "clearance factors"—see, eg,[20]). However, there is a lack of consensus as to whether such results can be extrapolated to endogenous, rather than spiked, infectivity. While reductions in endogenous infectivity can be demonstrated in rodent models, the low starting titers make it difficult in principle to demonstrate achievement of high clearance factors.*

tial.[‡] A large number of recipients would each be exposed to many thousands of donors per unit, in many cases also receiving many units over a prolonged period. This makes for a very large number of contacts within the population. Models were constructed using System Dynamics, an established way of modeling systems in which feedback may be important.[21-24] As with other communicable diseases, a large number of contacts means that even a very small infection risk per contact could have significant long-term effects. Even though many of those receiving plasma derivatives would be ineligible to donate (eg, hemophiliacs), "feedback" of infection within the population could be significant. In the worst case, vCJD might become self-sustaining. For any disease, this will occur if *on average* each person newly infected goes on to infect at least one other person. Under such conditions, the disease will spread until eventually limited by some other factor such as lack of exposure to blood or surgery.

The principle of a self-sustaining outbreak could be demonstrated fairly easily using System Dynamics models. While such scenarios might require rather pessimistic inputs on the infectivity of derivatives, these could not be ruled out definitively. On a precautionary basis, this made a compelling case for cutting the possible feedback of infection by sourcing plasma for fractionation from outside the UK. For similar reasons, it was also becoming clear that the identification of even relatively few blood donors with vCJD would necessitate large-scale recall of plasma products. Therefore, the decision was taken to import plasma for fractionation from the US—the most practical non-UK source—fractionation itself still being carried out within the UK. In view of later concerns, it should

---

[‡]*There is some evidence from animal models that very small infectious doses may lead to recipients entering a "carrier state" rather than developing symptomatic disease. However, this could still have significant implications for infection dynamics. The use of a no-threshold model was endorsed by SEAC and is commonly used as a precautionary assumption when there is little information on dose response.*

be noted that the rationale for this step does not depend on the prevalence of vCJD infection among US donors being zero. Rather, this is a risk reduction step requiring only that prevalence be substantially lower than among UK donors. A working assumption has been of at least a 100-fold differential: in view of the *relative* scale of BSE within the respective cattle populations, this still appears reasonable—even allowing for possible underreporting. The same comment applies to later decisions on the import of *Fresh Frozen* Plasma.

Following these initial steps, DH analysts undertook further work on the dynamics of infection via blood components, working in consultation with a range of external experts. This work considered how great the remaining risks might be and the potential impact of further precautionary measures. Of particular interest was the possible benefit of stopping those who had already received blood components from donating blood. Such a step would curtail the feedback of onward infection. But it would also carry risks. Any substantial impact on donation might endanger the sufficiency of the blood supply. Balancing these competing risks required further analysis of how great a reduction in vCJD transmissions might be achieved. This was done using System Dynamics models to consider the interplay between "stocks"—eg, of infective individuals in a given age group—and "flows"—eg, rates of birth, movement between age groups, infection, or death. Dedicated software was used to build up models including vCJD transmission via:

- primary (food-borne) infection
- receipt of plasma derivatives from UK donors prior to 1999
- receipt of Whole Blood, RBCs, Plasma, or Platelets from infective donors (treated as four separate routes)
- another unspecified secondary route, introduced to allow for other sources of infection, eg, reuse of surgical instruments

The first two were considered as historical routes. All secondary transmission routes are potential sources of feedback into donor prevalence. The basic structure of the model can thus be visualized as in Fig 9-1, a structure replicated for the various routes and for different age groups. All individuals were assumed to be susceptible to (at least secondary) vCJD infections, although this assumption could be varied.

Of the various factors affecting the dynamics of secondary infection, blood services staff were able to provide information on some.

At the time of analysis, annual usage of components in England was estimated to comprise roughly 2 million adult units of RBCs, 340,000 units of Fresh Frozen Plasma, and 210,000 adult therapeutic doses of Platelets. Platelet procurement was taken to be about 40% by apheresis of single donors, and 60% from pooling four separate donations. This is discussed fur-

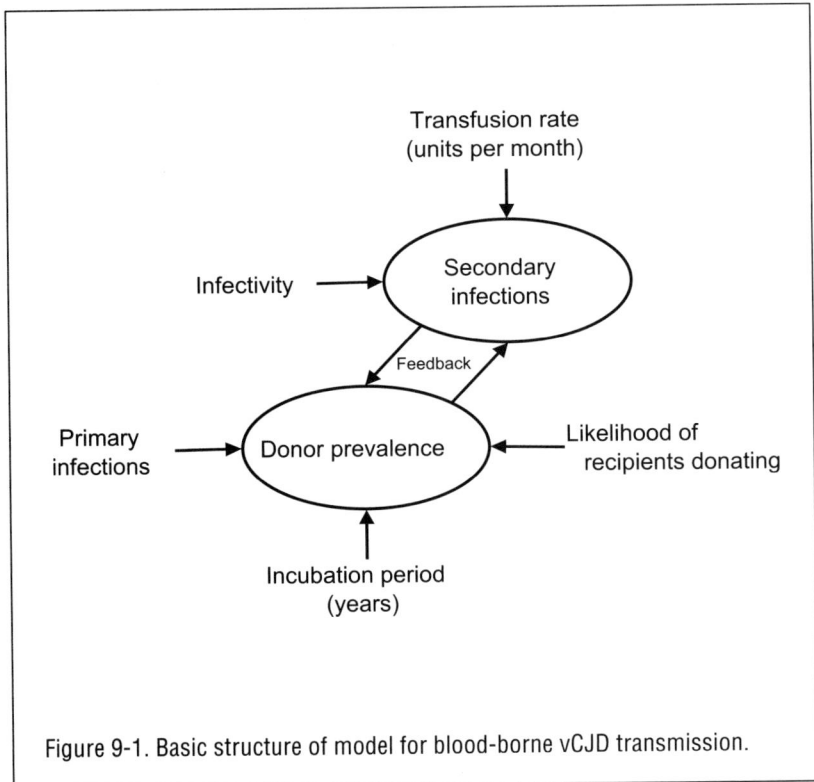

Figure 9-1. Basic structure of model for blood-borne vCJD transmission.

ther below. As a broad classification (and following the DNV study), usage was broken down into "chronic" and "acute," ie:

- transfusion of those suffering from known chronic illnesses (eg, chronic anemia) and already ineligible to donate blood.
- transfusion of other recipients in response to some acute condition (eg, blood loss), who might go on to donate.

Age distributions for both recipients and donors were available from blood services data. It is significant that recipients of blood tend to be older than donors, a point that reduces the potential "feedback" of infection within the population. On the question of posttransfusion survival, some published studies existed, and pilot results were also available from an ongoing large-scale (English) National Blood Service study.[25,26] While differing in detail, these present a similar general picture. Recipients often have conditions markedly reducing their immediate life expectancy. But after some years, survival increasingly becomes "normal for age." Reflecting this, the model divided recipients into two groups: "nonsurvivors" dying within 2 years of the transfusion episode and "survivors," taken to have a normal life expectancy for their age. Although a crude classification, this appeared sufficient for the purposes of analysis.[§] Infections among "nonsurvivors" were assumed never to result in *clinical cases* of vCJD, given that such individuals would almost certainly die of other causes first.

Other factors were much more uncertain, so the model was run using wide ranges of alternative assumptions. These included the relative likelihood of recipients going on to act as donors, if eligible to do so. The mean secondary incubation period was varied between 3 and 15 years: although there was no direct evidence on this at the time, subsequent events suggest that a figure within this range may be plausible, at least for re-

---

[§]Data on survival suggest that mortality rates from all causes level off substantially by about 18 months after transfusion, so although the choice of a 2-year cut-off is somewhat arbitrary, cut-offs of (say) 18 months or 3 years should yield roughly similar proportions of "survivors."

cipients susceptible to disease.[11] On the key question of the infectivity of blood components, baseline model runs were based on the "DNV scenario" already noted. This represents a worst case in the sense that a unit of any component sourced from an infected donor would contain a high enough dose to infect the recipient, even if leukocyte reduced. By the same token, these model runs showed the *greatest possible benefit* of recipient exclusion. Some working assumptions were also made about the primary vCJD outbreak. Infections were taken to have occurred between 1985 and 1995, peaking steeply around 1990-1991. This rough timing is common to most published studies, and minor variations did not significantly affect results. However, no assumption was made as to the number of primary infections: rather, the analysis concentrated on clarifying the *proportional* impact of blood-borne infection on the outbreak. Primary infections were taken to have a mean incubation period of up to 30 years. This is toward the maximum of the range generally suggested in the literature, so it was appropriate for exploring the maximum possible impact of blood-borne transmission: however, alternative assumptions were also explored.

Given these various inputs, the model generated dynamic scenarios for the vCJD outbreak as a whole, with or without interventions such as the exclusion of previously transfused donors. An *illustrative* example is shown in Fig 9-2, this particular example having an assumed mean secondary incubation period of 15 years. Note that this shows incidence of new infections, not clinical cases of vCJD. There would be significantly fewer clinical cases than infections, especially if secondary incubation periods are long (as in this example). The analysis could be extended to provide scenarios for secondary clinical

------

[11] *For comparison, the two recipients known to have developed vCJD after (presumed) blood-borne infection have had incubation periods of around 7 years. While firm conclusions cannot be drawn from just two instances, a somewhat higher estimate may be appropriate if cases with shorter-than-average incubation periods would be seen first.*

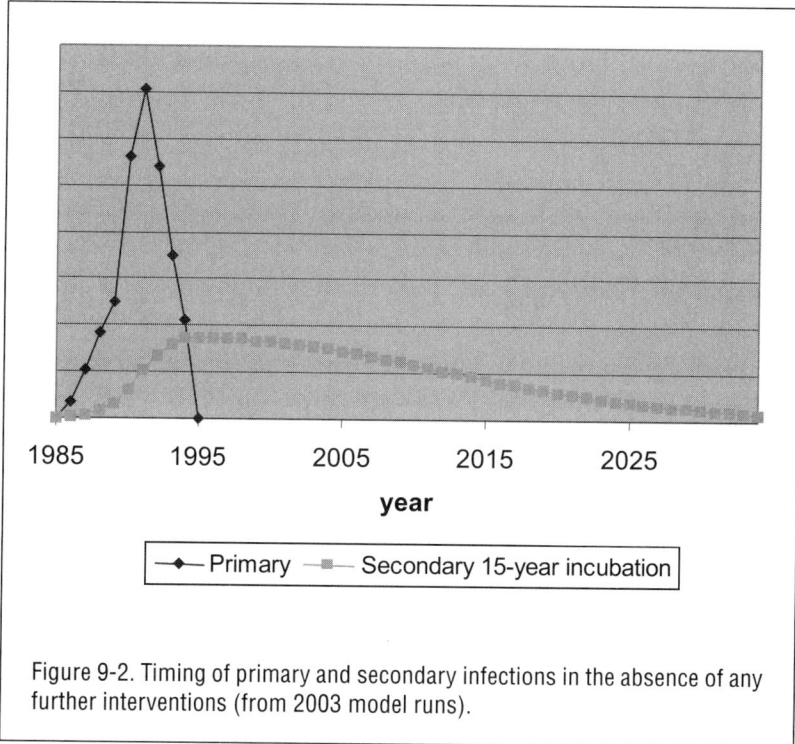

Figure 9-2. Timing of primary and secondary infections in the absence of any further interventions (from 2003 model runs).

cases, but these depend on quite detailed assumptions about the life expectancy of different patient types and the distribution of secondary incubation periods.

Model runs with wide ranges of inputs suggested some conclusions about the impact of transmission in different scenarios. The analysis demonstrated that transmission via blood components *could* contribute significantly to the final total of vCJD infections. In high-infectivity scenarios such as DNV's, blood-borne infections could eventually outnumber primary infections—even if recipients with very short life expectancy are discounted. However, this would require blood to be infective throughout a long primary incubation period, a point subject to a separate "reality check" outlined below. The effect of excluding previously transfused donors was found to be highly dependent on the *secondary* incubation period. In fact, the variation was very close to linear: with a 3-year mean incubation period, about 3% of *future* blood-borne infections would be prevented (this would also be roughly 3% of the number of primary infections). With a 15-year incubation period, the equivalent figure was approximately 16%. This dependency is to be expected, as longer incubation periods mean that infected individuals would survive longer as potential sources of infection. Consequently, the effect of excluding previously transfused donors would also be greater.

The different model runs also showed that results are much more sensitive to some changes than to others. For example:

- Shortening the mean primary incubation period has a roughly linear impact on secondary infections—eg, a mean period of 15 rather than 30 years would halve the expected blood-borne infections.

- The relative likelihood of recipients going on to donate also has a roughly linear impact. This parameter varied between 1 and 3, using a baseline value of 2 (implying that *surviving and eligible* "acute" recipients would be about twice as likely to donate as nonrecipients of similar age.) This was compatible with existing NBS donor survey data.

- By contrast, any historical transmissions via plasma derivatives appeared to have only small compounding effects—ie, they were unlikely to lead to additional transmissions via components. Results for component-related transmissions were therefore largely insensitive to inputs on plasma derivative infectivity.

Moreover, the model runs confirmed that the *timing* of infectivity in blood components is of key importance, rather than just the *level*. This was illustrated in a related exercise, which attempted to "calibrate" the transmission model against known data. The issue of concern was whether scenarios with high risks of vCJD transmission from an infected donor could be reconciled with the lack of evidence for actual blood-borne transmission, despite good surveillance. Until late 2003, there had been no known instance of a recipient of blood from a vCJD-infected donor also developing the disease. This raised the question of whether infectivity scenarios such as DNV's were too "pessimistic"—if blood was as infective as implied, should there not be more evidence of vCJD transmissions having occurred? Since then, two recipients of blood from a donor who later died from vCJD have developed the disease. (In addition, a recipient from another such donor was found to have signs of subclinical infection.) As discussed below, this shows beyond reasonable doubt that human blood can transmit vCJD. However, the quantitative question remains even in retrospect: *why were more instances of disease in both donor and recipient not seen earlier on?*

To check the transmission model against known data, two types of analysis were carried out in 2002-2003. One was to examine records of recipients known to have received blood from donors who went on to develop vCJD, using data from the same surveillance system that later identified the first (probable) blood-borne transmission.[17] "Over prediction" of transmission would be demonstrated if many recipients had survived longer than any plausible incubation period without developing vCJD. However, this line of inquiry allowed few firm conclusions. There were not many recipients of "implicated" blood components, and a high proportion had died of other causes quite soon after transfusion. A handful had survived several years (and a few remained alive), but one could not confidently say that these instances refuted a "pessimistic" transmission model.

A more fruitful approach was to use alternative infectivity assumptions in the model to provide "what-if" predictions of the *proportion of clinical vCJD cases* that would have been caused by blood-borne (rather than primary) infection. This proportion should be independent of the (unknown) scale of the whole outbreak. After due allowance for posttransfusion survival, such "predictions" could be compared with the proportion of actual cases with any history of transfusion. Some of these might thus be attributable to blood-borne infection: subject to any possible underreporting, *none* of the others could be. At the time of analysis, only five out of the 113 known vCJD cases in the UK had any reported transfusion history. This fact provided an upper limit of about 4% to 5% for the actual proportion of cases seen by the end of 2002 that could be due to blood-borne transmission. This could then be compared with the "predictions" given by varying assumed primary and secondary incubation periods[1] and with alternative infectivity assumptions. Although these were rough calculations, infectivity scenarios that predicted *substantially* greater impacts from blood-borne transmission might be rejected—or at least treated with skepticism.

These "calibration" runs suggested that using the "DNV" scenario did indeed lead to exaggerated predictions of the proportion of vCJD cases that could have been blood-borne. (With some inputs on incubation periods, the model predicted that most of the known cases would have been due to blood-borne infection, which is clearly unrealistic.) Furthermore, this finding appeared to be quite robust, in that even a substantial reduction in the assumed level of infectivity would still lead to some "over prediction." This conclusion is unaltered by the subsequent discovery of cases thought to have resulted from a transfusion, as model predictions were for clinical cases appearing by the end of 2002 compared with a reality of up to five "possibles" at that time.

However, model results are strongly dependent on *when* blood-borne infectivity appears, within the incubation period. A substantial delay in the onset of infectivity would affect the timing, as well as the numbers, of blood-borne infections. Because earlier infections would be removed, there would be a disproportionate reduction in "earlier" secondary clinical cases. This would make it much easier to reconcile the model runs with the case data, no matter how high the levels of infectivity

---

[1] *The proportion of blood-borne clinical cases will obviously be reduced for shorter primary and longer secondary incubation periods. However, there are limits to biologic plausibility here: in particular, it appeared unsatisfactory to reconcile the model with the data by assuming secondary incubation periods to be typically longer than primary periods.*

close to the onset of vCJD symptoms in the donor. Delayed onset of infectivity is also broadly consistent with various animal
models already cited, although these do indicate infectivity
being present substantially prior to the onset of clinical symptoms. Consistency with the case data may also be enhanced if
differentials between genotypes are considered. All clinical
cases seen so far are MM homozygous at Codon 129, as are just
under 40% of the population: it may be that exposed individuals of other genotypes develop clinical symptoms much later
or remain in some asymptomatic "carrier state." These hypotheses are discussed further below. Here, the key point is
that for a blood-borne vCJD transmission to occur *and to be detectable as a linked pair of clinical cases* might then require both
donor *and* recipient to be MM homozygotes, *and* the donation
to have been given in the latter part of the donor's incubation
period, *and* the recipient to have survived long enough to develop symptoms. This is a rather unlikely combination of
events.

These arguments show that high levels of blood-borne infectivity cannot be dismissed purely because more blood-
borne transmissions have not been observed. (Similar caveats
apply to the recent case-control finding[27] that blood transfusion does not appear as a risk factor for clinical vCJD.) It remains a prudent working hypothesis that infected blood components may contain high doses per unit, from some point
partway through the donor's incubation period. This hypothesis also has a key practical implication. If infectivity in blood
appears partway through the incubation period (and if the primary incubation period is long), it follows that a larger proportion of blood-borne transmissions have yet to occur. The
risks of transmission will rise as any infected donors reach the
infective stage of their incubation period. However, these future infections could still be avoided in principle. So while the
impact of blood-borne transmission could still be significant,
it may also still be possible to prevent many of these transmissions—despite the time that has elapsed since most primary
infections probably occurred.

Returning to the specific question of excluding previously transfused donors, it was difficult to predict how many donations would be lost by such a step. The estimated impact on vCJD risks—saving roughly 3% to 16% of future blood-borne infections, depending on the scenario used—was significant but not overwhelming. The vCJD risk was also seen to be "theoretical," given that no human transmission via blood had yet been seen. As noted, this changed in late 2003 with the first discovery of vCJD in both donor and recipient. Given the modeling work already done, this changed the balance of risk in favor of recipient exclusion. Concerns about sufficiency of supply, although real, were mitigated by the blood services' development of contingency plans to build up stock and recruit new donors as necessary. The first step, implemented from April 2004, was to exclude would-be donors of whole blood who reported themselves as having been transfused since 1980. To mitigate the effect on supply, the ban did not initially cover those who reported being uncertain of their transfusion status or those donating via apheresis. As the situation was monitored over the next few months, it became clear that the loss of donors was manageable, so the exclusion was extended to those groups also.

It is noteworthy that the successful introduction of exclusion took place against a background of declining demand for blood, reversing a long-term rising trend. There are thought to be several reasons for this: for example, reduced need for blood with newer surgical practices and the deliberate policy of encouraging "appropriate use."[28] In the present context, the point is that any reduction in unnecessary use of blood has a double benefit. First, there is a direct and proportionate impact on the risks of spreading vCJD—or indeed any other transfusion-transmitted infection. Second, an easing of demand allows other risk-reduction measures—especially those restricting the donor base—to be taken with less danger of a shortage of supply.

At the same time as analyzing the exclusion of previously transfused donors, the transmission model was used to assess other risk-reduction measures. These included:

- the importation of Fresh Frozen Plasma (FFP)—ie, plasma transfused in complete units, as distinct from being used for fractionation.
- reducing the plasma content of both RBCs (by choice of separation process) and Platelets (by increasing the use of additive solution).
- increased use of apheresis to procure platelets, rather than pooling buffy coats from four separate donations.

All of these would help to reduce the risk of vCJD transmission in at least some scenarios, and modeling helped clarify when and to what extent any advantage would be gained. There are limits to the feasibility of each, but some measures have been implemented. For example, it was not possible to import all the UK's requirement for FFP, it was found to be both feasible and cost effective to import FFP for the youngest recipients (ie, those born after January 1, 1996). These recipients also generally have good life expectancy, further increasing the life-years saved by each infection prevented. Compared with the rest of the population, they should also have less existing risk of vCJD through food-borne exposure, given the precautions implemented by 1996 to protect the food chain from BSE. The decision to import FFP for these selected recipients was therefore taken, and fully implemented in Spring 2004. Subsequent decisions have extended the importation of FFP for use in older children (up to age 16) and certain groups of adults with conditions requiring high and repeated use of FFP.

Reducing the level of plasma in RBCs and Platelets will be of value in reducing vCJD transmission risk if infectivity is associated with plasma rather than red cells or platelets as such, and is *not so high* as to infect for certain, even after plasma content has been minimized. Although the benefit is far from certain, reducing plasma content is thus appropriate where it can be done easily and without compromising the therapeutic quality of the pack.

In certain high-infectivity scenarios, sourcing platelets via single-donor apheresis rather than pooling four donations decreases the overall risk of vCJD infection across the population of recipients. This is because if significant levels of infectivity are associated with platelets and/or plasma, the recipient of a pooled unit would receive a dose sufficient to infect if *any* of the contributing donors were infective. However, this differential disappears in scenarios with lower infectivity, because the increased donor exposure per pooled unit is offset by the decreased dose received if one of the four donations is infective. Within the UK blood services, efforts are under way to increase the proportion of units sourced via apheresis.

## Assessments for Individual Incidents

Some rather different considerations come into play in analyzing individual incidents, as distinct from more general risks to public health. These typically occur when someone subsequently found to have vCJD has undergone certain forms of surgery, or has donated blood, organs, or tissues. The CJD Incidents Panel (CJDIP) is an expert committee set up in 2000 by the Department of Health to help deal with such situations. It advises hospitals, trusts, and public health teams throughout the UK on how to manage incidents, producing both general guidance[29] and case-by-case advice. Its focus includes all forms of CJD, although only vCJD is considered relevant in the context of blood-borne transmission.

One key role for the Panel is to recommend when people who might be at heightened risk of vCJD infection should be notified. Notification allows additional precautions to be put in place against further onward transmission. Such individuals may be asked not to donate blood (note that it is not permissible simply to discard donated blood without telling the donor why), and if they need to undergo surgery that might pose a transmission risk, the instruments can be discarded or quarantined afterward rather than reused. Decisions about notification need to strike a difficult balance. On the one hand, notification allows a reduction of any further risk to public health. But for the individual receiving this potentially alarming information, notification may be harmful. The risk of being infected cannot be fully quantified, and vCJD is a disease for which there is as yet no diagnostic test routinely available or any proven treatment. There are some important lines of research on diagnosis and treatment, and notified individuals might benefit from these in the future. But meanwhile there is no positive action for them to take, and there may be worries about practical matters such as life insurance/mortgage eligibility (although steps have been taken with insurers to mitigate these). All this worry may be quite unnecessary, in the sense that the individual may well not be carrying the infection—and even if carrying the infection, may never develop the disease.

There are obvious communication issues here, and a good deal of effort is put into handling notifications as sensitively as possible. But there is also the logically prior question of what level of risk should warrant notification. The Panel has adopted a general principle that people estimated to be at greater risk of carrying vCJD than the general population should be notified *unless the estimated risk is clearly below 1%.* This threshold was chosen partly to provide a simple and consistent approach to incidents of different types, and because it is at least an order of magnitude above the likely "background" prevalence of vCJD within the population. However, it also represents an implicit judgment about the balance of public health gain versus possible distress to individuals. In effect, failing to notify someone who is infected is judged to be 100 times worse than notifying someone who is not.[#]

---

[#]*This ignores the public cost of tracing and notifying the individuals concerned, which in some cases is quite a difficult task.*

Blood-related incidents considered by the Panel have included some in which a transfused *component* has been sourced from a donor later found to have vCJD. In line with the "DNV" scenario for blood-borne infectivity, these recipients are treated as being at high risk of infection: all are notified provided they are still alive and can be traced. Unfortunately, the need for this approach has been confirmed by the fact that one of these recipients has since also developed symptoms of vCJD. This has dispelled any residual doubt about the reality of blood-borne transmission. At the time of writing, there are now two instances of recipients developing vCJD after exposure to blood from a preclinical vCJD case, and another in which the recipient died of unrelated causes but was found to have signs of sub- (or pre-) clinical infection.

For the much more numerous recipients of *plasma derivatives*, the picture is more complex and uncertain. The Panel has taken a highly precautionary approach, basing the decision to notify on the most "pessimistic" scenario among those suggested by DNV. More detailed modeling carried out by the Health Protection Agency is used to estimate the maximum dose that might have been received, bearing in mind that some recipients (eg, hemophiliacs) often require the product on a repeated basis and may have received several doses from the same production batch. Recipients of plasma derivatives comprise the largest group of individuals notified so far, even though all the incidents involved relate to the use of UK-sourced plasma prior to 1999.

These analyses are concerned with "forward" risk assessments—ie, estimating the possible consequences for recipients if a donor had vCJD. More recently, the Panel has also faced the "reverse" situation as in Fig 9-3, in which the transfusion recipient later develops vCJD, with the donor (or donors) so far remaining free of symptoms. The diagram shows a number of individuals, all assumed to be exposed to some risk of primary vCJD infection through diet. One has donated blood, and one recipient of that blood (in component form) has developed vCJD. However, that individual was presumably also

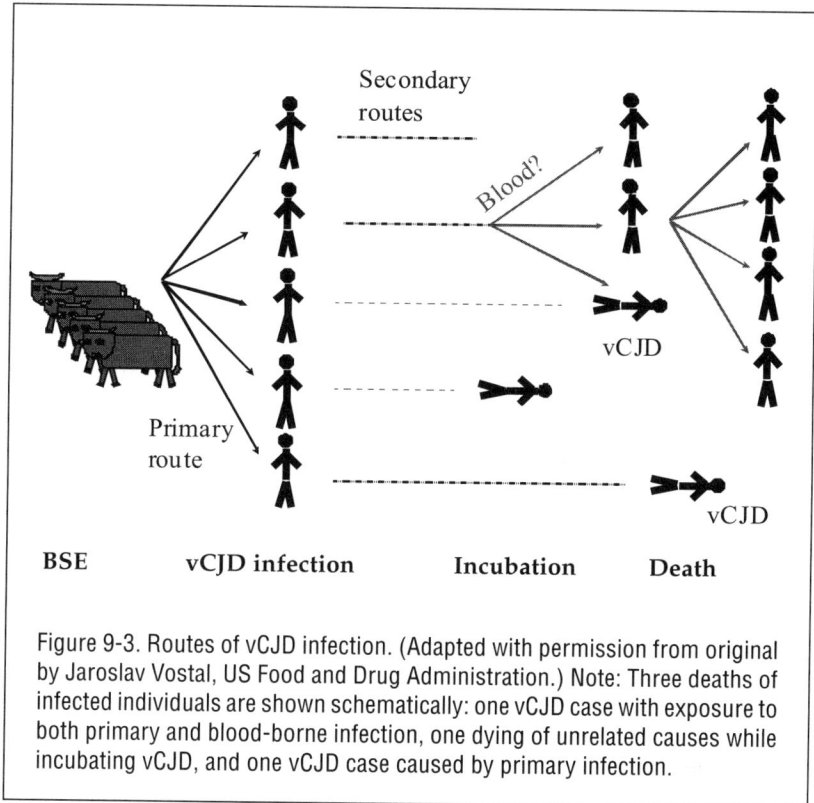

Figure 9-3. Routes of vCJD infection. (Adapted with permission from original by Jaroslav Vostal, US Food and Drug Administration.) Note: Three deaths of infected individuals are shown schematically: one vCJD case with exposure to both primary and blood-borne infection, one dying of unrelated causes while incubating vCJD, and one vCJD case caused by primary infection.

subject to dietary exposure to BSE, so there is no certainty that the infection was acquired via the donor. (Note that this is very different from the case in which both donor and recipient are found to be infected with vCJD.) The question here is whether such donors are at a high enough risk of carrying vCJD to warrant notification.

Clearly, a key consideration is the likelihood of the recipient's infection having come via the transfusion. This will depend on several factors, including the background risks of infection for both the recipient and the donor, and the chance of vCJD being passed to the recipient if the donor *is* infected. More formally, these probabilities are governed by the mathematics of *Bayes' Theorem*. This allows one to use the information of the recipient's infection to update the probability of the donor being infected. As shown in Fig 9-4, the theorem links the required probability—ie, the chance of the donor carrying vCJD infection *given that the recipient has vCJD* ("posterior probability" of D being infected given that R is)—with the following three factors:

- The chance of the donor being infected, given no information about the recipient (the "prior probability" of D being infected, regardless of whether R is).
- The chance of the recipient developing vCJD, regardless of whether the donor is infected (the total likelihood of R's infection occurring by any route).
- The chance of the recipient having vCJD if the donor is infected (the transmission probability, as calculated in the "forward" risk assessment).

Clearly, the chance of the donor being the source of the infection will depend on the infectivity scenario used. The implications for donors also depend critically on how many units the infected recipient had. The higher the number of donors, the greater the chance of the infection being blood-borne—but the smaller the chance of each individual donor being the source of infection. A more rigorous explanation of the model is provided at www.dh.gov.uk, but the basic logic can be set out as follows.

The simplest possible situation would be one in which an individual develops vCJD after receiving one unit of blood component from a single donor. To take the worst case, if the donor were infected, this would result in certain infection of the recipient (transmission probability = 1). Suppose also that there is nothing to differentiate the chance of this donor and this recipient being infected in the primary outbreak and that neither has any other known exposure, eg, via a surgical incident. It then follows that the recipient would be *equally likely* to have been infected directly through the dietary route or via the donor. Provided that the general prevalence in the population is low, the donor would have an implied risk of 0.5 of carrying vCJD.

*Prior Probability* = chance of hypothesis being true, prior to new event (evidence)

*Posterior Probability* = chance of hypothesis being true, after new event

*Likelihood ratio (for event)* = $\dfrac{\text{chance of event occurring if hypothesis is true}}{\text{"Total" chance of event occurring, regardless of hypothesis}}$

Then:

**Posterior Probability = Prior Probability * Likelihood Ratio**

In this context, let Prob [D] be the prior probability of D being infected. Then the probability of D being infected *given the event that R is* infected is given by:

**Prob [D/R] = Prob [D] * Prob [R/D] / Prob [R]**

Where Prob [R/D] is the chance of R being infected if D is and Prob [R] is the chance of R being infected anyway, regardless of whether D is.

Figure 9-4. Bayes' Theorem.

In reality, recipients are more usually transfused with more than one unit, each from a different donor. Extending the previous argument, and with the same simplifying assumptions, if someone with vCJD has received $n$ units of components (eg, red cells) from different donors, the chance of each individual donor carrying the infection is $1/(n+1)$. More formal use of Bayes' Theorem confirms these intuitive arguments and also allows modeling of more complex situations.

For example, suppose a recipient with vCJD has received blood from three donors, and the transmission probability from an infected donor is taken to be 0.5, rather than the worst case of 1. Let us also assume that the primary prevalence (p) is small, so there would be a negligible chance of being infected by more than one route. All else being equal, a first-order calculation is as follows:

- The prior probability of any individual donor being infected is simply p.
- If a given donor is infected, the probability of the recipient being infected is approximately 0.5.
- The total probability of the recipient being infected by any route (given no information about any of the donors) is approximately $3 \times 0.5\,p + p = 2.5\,p$.

So applying Bayes' Theorem as in Fig 9-4, the chance of each donor being infected, *given that the recipient is*, is $0.5 \times p\,/\,2.5\,p$ $= 0.2$. In other words, there would be a one in five chance of each individual donor being infected. Overall, there would be a three in five chance of the recipient's infection arising via transfusion, and a two in five chance of it having come from the primary outbreak.

There are also situations where recipients or donors might have different prior probabilities of being vCJD infected—eg, by not having been resident in the UK during the BSE outbreak. Or the recipient might have been transfused with a component from one donor and pooled products sourced from a number of others, leading to a different distribution of implied risk. In principle, the analysis can take further factors into account, for example the ages of recipients and donors, and their genotypes if known. The Panel has taken the view that insufficient evidence exists as yet about how these factors might affect the likelihood of vCJD infection. In the meantime, and using the Precautionary Principle, decisions should be based on there being a high risk of transmission. Nevertheless, the timing of the transfusion relative to the recipient's onset of symptoms is clearly relevant. Obviously, transfusion after the onset of symptoms cannot be the cause of an infection: the Panel has recommended that donations given less than a year prior to onset of symptoms should also be disregarded, as infection so close to onset would require an implausibly short incubation period. Perhaps most significantly, the model has helped explore the robustness of recommendations, by considering the implied risk for donors under a wide range of assumptions—especially as regards transmission probabilities.

To date, the Panel has had to consider three incidents involving donors of blood to recipients now known to be vCJD cases. Two of these recipients were each exposed to a few donors, while one was exposed to just over one hundred. The implied risk to donors in the first two groups clearly lay above 1% (unless the transmission probability is very small). The implied risk to each donor in the larger group lay just below 1%, but very close to the threshold if the transmission probability is assumed to be high. Given this, the Panel recommended that these donors should be traced and notified.

In each of these incidents, the donors in question had also given blood to other recipients. Since the 2004 exclusion of recipients from donating discussed earlier, these recipients should not pose an ongoing risk through blood donation. However, there might still be a risk of onward transmission via surgery. The chance of these individuals being infected can be modeled by a combination of the "reverse" risk assessment (to calculate the implied probability of each donor being infected) followed by a "forward" risk assessment (to calculate the probability of the infection being passed on). Results are more sensitive to the transmission probability than is the case

for the donors, as illustrated in Fig 9-5. This shows a hypotheti-
cal incident with 103 donors to a vCJD case. Fig 9-5A shows
how the implied risk of the donors being infected varies according to the assumed transmission probability (t): as can be

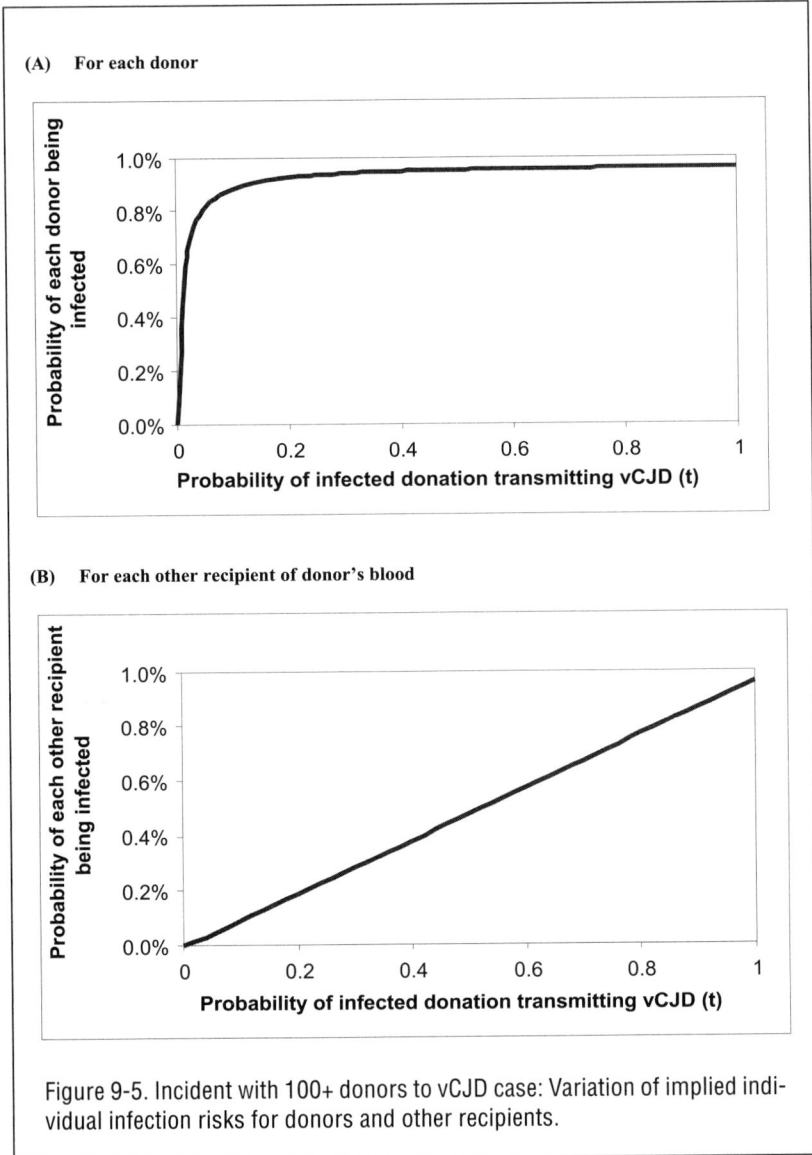

**(A)    For each donor**

**(B)    For each other recipient of donor's blood**

Figure 9-5. Incident with 100+ donors to vCJD case: Variation of implied individual infection risks for donors and other recipients.

seen, the estimated risk stays close to 1% as t is reduced from its "worst case" value of 1. By contrast, the implied risk to other recipients decreases much more rapidly (in fact, almost linearly) as t is reduced, as shown in Fig 9-5B. Based on these analyses, the Panel has recommended notifying only those recipients linked to the smaller groups of higher-risk donors. In part, this reflects the lower individual infection risks calculated for the recipients linked to the larger group. In addition, the balance between protection of public health and avoidance of individual anxiety is clearly somewhat different as between known donors (who may be highly likely to donate again) and recipients (who are now ineligible to donate).

## New Measures and Outstanding Issues

This chapter has presented an overview of the main issues tackled to date in the course of these risk assessments. Although more is known about vCJD than was the case even a few years ago, many key uncertainties remain. These affect the efficacy and cost-effectiveness both of measures already in place and potential new options.

A question on which all else depends is the prevalence of vCJD infection within the population in general and the donor base in particular. The original analysis made no specific assumption on this, and recent evidence has given cause for both optimism and renewed concern. For some while, deaths from vCJD have fallen year by year[30,31]—although 2004 saw an increase in new onsets. Independent efforts to model the primary outbreak mathematically have continued, and work on projected numbers of vCJD cases has given credence to less pessimistic scenarios. For example, published upper-limit predictions from the primary outbreak model developed at Imperial College (University of London) fell from an initial half-million cases to around 7,000 by 2002 and then to 540 by 2003.[32,33] Models produced elsewhere were also predicting fairly modest numbers of cases, as compared with earlier projections.[34,35]

However, these are projections of *clinical cases* rather than vCJD *infections*—the main driver for secondary transmission. The role of genetic factors remains unclear. As already noted, all vCJD cases seen so far are MM homozygotes at Codon 129. However, the second (presumed) blood-borne infection detected suggests that individuals of other genotypes are susceptible, at least for secondary transmission routes.[18] This lends weight to existing concerns that subsequent waves of clinical cases among other genotypes may be seen, although this remains speculative. Certainly, there is long-standing evidence both from animal models of prion diseases and from studies of kuru that differences in genotype can have significant effects on susceptibility and/or incubation periods.[36-39] (Individuals being less susceptible to clinical disease would not necessarily have a beneficial effect at a population level if they might still be infective.) Given that MM homozygotes make up a substantial minority of the population, susceptibility of the other groups would not necessarily imply a much larger overall outbreak.[40] The more basic concern is that while there might be a fairly small eventual number of primary cases, the number of primary infections might be significantly greater, feeding a larger secondary outbreak. This is given credence by a separate line of research testing stored tissue samples for prion protein accumulation. A retrospective study tested roughly 12,500 usable samples of appendix and tonsil tissue (mostly appendix). A single positive result in approximately 8000 was followed by two further positives in the full set.[41,42] These two show a pattern of prion accumulation unlike that seen in known vCJD cases, which raised some doubt as to their significance. However, the spleen samples taken from the recipient of vCJD-implicated blood show a similar pattern, making it more likely that the two appendix samples also indicate vCJD infection. Differences in appearance may be associated with different stages of incubation, or with genotypes, both these individuals being VV homozygotes.[43]

A smaller prospective study found no positives in 2000 tonsils sampled.[44] Collection of material for a much larger prospective study of tonsil samples has started, but the study is expected to take 2 years to complete. Meanwhile, the three positives found in the completed retrospective study suggest a best estimate for prevalence of just less than 1 in 4000, with a 95% confidence interval ranging from roughly 1 in 20,000 to 1 in 1400. These figures necessarily relate to the age cohort from which the samples were taken, mostly aged between 10 and 30 years at the time of their operations. This group may have been more heavily exposed to primary infection, making it overly pessimistic to apply the same figures to the whole population—the age distribution of primary infections being a research topic in its own right.[45,46] Conversely, the tissue survey would not necessarily have picked up all those carrying vCJD—although the risks of secondary transmission from patients with only localized prion accumulation might be less.

Clearly, significant uncertainties about prevalence of infection remain, and at present risk assessments generally consider illustrative scenarios of 1 in 1000, 1 in 10,000, and 1 in 100,000 across the UK population in general. In any case, the evidence from the retrospective survey can be reconciled only with small projected numbers of clinical cases by assuming that only a small minority of those infected ever go on to develop the disease. There is speculation that many might go into a long-term asymptomatic "carrier state," before eventually dying of other causes. If such individuals are nevertheless infective, the implications for secondary infection risks may be considerable. This concern is reinforced by very recent results[46] from experiments using transgenic mice expressing human PrP. These suggest that "for human-to-human vCJD infection, it should be assumed that all codon 129 genotype individuals (not just MM) can be infected, that long incubation times may occur and that a significant level of subclinical disease may be present in the population."

Aside from these longer-term concerns about the dynamics of vCJD, uncertainty about current prevalence makes it more difficult to evaluate the benefit of the two important new options that may soon become technically possible—the introduction of a screening test for vCJD and methods of removing prions more fully from donated blood. Vigorous research efforts are under way on both of these.

For the introduction of a screening test, one key issue is *specificity*—ie, the proportion of positive tests that are true indicators of infection. Unless specificity is *very* good—which would be unusual for any first-generation test—most of the "indicated positives" will actually be "false" rather than "true." The exact proportion is impossible to calculate against an unknown true prevalence of vCJD, but can be estimated for a range of scenarios. A test that yielded a large number of false-positive results could have an unacceptable impact on supply, as many donations would be unnecessarily discarded, as well as creating new dilemmas as to what to tell the donors concerned. It is therefore important that any screening test be used in conjunction with an independent confirmatory test applied to donations initially testing positive. In preparation for screening tests being offered commercially, the UK blood services have set up a Test Assessment Facility, with a large bank of samples against which the specificity of proposed tests can be evaluated.

Another key area of scientific innovation is the development of prion removal technologies to remove any residual vCJD infectivity from blood. Evaluation of these is subject to specific questions as to the most appropriate scenario for infectivity. In particular, it becomes of critical importance to consider how much of the infectivity in a donated unit would be associated with each component—while also remembering that components are not transfused in their pure form. For example, one model is of the infective dose per unit being split roughly evenly between leukocytes and plasma, with none associated with "pure" platelets[48] or red cells. In this view, the existing leukocyte reduction process would remove (almost all) cell-associated infectivity, but not that associated with the plasma.[49] The benefit of any new technology would then depend critically on its ability to remove the infective agent from the plasma—including the residual plasma present in units of

RBCs and Platelets. However, this is only one scenario, so far based primarily on rodent models. The situation would be very different were it to transpire that human blood can carry infectivity in "pure" red cells or platelets.

Aside from the scientific uncertainties involved, the cost-effectiveness of both screening tests and prion removal depends critically on the existing prevalence of infection. But the potential benefits of the two options are also interdependent: the introduction of either would reduce the benefit to be gained from the other. To that extent, these options compete with each other—unless some way is found of combining the two.

Three further factors affecting the dynamics of secondary infection warrant mention here. The first, already noted briefly, is the potential compounding effect of different transmission routes. While acknowledged in the existing dynamic models (and explored on a what-if basis), this is particularly difficult to quantify. For example, the chance of someone infected via blood or surgery going on to infect others will depend on how the probability of receiving blood affects, and is affected by, the chance of undergoing surgery on some separate occasion. To clarify this requires better longitudinal data on patients' long-term medical/clinical experiences. However, it is worth noting that because roughly half of all blood components are used in the course of surgery, exclusion of previously transfused donors should have the additional benefit of reducing any onward infection risk from donors infected via surgery.

A second, more specific point relates to the efficacy of the exclusion of previously transfused donors. As there is no centralized record of historical transfusions, exclusion is reliant on intending donors' self-reporting of transfusion status. Although this is true of other eligibility criteria for donation, self-reporting of transfusion status must be subject to strong caveats—especially for those who may have been transfused during surgery. For example, someone transfused while under anesthesia may be genuinely unaware of having received blood, and it is not universal practice to inform patients after the event. Others may simply forget, particularly given other pressures associated with undergoing surgery. The exclusion of those who report themselves as uncertain about their transfusion status addresses this issue to some extent. Nevertheless, those responding in this way when the measure was introduced were much fewer than anticipated from previous donor surveys. Some of these donors may have decided to exclude themselves prior to completing a health check questionnaire, and some individuals are known to have tried checking their records with their general practitioners. However, the main point is that without some systematic way of checking the reliability of self-reporting, it would be rash to assume 100% compliance.

A final topic currently under investigation concerns the distribution of blood-borne risks among individuals. Crudely, the additional exposure to vCJD infection for any recipient of blood components will be proportional to the number of units received. On blood service estimates, the median number of units per recipient is in the region of 3 to 4. However, this figure disguises a very skewed distribution. Some individuals receive many units of blood, often over a number of transfusion episodes. Examples include patients with thalassemia, who may need lifelong treatment, and those with thrombotic thrombocytopenic purpura (TTP). Such patients may receive blood components from hundreds of donors. It might be expected that patients receiving many units of blood would have poorer posttransfusion survival, and this may well be true of those undergoing surgical procedures—eg, organ transplants or treatment for massive accidental trauma. However, some groups (eg, TTP patients) are often relatively young and have good life expectancy. If someone in such a group were to be infected with vCJD, they might well survive long enough to develop the disease. Initial investigation in collaboration with the blood services suggests that most highly transfused individuals are hematology rather than surgical patients, with about 30% surviving more than 2 years. Further investigation is under way to clarify posttransfusion survival for different groups. Pending further research, the Incidents Panel has recommended that special precautions to prevent further onward transmission (via surgery) should apply to individuals exposed to 80 or more donors through transfusion of blood components. Meanwhile, these preliminary findings also suggest that the initial incident involving over 100 donors to a single recipient may not be as unusual as it first appeared.

To conclude, analysis of blood-borne vCJD risk remains a challenging task, both at an individual and a population level. This is an area in which there are some significant new policy options on the horizon, but many fundamental unknowns persist. The need to find proportionate responses in the face of uncertainty is likely to remain, as will the role of analysis in helping to make these responses as robust as possible.

# References

1. Department of Health (UK). Risk assessment for transmission of vCJD via surgical instruments: A modelling approach and numerical scenarios. London: Department of Health, 2001. [Available at http://www.dh.gov.uk.]
2. Department of Health (UK). Assessing the risk of vCJD transmission via surgery: An interim review. London: Department of Health, 2005. [Available at http://www.dh.gsi.gov.uk.]
3. Bennett PG, Hare A, Townshend J. Assessing the risk of vCJD transmission via surgery: Models for uncertainty and complexity. J Operat Res Soc 2005;56:202-13.
4. Department of Health (UK). Risk assessment for vCJD and dentistry. London: Department of Health, 2003. [Available at http://www.dh.gov.uk.]
5. Food and Drug Administration. Guidance for industry. Revised preventive measures to reduce the possible risk of transmission of Creutzfeldt-Jakob Disease (CJD) and variant Creutzfeldt-Jakob Disease (vCJD) by blood and blood products. Rockville, MD: CBER Office of Communication, Training, and Manufacturers Assistance, 2002. [Available at http://www.fda.gov/cber/gdlns/cjdvcjd.htm.]
6. Food and Drug Administration. Draft risk assessment: Potential exposure to the vCJD agent in United States recipients of Factor XI coagulation product manufactured in the United Kingdom. Rockville, MD: CBER Office of Communication, Training, and Manufacturers Assistance, 2005. [Available at http://www.fda.gov/ohrms.]
7. Anderson S. Risk analysis for TSE and plasma derivatives. Presented for the TSE Advisory Committee, Gaithersburg, MD, February 20,

2003. [Available at http://www.fda.gov/ohrms/dockets/ac/03 (accessed March 2, 2006).]

8. Public Health Agency of Canada. A cursory analysis addressing the question of the assessment of exposure to particular batches of variant Creutzfeldt-Jakob disease (vCJD) implicated Factor XI plasma product. Ottawa, Canada: Public Health Agency, 2005. [Available at http://www.phac-aspc.gc.ca.]

9. Agence Française de Securité Sanitaire des Produits de Santé. Risk analysis of new variant Creutzfeldt-Jakob disease transmission by blood and blood products. Paris: Agence Française de Securité Sanitaire des Produits de Santé, 2000. [Available at http://agmed.sante.gouv.fr/ang/pdf/mcj02.pdf.]

10. European Medicines Agency. CPMP position statement on Creutzfeldt-Jakob disease and plasma-derived and urine-derived medicinal products. London: European Medicines Agency, 2004. [Available at http://www.emea.eu.int.]

11. Australian Health Ministers' Advisory Council on Blood and Blood Products Committee. Report of the Working Party on the Supply and Use of Factor VIII and Factor IX in Australia. Canberra, Australia: Health Ministry, 2003. [Available at http://www.nba.gov.au.]

12. Brown P, Cervenakova L, McShane LM, et al. Further studies of blood infectivity in an experimental model of transmissible spongiform encephalopathy, with an explanation of why blood components do not transmit Creutzfeldt-Jakob disease in humans. Transfusion 1999; 39:1169-78.

13. Houston F, Foster JD, Chong A, et al. Transmission of BSE by blood transfusion in sheep. Lancet 2000;356:999-1000.

14. Ironside JW, Head MW. Variant Creutzfeldt-Jacob disease and its transmission by blood. J Thromb Haemost 2003;1:1479-86.

15. Hunter N, Foster J, Chong A, et al. Transmission of prion diseases by blood transfusion. J Gen Virol 2002;83:2897-905.

16. Llewelyn CA, Hewitt PE, Knight RS, et al. Possible transmission of variant CJD by blood transfusion. Lancet 2004;363:417-21.

17. Peden AH, Head MW, Ritchie DL, et al. Preclinical vCJD after blood transfusion in a PRNP codon 129 heterozygous patient. Lancet 2004; 363:527-9.

18. Det Norske Veritas for the Department of Health (UK). Risk assessment of exposure to vCJD infectivity in blood and blood products. London: DNV Consulting, 2003. [Available at http://www.dnv.com/binaries/vCJD_Update_Report_tcm4-74414.pdf (accessed April 19, 2006).]

19. Brown P, Rohwer RG, Dunstan BC, et al. The distribution of infectivity in blood components and plasma derivatives in experimental models of transmissible spongiform encephalopathies. Transfusion 1998;38:810-16.

20. Foster P. Removal of TSE agents from blood products. Vox Sang 2004; 87(Suppl 2):S7-10.

21.  Forrester JW. Principles of systems. Cambridge, MA: MIT Press, 1968.
22.  Senge PM. The fifth discipline. New York: Doubleday, 1990.
23.  Wolstenholme EW. System enquiry. Chichester, UK: Wiley, 1990.
24.  Dangerfield BC, Roberts CA, eds. Special issue: Health and health care dynamics. System Dynamics Review 1999;15(3).
25.  Vamvakas EC, Taswell HF. Long-term survival after blood transfusion. Transfusion 1994;34:471-7.
26.  National Blood Service/Medical Research Council. Transfusion medicine epidemiology pilot study report. (NBA Grant Award BS00/ RB00). Cambridge, UK: NBS/MRC Clinical Studies Unit, 2002.
27.  Ward HJT, Everington D, Cousens S, et al. Risk factors for variant Creutzfeldt-Jakob disease: A case-control study. Ann Neurol 2006; 59:111-20.
28.  Department of Health (UK). Better blood transfusion: Appropriate use of blood. Health Service Circular HSC 2002/009. London: Department of Health, 2002.
29.  CJD Incidents Panel. Management of possible exposure to CJD through medical procedures: A consultation paper. London: Department of Health, 2001.
30.  Andrews NJ, Farrington CP, Ward HJ, et al. Deaths from variant Creutzfeldt-Jacob disease in the UK. Lancet 2003;361:751-2.
31.  Andrews NJ. Incidence of variant Creutzfeldt-Jacob disease onsets and deaths in the UK. London: Statistics Unit, CDSC, Health Protection Agency, 2005.
32.  Ghani A, Ferguson NM, Donnelly CA, Anderson RM. Factors determining the pattern of the variant Creutzfeldt-Jakob disease (vCJD) epidemic in the UK. Proc Biol Sci 2003;270:689-98.
33.  Ghani A, Donnelly CA, Ferguson NM, Anderson RM. Updated projections of future vCJD deaths in the UK. BMC Infect Dis 2003;3:4.
34.  d'Aignaux JN, Cousens SN, Smith PG. Predictability of the UK variant Creutzfeldt-Jakob disease epidemic. Science 2001;294:1729-31.
35.  Valleron AJ, Boelle PY, Will R, Cesbron JY. Estimation of epidemic size and incubation time based on age characteristics of vCJD in the United Kingdom. Science 2001;294:1726-8.
36.  Cervenakova L, Goldfarb LG, Garruto R, et al. Phenotype-genotype studies in kuru: Implications for new variant Creutzfeldt-Jakob disease. Proc Natl Acad Sci U S A 1998;95:13239-41.
37.  Lee HS, Brown P, Cervenakova, L, et al. Increased susceptibility to kuru of carriers of the PRNP 129 methionine/methionine genotype. J Infect Dis 2001;183:192-6.
38.  Cervenakova L, Yakovleva O, McKenzie C, et al. Similar levels of infectivity in the blood of mice infected with human-derived vCJD and GSS strains of transmissible spongiform encephalopathy. Transfusion 2003;34:1687-94.
39.  Hill AF, Collinge J. Subclinical prion infection in humans and animals. Br Med Bull 2003;66:161-70.

40. Clarke P, Ghani AC. Projections of the future course of the primary vCJD epidemic in the UK: Inclusion of subclinical infection and the possibility of wider genetic susceptibility. J R Soc Med 2005;2:19-31.

41. Hilton D, Ghani A, Conyers L, et al. Accumulation of prion protein in tonsil and appendix: Review of tissue samples. BMJ 2002;325:633-4.

42. Hilton D, Ghani A, Conyers L, et al. Prevalence of lymphoreticular prion protein accumulation in UK tissue samples. J Pathol 2004;203: 733-9.

43. Ironside JW, Bishop MT, Conolly K, et al. Variant Creutzfeldt-Jakob disease: Prion protein genotype analysis of positive appendix tissue samples from a retrospective prevalence study. BMJ 2006;332:1186-8. (Epub 2006 April 10.) [Available at http://bmj.bmjjournals.com/cgi/content/full/332/7551/1186 (accessed May 22, 2006).]

44. Frosh A, Smith L, Jackson C, et al. Analysis of 2000 consecutive UK tonsillectomy specimens for disease-related prion protein. Lancet 2004;364:1260-2.

45. Cooper JD, Bird SM. Predicting incidence of vCJD from UK dietary exposure to BSE for the 1940 to 1969 and post-1969 birth cohorts. Int J Epidemiol 2003;32:684-791.

46. Boelle PY, Cesbron JY, Valleron AJ. Epidemiological evidence of higher susceptibility to vCJD in the young. BMC Infect Dis 2004;4:26 [Available at http://www.biomedcentral.com/1471-2334/4/26 (accessed March 2, 2006).]

47. Bishop MT, Hart P, Aitchison L, et al. Predicting susceptibility and incubation time of human-to-human transmission of vCJD. Lancet Neurol 2006;5:393-8.

48. Holada K, Vostal JG, Theisen PW, et al. Scrapie infectivity in hamster blood is not associated with platelets. J Virol 2002;76:4649-50.

49. Gregori L, McCombie N, Palmer D, et al. Effectiveness of leucoreduction for removal of infectivity of transmissible spongiform encephalopathies from blood. Lancet 2004;364:529-31.

In: Turner ML, ed.
*Creutzfeldt-Jakob Disease: Managing the Risk of
Transmission by Blood, Plasma, and Tissues*
Bethesda, MD: AABB Press, 2006

# 10

# Risk Management in the Face of Uncertainty

## MARC L. TURNER, MB, CHB, PHD, FRCP, FRCPATH

SEVERAL KEY UNCERTAINTIES and assumptions remain with respect to assessment of the potential risk of transmission of transmissible spongiform encephalopathies (TSEs) or prion diseases by blood, plasma, cell and tissue products, and organs in humans.

## The Nature of the Infectious Agent

In Chapter 1 of this book, Wadsworth and Collinge review the molecular pathology of prion diseases, and, in Chapter 2, Bruce reviews the data on peripheral pathogenesis. These two chapters reflect the continuing dialogue in the field between different approaches to establishing the nature of the infectious agent. To what extent should this debate concern those of us charged with the assessment and management of risk in

*Marc L. Turner, MB, ChB, PhD, FRCP, FRCPath, Senior Lecturer in Immuno-
hematology and Transfusion Medicine, University of Edinburgh, and Clinical Director, Edinburgh Blood Transfusion Centre, Edinburgh, United Kingdom*

blood services? The molecular characteristics of the infectious agent affect the pathophysiology of the disease—ie, the rate at, and mechanism by which, the infection develops and spreads; the distribution of infectivity in blood, plasma, and tissues (see Chapters 4 and 8); the extent to which infectivity is detectable in blood and peripheral tissues and, in particular, the degree of correspondence between abnormal conformation of the prion protein and infectivity (see Chapter 5); and the extent to which transmissibility is likely to be mitigated by risk-reduction measures such as leukocyte reduction (see Chapter 6). Differences in the methods used to assess the level of infectivity affect the assumptions that underpin risk assessment and risk management.

## The Prevalence and Distribution of Subclinical Disease in the Donor Population

Ironside reviews the clinical and neuropathologic features of human TSEs in Chapter 3. In sporadic Creutzfeldt-Jakob disease (CJD), there is little evidence overall of a prolonged subclinical phase of disease, although incubation periods in iatrogenically transmitted sporadic CJD can range from a median of 2 years for centrally transmitted disease to 13 to 15 years for disease transmitted peripherally via cadaveric pituitary hormones. This large span suggests the potential presence of a cohort of subclinically infected persons who either have not yet developed or may never develop clinical neurologic disease. The latter persons are, however, relatively easy to define on the basis of exposure to neurosurgical instrumentation or high-risk tissue products (see Chapter 8).

Historically, it proved very difficult to assess the likely incidence of variant CJD (vCJD) on the basis of the magnitude of the bovine spongiform encephalopathy (BSE) epidemic, because the extent of transmissibility of BSE between cattle and man was (and remains) uncertain. Early projections, which were based on the incidence of clinical vCJD, showed very wide confidence limits because of the small number of cases.

The future incidence of clinical disease is now projected within much narrower confidence limits, although recent small increases in numbers and geographic dispersion are of some concern.

However, two important discrepancies in the epidemiologic data require explanation. The first of these discrepancies is the observation that the average age at onset of clinical vCJD has not altered over the past decade, as would be expected if all persons were subject to infection at a similar point in time. The mathematical models that best fit this observation[1] suggest an age-related susceptibility or exposure between the ages of 10 and 20 years; a cohort of that age in the past decade would now be aged 25 and 35 years and will gradually progress through the donor population. The second discrepancy is that current projections of the likely future incidence of clinical vCJD are inconsistent with those based on a retrospective study of tonsils and appendixes in the United Kingdom (UK).[2] Again, the mathematical models that best fit these data at present suggest that 90% to 95% of infected persons could have long-term preclinical or true subclinical disease,[1,3,4] which potentially is related to heterozygosity or valine homozygosity at codon 129 of the *PRNP* gene. This finding would be consistent with some of the experimental data[5] and also with clinical findings in some other human prion diseases, such as kuru, and in the human growth hormone transmissions, although, in these conditions, there was early dovetailing of heterozygotes with homozygotes, which has not happened with vCJD. More definitive data on the prevalence of subclinical vCJD are awaited from a prospective study of tonsils and appendices in the UK and smaller-scale ongoing studies in other countries (M Glatzel, personal communication).

In the meantime, extrapolation from current clinical vCJD data would suggest that the prevalence of subclinical disease is likely to be higher in Scotland than in England, that the Republic of Ireland may have a prevalence 25% of that in the UK (2 indigenous cases per 3 million population, which equates to ≈40 cases in a population of 60 million), and that the prevalence in France is 10% of that in the UK (17 cases in a population of 60 million). The presence of single cases (or the absence of cases) does not permit predictions about the prevalence of subclinical disease in other countries, but it is likely to be significantly lower than that in the above-noted countries. Further studies of the prevalence of subclinical disease in other affected countries would inform these estimates and provide a more accurate basis for risk assessment. Such risk assessments are a primary consideration in decisions about donor exclusion criteria (those based on geographic criteria or on previous blood component exposure) and on the costs and benefits of implementing risk-reduction measures such as universal leukocyte reduction, prion-reduction filters, or vCJD assays (see below).

## Distribution of Infectivity in the Peripheral Tissues in Prion Diseases

Brown reviews the data on blood infectivity in Chapter 4. In addition, the World Health Organization recently reviewed the distribution of infectivity and PrP$^{TSE}$ in peripheral tissues and organs in vCJD and other human TSEs and in naturally and experimentally infected animal TSEs (see Chapter 8, Tables 8-3, 8-5, and 8-6). Many tissues have not yet been tested. In addition, there are significant limitations in the sensitivity of the available assays. For biologic assays, intracranial injection limits the amount of tissue that can be assayed, which leads to the requirement for large numbers of animals to detect low levels of infectivity.[6-8] In human disease, there is the additional difficulty of a species barrier between the person and the test animal, which further reduces the sensitivity of detection of infectivity. Most biochemical assays are below the level of sensitivity of infectivity assays (see Chapter 5). The current working assumption is that the level of infectivity in the peripheral blood during the incubation period is in the order of two intravenous median infectious doses $(ID_{50})/mL$[6,7] or one infectious dose $(ID)/mL$.[8]

The spatial distribution of infectivity among different components of blood remains somewhat uncertain. Two sets of studies pertain. Brown et al[6,7] used the Fukuoka 1 strain of Gerstmann-Sträussler-Scheinker disease in mice and a separation technique that mimics to a certain extent that used in the United States for clinical blood component separation. They found a level of infectivity in the buffy coat (containing both the leukocytes and platelets) 4 to 5 times that in the plasma. Gregori et al,[8] in studying purified components in the 236K hamster scrapie model, concluded both that red cells and platelets themselves have very little associated infectivity and that ≈60% of the infectivity was associated with the plasma and 40% with the leukocytes. Further work (RG Rohwer, personal communication) suggested that most of the leukocyte-associated infectivity can in fact be washed off and that up to 95% of the infectivity may be plasma based. These possibilities raise two interesting and important points. First, infectivity does not track normal prion protein expression in relevant animal models.[9] Second, as suggested by Silveira et al,[10] maximum infectivity in hamster brain homogenates is associated with particles estimated to contain only 14 to 28 PrP molecules. This hypothesis is consistent with the data from Brown et al[6,7] showing no effect of leukocyte reduction on plasma infectivity and data from Gregori et al[8] suggesting that leukocyte reduction removes only 40% to 70% of whole blood infectivity.

It is not known how infectivity develops in humans during the incubation period. As Bennett and Dobra point out in Chapter 9, there are three a priori possibilities. The first of these possibilities, that infectivity is very low during the incubation period and does not begin to rise until clinical disease develops, is not consistent with either experimental animal data or sheep and human clinical transmissions (see below). The two remaining scenarios—a linear increase during the incubation period and an early increase followed by a plateau—are both plausible and difficult to resolve on the basis of current experimental data. However, the first scenario is a more conservative assumption from a risk assessment and management perspective because it suggests that 1) fewer transmissions would occur in the earlier than in the later part of the incubation period, 2) the small number of clinical transmissions observed thus far may be superseded by those still to come, and 3) there is therefore much at stake in putting in place further precautionary measures as they become available.

## Transmissibility of Prion Diseases by Blood and Tissues

Transmission of infection by the transfusion of blood drawn from a person during both the incubation and clinical phases of the disease has been shown in sheep naturally infected with scrapie and experimentally infected with BSE.[11] In sporadic CJD, there are a handful of reports of patients who developed CJD after exposure to blood transfusion, but these reports are poorly substantiated in terms of establishing a link with CJD in the donor. In comparison, over the past 25 years, a large number of epidemiologic case-control, look-back, and surveillance studies have shown no statistically significant linkage between CJD and blood transfusion, no greater risk of sporadic CJD in patients exposed to blood components or plasma products from donors who have developed sporadic CJD, and no increase in the incidence of CJD in sentinel populations, such as hemophiliacs who have received large volumes of plasma products.[12] Clearly, CJD is a rare disease, however, and occasional cases of transmission could be missed by these studies.

The Transfusion Medicine Epidemiology Review was established in the UK to track potential linkages between CJD in donors and recipients. In the forward arm, when subjects develop CJD, the Blood Services are notified, so that they can establish whether the person has been a blood donor; if so, the recipients of his or her blood are traced and informed. In the reverse arm, it is checked whether subjects who develop CJD have themselves received blood; if so, their donors are traced and notified. Again, no link has been described between sporadic or familial CJD in donors and recipients. However, 18 blood donors have gone on to develop vCJD and, of the 66 identifiable recipients of their blood (26 of whom are still alive), 2 have developed vCJD and 1 had evidence of subclinical infection at postmortem (she died of an unrelated condition) (see Chapter 4). The clinical transmissibility of variant CJD by blood components is therefore established beyond doubt. Although 9 of the above 18 donors also contributed to 23 plasma pools, from which 174 plasma product batches were manufactured before the UK moved to the use of imported plasma in 1999, no recipients of the implicated products thus far have developed clinical vCJD, although all are treated as "potentially at risk for public health purposes."

Cells, tissues, and organs are transplanted much more rarely than blood components are transfused, and many of these components are derived from brain-stem-dead or non-heart-beating donors. Without systematic testing of neural or lymphoid tissues, it is not possible to know whether such persons were incubating vCJD at the time of death (see Chapter 8). As far as can be ascertained, no patients who have developed vCJD have received cell, tissue, or organ transplants. As noted in Chapters 8 and 9, the mass of tissue transferred during a blood transfusion or tissue or organ transplant is normally so large that a very low concentration of infectivity (per mL or g of tissue), well below the level of sensitivity of current assays, would suffice to transmit infection by the transplanted tissue as a whole. Therefore, negative infectivity or biochemical assays cannot be interpreted as meaning that the disease is not transmissible via this route. The transmission of clinical vCJD by blood components in the absence of detectable infectivity by bioassay reinforces this argument. The UK Blood Services are conducting a study of the feasibility of using Western blot to test tonsil tissue from cadaver donors to ascertain whether that approach could be used to screen the cadaver donor population for preclinical vCJD. Clearly, such testing would not be applicable to live donors or to organ transplant donors, because transplantation normally proceeds within several hours of the death of the donor.

# Risk Management Approaches

In the face of the significant uncertainties outlined above, the most appropriate risk management approaches are those that have some impact over a wide range of plausible scenarios, as noted in Chapter 9.

## Donor Selection

Risk management through donor selection criteria is driven by the likelihood of a different prevalence of subclinical disease in specific sectors of the population. Such groups may be defined on the basis of geography, age, lifestyle, or exposure to specific surgical or medical procedures. The limitations of such measures are driven by the "sensitivity" (ie, the likelihood that such persons will be identified or will identify themselves) and the "specificity" (ie, the extent to which subclinical disease is associated with the sector of the population circumscribed by the deferral criterion) of the criterion.

Residence in the UK and, to a lesser extent, in Ireland, France, and other Western European countries is clearly a risk factor in terms of the likely higher prevalence of subclinical disease in the donor population, and this risk is reflected in the donor exclusion criteria applied by many other countries. Most countries apply a cumulative deferral criterion predicated on the differential risk in the target population compared to the general population, which is balanced against the negative impact on the blood donor base, which in turn is determined by the frequency with which residents in the country in question visit the UK and their average duration of stay. Most countries have applied a phased approach to manage donor loss.

In the UK itself, apart from a small cluster around Leicester and the different prevalence in the northern and southern parts of the UK, no clear high-risk epidemiologic groups have been identified. As discussed by Bennett and Dobra (see Chapter 9), mathematical modeling suggests that blood transfusion in and of itself is unlikely to give rise to a self-sustaining outbreak, but it is possible that compounding with other routes of transmission (eg, tissue transplantation and surgical or medical instrumentation) could do so. To reduce the risk of tertiary and higher-order transmissions and the possibility of a self-sustaining outbreak, the confirmation of clinical transmission of vCJD by blood transfusion led to the deferral of donors who have definitely or probably received blood components. In the UK, this step led to a loss of 5% to 10% of blood donations.

However, one ought to be mindful that donor selection remains, at best, a blunt tool, because of genuine ignorance and failures of recollection among donors; for example, some studies reveal up to 20% inconsistency in answering questions about blood donation history (P Hewitt, personal communication). Additional measures therefore are clearly necessary.

## Blood Donor Screening Assays

Several approaches to the detection of subclinical vCJD in donor populations are under development, as reviewed by Minor and Brown in Chapter 5. Broadly, these can be divided into surrogate assays, biochemical assays for abnormal prion protein (PrP$^{TSE}$), and infectivity assays. Surrogate markers represent nonspecific evidence of neurologic or peripheral tissue dysfunction, and, as such, their sensitivity and specificity for subclinical human TSEs are likely to be poor. Nevertheless, under some circumstances, they could represent a first-pass deferral criterion.

Much research is focused on the detection of PrP$^{TSE}$ (see Chapter 5). The sensitivity of such assays is a major challenge: on the basis of a comparison of the amounts of infectivity and PrP$^{TSE}$ in hamster brain, it has been estimated that the threshold of detection may need to be as low as 0.1 to 0.01 pg/mL.

However, it was pointed out that different tissues and different species could show different ratios that result in a less stringent threshold. Specificity is also a significant problem, in that, broadly speaking, it has proved difficult to generate monoclonal antibodies with a sufficiently high degree of specificity to the abnormal conformer. Many assays therefore rely upon differential proteinase digestion of PrP, although that may not correlate well with infectivity. Recent data suggest that infectivity can be present in the absence of PrP$^{TSE}$ and that PrP$^{TSE}$ can also be present in the absence of infectivity or clinical disease, which would indicate that the relationship between the abnormal conformer and infectivity is not simple (J Manson, personal communication). Figure 10-1 outlines the theoretical position of implementing an assay with 99% sensitivity and specificity; one can see that, although small numbers of persons would be missed because of the lack of sensitivity (negative predictive value, 99.99989%), the relative lack of specificity (positive predictive value, 0.98%) would lead to large numbers of false-positive donors.

The general approach to blood donor screening involves the use of assays with a high degree of sensitivity in an effort to miss as few true positives as possible and compensate for the relatively low level of specificity by using confirmatory as-

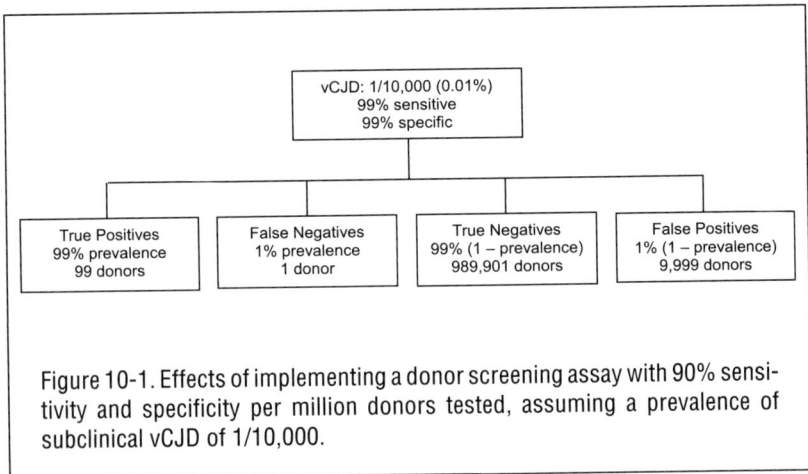

Figure 10-1. Effects of implementing a donor screening assay with 90% sensitivity and specificity per million donors tested, assuming a prevalence of subclinical vCJD of 1/10,000.

says—ie, assay techniques based on methods other than that of the screening assay. The need, therefore, is not merely for a single assay but for a series of assays, including some that show infectivity in vitro, in vivo, or both.

This need brings up a further series of considerations, including the problem of validating such assays. Normally, validation is carried out by using blood from patients known to have the disease in question, but people with subclinical vCJD are, by definition, currently not identifiable as CJD patients. It seems unlikely that large numbers of persons with clinical vCJD will be available for or capable of donating large volumes of blood; therefore, much of the development and validation of assays will have to be carried out on spiked brain homogenates and/or endogenously infected animal models. Given the issues concerning the applicability and relevance of spiking studies to endogenous infectivity and the known variations in the level and distribution of infectivity between different strains of TSE in different species of animals, assays will have to be evaluated and cross-referenced against several models if a generalizable evaluation is to be carried out.

Finally, the impact of screening (among both the donor population as a whole and those who test positive) should be considered. Doubt will exist about the applicability of the assay to human disease, about the discrimination of false positives from true positives, and about the implications of a true-positive result for the patient. Donors have to be informed both that they are to be screened and that they had a positive result when one arises, even though the implications of the result may be uncertain. The psychological and social effects on such persons are likely to be high, which reinforces the need for deeper consideration of the ethical issues and provision of adequate counseling and support resources.

## Blood Component and Tissue Processing

In Chapter 6, Cardigan and Williamson discuss current and potential future blood component procurement and processing methods. It is relatively clear that, in most scenarios, a reduction in exposure to leukocytes and plasma is likely to reduce the level of infectivity. Universal leukocyte reduction has been implemented in a number of countries on the basis of the assumption that, if infectivity is present in blood, it would most likely be associated with the mononuclear leukocytes. The evidence suggests that this is only partially true (see above) and that leukocyte reduction is likely to have only a partial impact on the level of infectivity and perhaps a small or negligible impact on transmission rates.

Reduction in exposure to plasma may have an additional impact; in the UK, this possibility has led to the importation of Fresh Frozen Plasma for use in children under the age of 16 years, and some high-risk groups, such as patients with thrombotic thrombocytopenic purpura, who are exposed to large volumes of plasma. Blood component processing can reduce residual plasma through the suspension of red cells in an optimal additive solution, leading to 10 to 20 mL residual plasma per component. Given that it is estimated that there are 2 intravenous $ID_{50}$/mL of infectivity in plasma, there would still be sufficient infectivity to transmit disease to the recipient.

Two companies are developing prion-reduction filters for red cell concentrates that promise a reduction up to an additional 3 log in infectivity. Risk assessment suggests that such a reduction would have a significant impact on the risk of transmission of the disease, particularly if associated with leukocyte and plasma reduction. However, there are downsides, including the loss of an additional 40 to 50 mL of blood in the dead volume of the additional filter, which could lead to the need for extra transfusions in some patients and have a potential negative effect on the quality and safety of the product itself. Again, there are concerns about the evaluation of these technologies and their applicability to the human situation, given that they have been developed with the use of spiked homogenates and endogenous infectivity in animal models. The UK Blood Services have developed a series of quality, efficacy, and operational specifications, and they intend to carry out an independent evaluation using spiked 263K hamster brain homogenate and 301V murine spleen along with endogenous infectivity studies.

Foster reviews the position with respect to plasma products in Chapter 7. Early theoretical models based on considerations about the likely physicochemical nature of the infectious agent and the known partitioning effects of the processes used in plasma fractionation suggested that a significant reduction in infectivity should occur and should lead to a relatively low risk from plasma products, particularly immunoglobulins and albumin. Studies with spiked brain homogenates tend to bear out these predictions, although they carry the limitation that such preparations are unlikely to accurately reflect the physicochemical nature of the infectious agent in plasma. A smaller number of endogenous infectivity studies in animal models support the general premise but are unable to show a reduction of more than 1 to 2 log because of low levels of infectivity in the starting material. Surveillance of sentinel populations exposed to large volumes of plasma products, some of which are known to have been manufactured from pools that include a contribution from a donor who subsequently developed CJD, have not shown yet any evidence of transmission of either sporadic or vCJD. Continued vigilance is, of course, critical in this regard.

The position with respect to cell and tissue products is reviewed by Galea and Turner in Chapter 8. Broadly speaking, processing that reduces the amount of residual cellular material while avoiding pooling is likely to be of benefit, and studies into the applicability of washing methods to bone processing are ongoing.

Several approaches have proved effective in the decontamination of surgical instrumentation but are inapplicable to cells, tissues, or organs requiring viable tissues. Some human tissue products such as morselized bone and tendon are largely used in an acellular form; hence, some of those approaches may be applicable in this setting. Many other compounds have been identified that may interfere with infectivity and would benefit from further exploration,[13] although it should be observed that the potential side effects of the infusion of such compounds into patients should be given appropriate consideration.

## Optimal Use of Blood and Tissues

One of the most effective risk management processes is to ensure that blood, tissues, and organs are transfused or transplanted only when there is clear clinical need and when the potential benefit outweighs the risk. Studies show that a great deal of variation in clinical practice remains. Much further research, education, and audit should be carried out to build the evidence base in transfusion and transplantation medicine and to ensure a high standard of prescribing practice.

# Conclusions

Most of the straightforward, low-risk, and low-cost options for risk management have been implemented. Further risk management strategies are likely to incur detriment in terms of damage to the donor base, potential damage to the quality of the product, or high cost. The weighing of these measures against other health service priorities is highly problematic and must be balanced against the risk posed by vCJD in the donor population and other priorities and risks. Such decisions will continue to prove highly challenging for the foreseeable future.

# References

1. Clarke P, Ghani AC. Projections of the future course of the primary vCJD epidemic in the UK: Inclusion of subclinical infection and the possibility of wider genetic susceptibility. J Royal Society 2005;2: 19-31.
2. Hilton DA, Ghani AC, Conyers L, et al. Prevalence of lymphoreticular prion protein accumulation in UK tissue samples. J Pathol 2004;203: 733-9.
3. Copper JD, Bird SM. Predicting incidence of variant Creutzfeldt-Jakob disease from UK dietary exposure to bovine spongiform

encephalopathy for the 1940-1969 and post-1969 birth cohorts. Int J Epidemiol 2003;32:784-91.

4. Boelle PY, Cesbron JY, Valleron AJ. Epidemiological evidence of higher susceptibility to vCJD in the young. BMC Infect Dis 2004;4: 26-33.

5. Wadsworth JD, Asante EA, Desbruslais M, et al. Human prion protein with valine 129 prevents expression of variant CJD phenotype. Science 2004;306:1793-6.

6. Brown P, Rohwer RG, Dunston BC, et al. The distribution of infectivity in blood components and plasma products in experimental models of transmissible spongiform encephalopathy. Transfusion 1998;38:810-16.

7. Brown P, Cervenakova L, McShane LM, et al. Further studies of blood infectivity in an experimental model of transmissible spongiform encephalopathy, with an explanation of why blood components do not transmit Creutzfeldt-Jakob disease in humans. Transfusion 1999; 39:1169-78.

8. Gregori L, McCombie N, Palmer D, et al. Effectiveness of leuco-reduction for removal of infectivity of transmissible spongiform encephalopathies from blood. Lancet 2004;364:527-31.

9. Barclay GR, Houston F, Halliday S, et al. Comparative analysis of normal prion protein expression on human, rodent and ruminant blood cells using a panel of anti-prion antibodies. Transfusion 2002;42:517-26.

10. Silveira JR, Raymond GJ, Hughson AG, et al. The most infectious prion protein particles. Nature 2005;437:257-61.

11. Hunter N, Foster J, Chong A, et al. Transmission of prion diseases by blood transfusion. J Gen Virol 2002;83:267-71.

12. Turner ML, Ironside JW. New variant Creutzfeldt-Jakob disease: The risk of transmission by blood transfusion. Blood Rev 1998;12:255-68.

13. Head MW, Farquhar CF, Mabbott NA, Fraser JR. The transmissible spongiform encephalopathies: Pathogenic mechanisms and strategies for therapeutic intervention. Expert Opin Ther Targets 2001;5:569-85.

# Index

importation of, 179-180, 249,
253-255, 265, 296
nanofiltration, 203-205
plasma fractionation,
191-198, 297
prion reduction technologies,
167-174, 296-297
for transplantation, 229,
231-240
appropriate cell and tissue
use, 239-240
avoiding cross-contamina-
tion, 231-232
CJD testing on donors,
236-237
decontamination regimens,
239, 297-298
donor selection, 232-235
importing tissues, 235-236
pooling and tissue processing, 238-239
Rodent studies. *See* Animal studies
Routes of infection, 268-269
compounding effects of, 251,
279
and infectivity levels, 152
primary, 258, 275-276
in rodent models, 38-39, 103,
152
secondary, 247-248, 249, 258
Rov9 murine cell line, 140-141

**S**

S100 protein, 64, 83
SAG-M (saline-adenine-glucose-mannitol) solution, 163, 166
Schwann cell culture, 141-142
sCJD. *See* Sporadic CJD
Scrapie
animal infectivity studies, *97,
99,* 104-105, 120
blood infectivity titers, 105, *108,*
109
effects of FDC ablation on,
43-44

lymphoid involvement in, 38
mechanism of FDC infection in,
44-45
normal and pathologic PrP in,
40-41
role of FDCs in, 42-43
routes of infection in, 38-39
spread of infectivity in, 47-50
susceptibility to, 52
time-course studies in, 105, *106,*
109, *110*
uptake and transport of
infectivity in, 46
Screening for intensely fluorescent
targets (SIFT), 138
Screening tests, 278, 293-295. *See
also* Testing
Secondary transmission, 247-248,
249
and compounding transmission
routes, 279
effect of genetic factors on, 276
factors affecting, 256-258
scenarios for, 258-263
timing of, 257, 258- 260, 262-263
Secretions, infectivity in, *225*
Sensitivity of detection methods,
103, 142-143, 210, 288, 293-294
Seprion ligand, 132
Sheep models. *See* Animal studies
Sickle cell trait, 159
SIFT (screening for intensely fluorescent targets), 138
Skin grafts, 240
Sleep disorders
fatal familial insomnia, 65,
76-77
sporadic fatal insomnia, 74
SMB murine cell line, 140
Solvent/detergent-treated FFP, *181,*
183
Species barriers, 23-25, 96, 103, 288
Specificity of testing, 142-143, 278,
293-294
Spleen, 38, 39, 40, 237